D1708963

THE NATIONAL UNDERWRITER COMPANY

BUILDING A FINANCIAL SERVICES CLIENTELE, 11th EDITION

Alfred Granum, CLU; Barry Alberstein, MBA, Ph.D., and Delia Alberstein, CLU, ChFC

This newly revised book contains some of the most important updates ever made to this highly popular publication. This edition of *Building a Financial Services Clientele* brings the proven One Card System ("OCS") to life in a contemporary, high-tech context—penetrating the mechanics of the system itself to expose why the approach works and how you can take advantage of today's tools and technology while still employing the remarkably effective OCS system.

Enhancements to the 11th Edition

- The benefits of new technology for the financial services representative

- Learn how Facebook, Linked In, Copytalk, Google, and other tools enhance the effectiveness and ease of this client-acquisition system

- Useful tools for increasing industry knowledge and skills

- Using social media to increase success with prospecting for new clients

- Scripts for the six-step prospecting approach to gaining more clients

- Effective communication techniques for today's producer

- Tools for customer-relationship management and practice management

- Setting goals and refining work plans

- Analyzing and managing activity and production

- Scheduling the ongoing contacts that build relationships, capture cross-sales and lead to a growing base of clients and referrals

- Improving soft skills for prospecting, scripts for the initial approach, and better closing techniques

Building a Financial Services Clientele, 11th Edition, remains the single source for access to the proven OCS client-acquisition system. And this new edition still provides time-tested step-by-step instructions on how to:

- Become the one and only trusted financial advisor for your clients

- Capture 40 percent of deferred business, increase case size, and obtain quality referrals

- Continually find and acquire new, dedicated clients

Whether you're a beginner or an established professional, this book will help you master the proven techniques that turn prospects into long-term clients.

To place orders for ***Building a Financial Services Clientele*** or any of our products, or for additional information, contact Customer Service at **800-543-0874**.

11th Edition

Building a
Financial Services Clientele

The Ultimate Guide to the One Card System

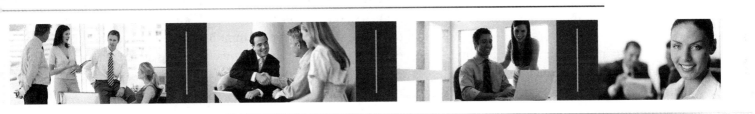

O. Alfred Granum, CLU
Barry Alberstein, MBA, Ph.D.
Delia Alberstein, CLU, ChFC

One Card System®

ISBN 978-1-936362-53-0

Eleventh Edition

2012

THE NATIONAL UNDERWRITER COMPANY
5081 Olympic Blvd., Erlanger, KY 41018

Copyright 1968, 1972, 1974, 1975, 1977, 1985, 1990, 1993, 2001, 2006, 2012

Printed in the United States of America

ABOUT SUMMIT BUSINESS MEDIA

Summit Business Media is the leading B2B media and information company serving the insurance, financial, legal and investment advisory markets. Summit strives to be "The Next Generation of Business Information" for executives and practitioners by providing breaking news and analysis, in-depth practice management strategies, business-building techniques and actionable data. Summit services the information needs of its customers through numerous channels, including digital, print, and live events. Summit publishes 16 magazines and 150 reference titles, operates 20 websites and hosts a dozen conferences, including the world's largest mining investment conference held each year in South Africa. Summit's Marketing Data division provides detailed information on millions of benefits plans, agents and advisors in the U.S.

Summit employs 350 employees in ten offices across the United States. For more information, please visit www.summitbusinessmedia.com.

ABOUT THE NATIONAL UNDERWRITER COMPANY

For over 110 years, The National Underwriter Company has been the first in line with the targeted tax, insurance, and financial planning information you need to make critical business decisions. Boasting nearly a century of expert experience, our reputable Editors are dedicated to putting accurate and relevant information right at your fingertips. With Tax Facts, Tools & Techniques, National Underwriter Advanced Markets Reference Service, Field Guide, FC&S®, and other resources available in print, on CD, and online, you can be assured that as the industry evolves National Underwriter will be at the forefront with the thorough and easy-to-use resources you rely on for success.

The National Underwriter Company Update Service Notification

This National Underwriter Company publication is regularly updated to include coverage of developments and changes that affect the content. If you did not purchase this publication directly from The National Underwriter Company and you want to receive these important updates sent on a 30-day review basis and billed separately, please contact us at (800) 543-0874. Or you can mail your request with your name, company, address, and the title of the book to:

The National Underwriter Company
5081 Olympic Boulevard
Erlanger, KY 41018

If you purchased this publication from The National Underwriter Company directly, you have already been registered for the update service.

National Underwriter Company Contact Information

To order any National Underwriter Company title, please

- call 1-800-543-0874, 8-6 ET Monday – Thursday and 8 to 5 ET Friday

- online bookstore at www.nationalunderwriter.com, or

- mail to The National Underwriter Company, Orders Department, 5081 Olympic Blvd, Erlanger, KY 41018

Preface

In this book you will learn a proven system – thoroughly tested and refined during the past several decades – that you can use to for developing a long-term supply of financial services clientele.

It won't always be easy. In fact, the first few years will be challenging. It will take a lot of hard work and dedication. You will, however, learn methods of organization and activity to keep you on track in meeting your predefined goals. You'll find yourself wondering, "How can I see everyone I promised to call this year?" By carefully following the concepts of this system, you will have the power to control your own destiny and attain success beyond your highest expectations.

Always remember – your goal is not merely to meet people and make sales. You are developing Clients whom you will see and sell many times throughout your career. Your Clients will be people with whom you will develop close relationships over the years. You will have a profound effect on the lives of thousands of people, even on future generations.

It's been said that the person who knows *how* to do the work well will always have a job. The person who also knows *why* will usually be the master. This book can help you acquire a firm grip on both the *how* and the *why*. When you understand *why* certain activities are important, you will be in the position to excel. As such, this guide presents the original approach to the One Card System to teach you the *why* so you can incorporate today's tools to take your performance to new levels.

To this end we have reformatted this book into three sections: 1) why the research and original approach are still valid today; 2) taking advantage of today's tools and technology to succeed with the system; and 3) critical soft skills for gaining new clients and closing more sales.

This edition also contains two new chapters. The first discusses new tools now available to the financial representative and how to utilize them in building a clientele. The second chapter is a review of the new web based Career Activity Management (CAM) System™ with an eye toward demonstrating how such a system can harness the power of the new mobile technology to manage and build your practice while using the theory of the One Card System.

This is truly an exciting time to be a part of the financial services industry and we are pleased to present a system that can help you stand apart from your peers and reach higher levels of achievement. Wishing you the best of luck as you help your clients achieve financial security and peace of mind.

O. Alfred Granum
Barry and Delia Alberstein
November 1, 2011

Introduction

What is the best way to use this book and system?

There are several steps in mastering this critical material.

1. Read the entire book all the way through making notes or highlighting important points you want to remember and return to later. Consider outlining the book by hand. We learn best when we record our thoughts, so this is a great way to program your subconscious and truly learn the material.

2. While the hand-written cards and file box are often replaced by automated data collection today, the original techniques are presented to give you a thorough understanding of the process. It is recommended that you use the cards for the first ninety days while you build a clear understanding of how to use the system. Many of today's most successful producers continue to use the cards and file box and find this approach much simpler than automated systems.

3. Lay out an action plan for implementation. You will probably need to re-read some of the text to accomplish that. Identify the supplies you will need and set a date to begin using the system. The use of the annual OCS Productivity Planner calendar is highly recommended to record all activities for easy review during the weekly planning process. Combined with current technology, such as the Alberstein CAM System, you'll have a powerful process that virtually guarantees success.

4. Master the verbal scripts in the section on Soft Skills. Practice reading them. Record them and play them back. Continue this process until you feel completely comfortable. Remember, professionals are well prepared; ad-libs are for amateurs.

5. Continually refer back to the book as questions come up. In this way you can fully understand how the system was actually designed to be used rather than allowing the slow dilution of its power by small mistaken alterations.

Please note: The terms "Suspect" and "Qualified Suspect" are used interchangeably throughout this book. All Suspects are Qualified Suspects. It is also important to note that the section entitled, "Six Step Prospecting and Three Step Promotion" is referring to the process of acquiring new Qualified Suspects, sometimes known as Suspecting.

Today's Financial Professional is referred to by a growing number of titles. These include Agent, Financial Representative, Producer, Associate, Broker, Financial Advisor, and Financial Consultant among others. For the purposes of this text all of these will be referred to as "Financial Services Professionals."

The Authors

O. Alfred Granum, CLU

Al Granum is a living legend in the life insurance business and many would argue that he has had more of an influence on the way financial professionals work than any other person in the past 50 years. Here are a few items from his phenomenal list of accomplishments.

O. Alfred Granum, Chartered Life Underwriter (CLU) and Lifetime Million Dollar Round Table (MDRT) member, graduated Phi Beta Kappa from the University of Wisconsin with simultaneous BA and MA degrees in life insurance. Starting as an agent for the Northwestern Mutual in Amery, Wisconsin, he worked his way up to agency officer, production manager and general agent in Chicago.

Leadership was a habit with his agency. It ranked number one in Northwestern Mutual for volume in 18 out of his last 25 years and was the first in NML to break numerous volume record benchmarks. Mr. Granum did not have a giant agency in terms of numbers. The 45 people in the agency for more than one year produced an average premium which was the highest known in any large agency in the world. Within that group there were 28 CLUs and 42 Provisional Applicants or members of the MDRT. In addition, there were 6 CLUs and 4 MDRT members among the distinguished Emeritus agents. Two of his agents, Dave Hilton, Sr. and John Cruikshank, became Presidents of the MDRT.

The agency's steady growth, which was phenomenal in a business where many agents tend to level off and retrogress too early, was due in no small measure to the agency's continuous emphasis on Client Building. The well-known One Card System (OCS), which has been featured in the MDRT's *Personal and Office Efficiency Manual*, was developed in this agency.

Al has given of himself by participating in countless programs for the National Association of Insurance and Financial Advisors (NAIFA), the General Agents and Managers Association (GAMA), MDRT, CLU Institutes, Louisiana State University Insurance seminars and sales congresses, career schools and management seminars. He has spoken in every state in the US, every Canadian province, in several European countries, Australia and Asia. *The Science...The Art of Building a Life Insurance Clientele* and the subsequent *Building a Financial Services Clientele* communicate his message. In addition, Granum is the author of numerous audio and video presentations and magazine articles. Al's original text, which has seen ten editions since 1968, has been translated into French, Spanish, Japanese, Korean, Mandarin and Polish. In recent years, Al Granum has specialized in seminars and consultations for industry groups, companies and agencies as well as serving as a faculty member at Bryn Mawr for the MDRT's "Fast Track" program.

Mr. Granum has been awarded the highest honors of the industry, to include the John Newton Russell Award from NAIFA and the Huebner Gold Medal from the American College in Bryn Mawr. He has been elected to the National General Agent's and Manager's Hall of Fame. Additionally, his fellow general agents have honored him by endowing the Professorship Chair in Management in Al Granum's name at The American College.

Barry Alberstein, MBA, Ph.D.

Dr. Barry Alberstein is a Clinical and Consulting Psychologist with a Masters Degree in Business Administration. He has consulted extensively with the life insurance and financial services industry for the past 30 years on the psychology and administration of practice management, the consultative sales model, and building trusting client relationships.

He is featured speaker at many domestic and international industry meetings, including multiple presentations to the *Million Dollar Round Table (MDRT)*. Dr. Alberstein has authored numerous articles on various aspects of the financial services career and is on the faculty of The Fastrack Academy for the Northwestern Mutual Financial Network. He maintains an active performance coaching practice and has had the privilege of personally conducting over 3,500 Client Builder (productivity enhancement) meetings, which included the opportunity to listen to and analyze more than 20,000 monthly activity and production reports from advisors.

Dr. Alperstein's unique combination of clinical, business, and consulting experience has provided valuable insights into the elements of a successful career. These, in turn, have enabled continuing contributions to the better understanding and implementation of the One Card System as well as the creation of the Career Activity Management (CAM) System, a web-based practice management program designed specifically for the financial services industry.

Dr. Alberstein obtained his Ph.D. in Clinical Psychology from the University of Washington in Seattle, having previously received his MBA from Northeastern University in Boston, and his BA in Communication from the University of California at Berkeley.

Delia Alberstein, CLU, ChFC

Delia Alberstein has an extensive background in the life insurance and financial services Industry. She was a successful financial advisor for twelve years and served four years in agency management as the Associate General Agent for Connecticut Mutual in Seattle, Washington. There her duties included recruiting, selection, initial and advanced training, as well as field and office supervision of advisors. In that capacity, she brought their new organization from 44th to 5th in the company within three years, and received Connecticut Mutual's prestigious Management Council Award each year.

In 1994, Delia joined Barry full time in their consulting practice, providing a practitioner's perspective. She has developed and conducted numerous training programs for managers and advisors, and has co-authored the development of the web-based Career Activity Management (CAM) System. Possessing a thorough understanding of the One Card System, Delia is a professional trainer who truly understands what it takes to develop a successful financial services practice, a thriving agency and enduring careers.

Table of Contents

Part 3: Critical Soft Skills for Client Building

The Touch of the Master's Hand

'Twas battered and scarred, and the auctioneer
Thought it scarcely worth his while
To waste much time on the old violin,
But he held it up with a smile:
"What am I bid, good folks," he cried,
"Who'll start the bidding for me?"
"A dollar, a dollar," then "Two! Only two?"
"Two dollars, and who'll make it three?"

"Three dollars once, three dollars twice;
Going for three—" But no,
From the room, far back, a gray-haired man
Came forward and picked up the bow:
Then wiping the dust from the old violin,
And tightening the loose strings,
He played a melody pure and sweet
As a caroling angel sings.

The music ceased, and the auctioneer,
With a voice that was quiet and low,
Said, "What am I bid for the old violin?"
And he held it up with the bow.
"A thousand, and who'll make it two?"
"Two thousand, and who'll make it three?"
"Three thousand once, three thousand twice,
And going, and gone, said he.

The people cheered, but some of them cried,
"We do not quite understand
What changed its worth." – Swift came the reply:
"The touch of a master's hand."
And many a man with life out of tune,
And battered and scarred with sin,
Is auctioned cheap to the thoughtless crowd,
Much like the old violin.

A "mess of pottage," a glass of wine,
A game – and he travels on.
He is "going once," "going twice,"
He's "going" and almost "gone."
But the MASTER comes, and the foolish crowd
Never can quite understand
The worth of a soul and the change that's wrought
By the touch of the MASTER's hand.

— Myra Brooks Welch

Part 1

Why the Research and Original Approach Are Valid Today

Chapter 1

Building a Long-Term Career

You're in Control

What is it about a sales career in financial services that attracts people? The magnitude and range of skills required to succeed are clearly daunting. Yet, the career continues to attract a steady stream of energetic, entrepreneurial people. What is the appeal? The answer is the unique combination of rewards the career offers such as:

Rewards and Opportunities

- Financial potential;

- Independence;

- An opportunity to truly help people in a significant way; and

- Intellectual stimulation.

Financial Potential – Earnings Commensurate with Your Talent and Effort

Many believe the financial potential of this career is "unlimited." Perhaps this is a bit of a stretch, but it is clear that a financial services professional can earn compensation in direct proportion to his or her talent and effort. Think about it. Most career opportunities have clear limits on what someone can earn in a given time period. How many other careers are as free from the restrictions of internal corporate politics? In most financial services companies the territories, markets, and types of accounts are open to every producer. It's really you and the world – you're in control! The opportunity to achieve is truly exceptional.

Personal Independence

The initial relationship between you and your company is one of interdependence.

The poet Christopher Morley once wrote, "There is only one success... to be able to spend your life in your own way." It appears that most people who are attracted to the financial services industry have a strong desire to be self-directed and Captain of their own ship. Experienced, successful financial services professionals have an unusual amount of independence in the structuring of their professional lives. They control their own calendars and time schedules. They have the luxury of being able to choose their own travel commitments. They can schedule around family events and, to a large extent, control their own destiny.

As success is earned, so is increased independence. Perhaps it would be more accurate to describe the initial relationship between new Financial Services Professionals and their companies as one of *interdependence*. Nonetheless, the combination of earning potential and independence creates an opportunity for personal freedom that few careers can match.

An Opportunity to Be of Service to Others

Your contribution to your Clients' financial security will flow through generations.

Another appealing feature of a financial services career is the genuine opportunity to help other people in a significant way. It is difficult to overstate the human benefit that flows from your work. Programs providing an intelligent mix of insurance and investments provide both peace of mind and personal confidence. Knowing that the financial well being of one's family and business is protected is both satisfying and enormously important. Furthermore, your contribution to your clients' future doesn't stop with the immediate family. It flows through generations and has a lasting mark on the course of the lives of children and grandchildren. Communities also benefit through capital accumulation and business longevity. The financial services professional truly makes a substantial and lasting difference in many, many lives.

Continual Intellectual Stimulation and Challenge

Finally, the ever-changing nature of the economy, tax laws, and the industry offer continual intellectual stimulation. While this career choice is not without its challenges, it is never boring.

The Client Building Philosophy

The Profit Is in the Relationship, Not in the Sale

The key to achieving this combination of compensation, individual freedom, and service to others centers around the process of obtaining and sustaining a client base. Clients – not just sales – bring both freedom and the opportunity to be of genuine service.

Who, then, is a Client? A Client is a person, household or business that has purchased insurance or other financial products as a result of an in-depth Fact Finding Interview. In other words, a Client is a *paying entity* in which the decision maker has a relationship with you that is based upon a thorough discussion of his or her situation. A Client is probably best defined not by what he or she has bought, but by the *process* that was used to determine the purchase. Simply put, a Client is someone who has shared personal and financial information with you and feels a sense of trust and continuity into the future. A Client is considered to be *active* when he or she is likely to buy from you again as his or her situation changes over time.

You know you have a true Client when, if asked whether they have a trusted financial professional, they name you!

Your Client Base

What is a client base? Since Active Clients are people or businesses that will continue to buy from you in the future, a client base is best viewed as a reservoir of long-term relationships and repeat sales. Unfortunately, the reservoir is somewhat leaky. That is, Clients die, move, divorce or are lured away. Some just become satisfied and saturated, so steady but slow attrition is inevitable. The goal is to fill the reservoir with new Clients faster than the reservoir drains.

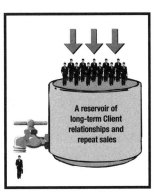

A reservoir of long-term Client relationships and repeat sales

Client vs. Policyholder or Investment Account Holder

A *Client,* in One Card System (OCS) terminology, is not the same as a *policyholder* or *investment account owner.* A policyholder or account owner is a person who has engaged in a sales transaction with a producer but feels no particular sense of trust or loyalty. This person often buys a product focusing on cost or potential gain. The producer is often viewed as a vendor selling a commodity. A true Client is buying *you and your services as a trusted Financial Services Professional.* You know you have true Clients when, if asked if they have a trusted Financial Services Professional, they will name you!

A "Client" in OCS terminology is defined as a paying entity, and may include more than one policyholder or investor.

The Economic Value of a Client

Remember, for One Card System purposes, a Client is defined as a *paying entity*. Each Client represents an account or a checkbook. For example, I might buy one life insurance policy on myself, another on my spouse, and two mutual funds for our children. That would be four sales but, since they all came from one checkbook, you would have *only one Client*.

Additionally, Clients buy repeatedly. Statistics reveal that life insurance Clients will buy additional coverage an average of five to seven times. These subsequent life insurance sales have a tendency to increase in commission value. When other insurance products and potential equity sales are added to the relationship, the total number of sales can go much higher.

A good Client, properly serviced, can be a tremendous contribution to your reservoir. Whether the Client is an individual, a household, or a business, a true Client will continue to buy from the professional who understands and responds over time to the Client's changing needs. Furthermore, making the repeat sale is much faster and easier than the time and effort required to obtain a new Client.

Need Based vs. Transaction Based Selling

The Client Building Philosophy stresses that a client base is built through a need based, relationship driven sales process rather than a transaction based, product driven sales process. Transaction based selling focuses on selling a specific product or range of products to customers by emphasizing price, features, and benefits. The idea is to make a sale – to engage in a successful transaction. Client Building stresses making the individual a Client by first listening to and focusing on his or her needs. The specific product is secondary to the act of fulfilling the Client's needs and laying the groundwork for a long-standing relationship.

Becoming Bulletproof

The Magnificent Obsession – To obtain 1,000 Clients in your career.

A clear vision of the benefits of the career requires a sincere desire to build a significant Client base. But how many Clients are necessary to obtain personal freedom? While the exact number is difficult to identify, it is safe to say that obtaining between 500 and 1,000 Clients will probably do the job. The burning desire to acquire 1,000 Clients is what we refer to as *The Magnificent Obsession*. Building a client base of between 500 and 1,000 Clients not only brings you the dual benefits of repeat sales and helping people, but it also creates a tremendous opportunity to control your own destiny.

It can be said that the process of obtaining between 500 and 1,000 Clients makes you *bulletproof*. A large, diverse Client base protects the security and continuity of your practice. You are protected from unfavorable changes in politics or products as well as changes in tax law, interest rates, and the fluctuations of the economy. Certainly, economic and political changes will affect some of your Clients, but the size and diversity of the client base, with its repeat purchasing power, protects you against the variations and declines encountered in many other professions.

A Rewarding Career!

This profession remains unique, challenging, and full of lucrative rewards. It offers self-direction, substantial compensation, and a chance to help people in a truly meaningful way. Rewarding and satisfying Client relationships remain the key to realizing the benefits of the career and establishing the path to personal freedom. Conscientiously implemented, the One Card System will take you as far as your talent, effort, and imagination allow.

Chapter 2

The Goal:
Build a Lifelong Supply of Clients

Documentation Is the Foundation

To fully appreciate the OCS, it helps to understand the background of its creator, O. Alfred Granum, CLU. Al Granum was manager and General Agent for The Northwestern Mutual Life Insurance Company in Chicago for twenty-eight years. During that time he developed and managed what many have described as the most successful agency in the world. His agent productivity records are still unequaled.

During his tenure as General Agent, his agents recorded and documented their sales activities and results over a twenty-five-year span. Al Granum conducted major analyses of the records at the fifteenth, twentieth and twenty-fifth years. The results of this longitudinal study served as a phenomenal base of data that developed both the science and the art of building a clientele, and ultimately became the One Card System – one of the most effective tools ever used in the financial services profession.

The Development of the 10-3-1 Ratio

Al Granum scientifically quantified exactly what it takes to achieve measurable success in the business. He identified the conversion ratios that clearly describe the numbers of candidates (Ten Qualified Suspects) who grant Fact Finding Interviews (Three Prospects) and who ultimately become Clients (One New Client). This is the famous 10-3-1 ratio of Client Acquisition.

It might be true that as product mixes and technologies change, new Client Acquisition ratios may also change somewhat. What remains critical, however, is that you have a practice administration system that allows you to monitor exactly what is true for you. As Al Granum has often said, "You must know the truth of your situation and then take appropriate action." If you have no way of determining the truth of your business situation, you will have no way of determining the appropriate action.

The One Card System is time tested and solid; it teaches the true fundamentals of the profession. In today's business environment, it remains a virtual blueprint for success.

While the original data goes back some forty years, it is interesting to note that a recent study of new client acquisition completed in the Japanese life insurance industry confirmed Granum's findings are still valid today.

The research clearly shows that the way to achieve the goals that brought you into the business is through building your clientele. Your mission – or the *Magnificent Obsession* – is to obtain 1,000 Clients. In order to accomplish this, three areas of expertise are necessary:

1. Knowledge – An understanding of the *science* of the business that allows you to predict future outcomes based upon today's activities.

2. Administration and Organization – A system that guides your activities on a daily, monthly, and yearly basis and is based upon the predictable relationships that govern the business. This is the One Card System.

3. Soft Skills – Mastery of the Sales Cycle skills that allow you to better control the outcome of sales interactions. This is the *art* side of the business.

The Science and the Art of Client Building

There's more to a building client base than just seeing more people

The Science	The Art
• The activity to sales ratios • A system to guide business activities • Organization and time control	• Sales Cycle mastery • Relationship skills • The Persuasion skills that move people to action

1) Understanding the Science – The Knowledge

It is one thing to want to build a large client base for your career. It is another to know how to do it. Most Financial Services Professionals' understanding of the science side of the business is usually handled by the directive, "Just see more people."

Predict and control

The philosophy of science tells us that true *understanding* comes when we can both *predict and control* events in a given situation. A true understanding of the financial services business requires that we are able to at least predict how much activity is required to produce the desired results. In other words, how many new people must be identified in order to make a sale? If we know the basic conversion ratio we can then predict the outcome of our efforts.

Predictable relationships, however, don't offer complete scientific understanding. We must be able to *control* the outcome as well. To do this, we must be able to make a fine grained analysis of the process that guides us from the identification of new people to the ultimate sale. When we understand the Sales Cycle and how many people it takes to move through each step, we increase our ability to control the process.

2) An Organizational System

An organizational system to guide your daily, monthly, and yearly activities can take your performance to higher levels. This system must be based upon the scientific truths that underlie the business. *The OCS was specifically designed around those truths.* It is the ideal administrative system. Ultimately, the goal is not to drive the system, but to have the system drive you. When all of that is in place you will have the understanding, the skills and the method to build a great clientele. If you add strong personal motivation, health, talent, and sufficient self-discipline to the formula, you have everything required for a long-term successful career.

The Wheel of Client Acquisition

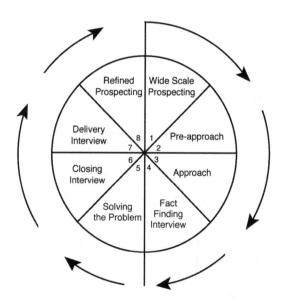

3) Understanding the Art – The Soft Skills

Understanding the structure of the Sales Cycle

Obviously, our ability to move people through the process will depend upon our mastery of the required sales skills. Excellent selling skills alone aren't enough. You must also know when and how often to apply those skills. In other words, you must understand how the sales process is structured. The model for the structure is called the Sales Cycle. *When you have mastered the Sales Cycle, you can combine the art and the science to be your best.*

Twenty-Five Years of Research – Still Valid Today

The One Card System is not based upon opinion, personal sales experiences or sales truisms. It is based upon twenty-five years of meticulous collection and analysis of activity and production data from *successful* life insurance Agents. The research was conducted at the Northwestern Mutual Life Insurance agency in Chicago, Illinois, from 1958 through 1983. During those years the agents in the Granum Agency were considered among the most productive agents in the world.

*Meticulous collection and analysis of activity and production data from **successful** life insurance Financial Professionals*

You may ask, "If the financial services industry has changed, how can the research data from professionals who only sold life insurance be meaningful today?" There are at least two important answers to that question. The first is that the research shows how you quantify your business. Regardless of the specific financial product, it shows you what data is critical to your business and how to collect it so you can answer your business questions. It shows you how to gain a scientific understanding of your business. Again, it is the process that is crucial, not the specific product being sold.

The second answer to the question is that the results of the original research comprise the most complete longitudinal study available today on the financial services career. As product mixes change the statistics of New Client Acquisition *might* change. You'll note the emphasis on *might* change. The most recent study conducted in Japan in 2004-2005, with over 200 Financial Services Professionals, replicated the Granum research results (the 10-3-1 Ratio). As a starting point for our understanding of what it takes to acquire a New Client, the Granum data is the most extensive and complete available. The goal is to inspire you to collect your own data on your business. Then you can both predict and control your business outcomes, no matter which collection of financial services you present.

Collect the data on you and your business so you can both predict and control your business outcomes

Understanding the OCS Terminology

Key OCS definitions:
- *Suspect*
- *Prospect*
- *Client*
- *Active Client*

Before exploring the research in-depth, you must understand the definitions that were used in the research. These are the same definitions that are used today in the One Card System.

Suspect

The words "Suspect" and "Qualified Suspect" are used interchangeably and refer to an entity that could be a person, a business or an organization. This entity has enough going for it that you *suspect* it is worth pursuing. That is, you have sized up the entity (either personally or through a referral) and think you could turn it into a Prospect and, eventually, into a Client. If the entity isn't qualified then it is only a name" or "identity." The entity isn't called a Suspect until it has been qualified, meaning you have identified the:

- Name and age;

- Business telephone number and address;

- Occupation and Title; and

- Approximate income.

Prospect

A *Prospect* is a Qualified Suspect who has participated in a full Fact Finding Interview with you. This is an important distinction. Many people in the business refer to a Prospect as someone the Financial Services Professional is interested in pursuing. However, it is important to remember that the OCS Financial Services Professional will only use the term Prospect to refer to someone who has engaged in a Fact Finding Interview. You will see that the process of gathering facts is the key to establishing trust and is central to the behavior that distinguishes you as a true Financial Services Professional.

Client

A Prospect becomes a Client when "It" buys. The Client is the paying entity or account. A Client may be an individual, a corporation, a trust, a partnership, or a grandparent. Each is the paying entity or the account from which the funds are provided.

Active Client

An Active Client is a Client whom you believe will buy additonal products from you in the future. That is, you feel the Client has additional needs and means, and you believe the relationship is strong enough that he or she will purchase again from you.

The Research

The Research Questions

As a basis for the research project ten basic questions were asked. The first three covered the broad conversion from Suspects to Clients. The last seven made a finer granular analysis of the process.

1. Given a known number of Qualified Suspects, how many of this original group will eventually buy and become Clients?

2. When, if ever, is the individual finally sold?

3. How long will it take to completely process or digest a given group of Suspects? That is, how long before all of the Suspects who are going to become Clients finally do so?

4. How many of the Suspects will ultimately become Prospects by divulging Facts?

5. What happens to the Suspects who do not give Facts? How many agree to "keep in touch" and how many will be discarded or dead filed?

6. Given a known number of Prospects, how many will become Clients?

7. When, if ever, is the Prospect finally sold?

8. How long will it take to completely process or digest a given number of Prospects? That is, how long before all of the Prospects who are going to become Clients finally do so?

9. What is the closing ratio (cases sold divided by cases opened) when selling to New Clients versus repeat sales to existing Clients?

10. What is the average number of sales that can be expected from each New Client over time?

The Critical Understanding

Understanding the answers to these questions provides the critical information necessary to guide your career. You will then know the conversion ratios required to set up an appropriate activity program. You will know how many Suspects you will need to obtain a New Client.

Interpreting the research answers guides your success

You will know the approximate time frame for processing Suspects. Finally, you can predict how many Suspects will become Prospects and, ultimately, Clients.

This kind of information is vital to a true understanding of the business. The answers, however, took time and effort to obtain.

How Were the Agents Involved in the Research?

During a period of over twenty-five years, an exceedingly capable group of life insurance Agents (Agents who experienced the highest median productivity of any Agents in any large agency in the world) maintained accurate, detailed records on over 150,000 Qualified Suspects and sifted them through to ultimate success or elimination. The records included the name of each Suspect, the date and circumstances under which the name was obtained, the strength of the introduction, and what happened as a result of the first contact.

The Agents continued to track and record what happened to each Qualified Suspect as he or she moved through the Sales Cycle process. Additionally, the Agents coded the type and results of all of the cases they opened. This information was recorded and tabulated year by year.

All of the individual Agents' records were collected, tabulated and analyzed after ten, fifteen, twenty, and twenty-five years. That was a massive undertaking and involved many thousands of hours on the part of the agency staff members.

The Tabulation Process

Step One – Tracking the Suspects

Information on 150,000 Suspects

The information gathered on 150,000 Suspects was recorded, tabulated and correlated. The actual names of the Suspects were first recorded in dozens of ruled notebooks and later in what became the Agents' *Success Manuals*. The tables that were used to record the data are reproduced in the Annual Review and Planning section of the *Success*

Manual. Those tables are still available in the OCS Productivity Planner to record and study your own results from year to year and compare your records with those of other Financial Services Professionals. The results for an Agent who got off to a fast start and qualified for the MDRT (Million Dollar Round Table) in his first year are shown in the next illustration.

Suspect illustration

TOTAL "SUSPECTS" PROCESSED EACH YEAR

YEARS ELAPSED SINCE "SUSPECTS" INITIALLY OBTAINED

YEAR	TOTAL	1		2		3		4		5		6	
		Sold	%	Sold	%	Sold	%	Sold	%	Sold	%	Sold	%
1st	826	25	3.0	56	6.8	66	8.0	72	8.7	74	8.9	74	8.9
2nd	522	26	4.9	47	9.0	50	9.6	53	10.1	53	10.1	53	10.1
3rd	410	24	5.8	43	10.5	50	12.1	53	13.0	56	13.6	58	14.1
4th	280	15	5.3	31	11.1	32	11.4	35	12.5				
5th	356	11	3.1	22	6.2	25	7.0	26	7.3				
6th	494	21	4.3	43	8.8	43	8.8	45	9.1				
7th	434	23	5.2	31	7.1	33	7.7	35	8.1				
8th	346	14	4.0	31	9.0	37	10.8	40	11.6				
9th	486	32	6.5	53	11.0	63	12.9						
10th	353	24	6.7	44	12.4								
11th	350	25	7.1										
	4,857	240		401		399		359		183		185	
Averages (%)			4.9		8.9		9.6		9.8		10.4		10.5

The columns for this Agent show that in the first year he acquired 826 Qualified Suspects (actually wrote the names in his *Success Manual*), and sold twenty-five or 3 percent of them. By the sixth year a total of seventy-four, or 8.9 percent, of the Suspects had been sold. Yet, looking at the bottom line totals for the first three years, we can see that this Agent wrote an average of 4.9 percent of his Suspects by the end of year one, 8.9 percent through year two and 9.6 percent through year three. Note that the results show how many of the Suspects became Clients, not the total number of lives sold.

Step Two – Tracking the Facts

The second phase of the study involved tabulating and analyzing the results of more than 45,000 Facts interviews. A Facts (Confidential Questionnaire) interview is *only recorded one time* (the first time it is done) in the *Success Manual*. The tens of thousands of reviews and updatings of previously completed Facts are not counted as additional Facts. These records were obtained by counting the number of "New

Facts" boxes used in the Agents' *Success Manuals* and transferring the data to the table in the back of the manual. Again, you have access to these same tables in the *Success Manual* section of the *Productivity Planner* and are encouraged to keep your own records for analysis and comparison.

Records were maintained on over fifty Agents until each of the initial Facts (Confidential Questionnaire) interviews had been resolved by sale or elimination. This process was originally followed for up to eleven years with some Agents. It has now been determined that four years is long enough. The results for another "fast start" Agent are shown in the next illustration.

Facts illustration

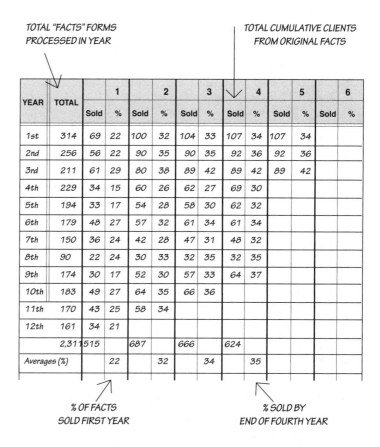

TOTAL "FACTS" FORMS
PROCESSED IN YEAR

TOTAL CUMULATIVE CLIENTS
FROM ORIGINAL FACTS

YEAR	TOTAL	1		2		3		4		5		6	
		Sold	%	Sold	%	Sold	%	Sold	%	Sold	%	Sold	%
1st	314	69	22	100	32	104	33	107	34	107	34		
2nd	256	56	22	90	35	90	35	92	36	92	36		
3rd	211	61	29	80	38	89	42	89	42	89	42		
4th	229	34	15	60	26	62	27	69	30				
5th	194	33	17	54	28	58	30	62	32				
6th	179	48	27	57	32	61	34	61	34				
7th	150	36	24	42	28	47	31	48	32				
8th	90	22	24	30	33	32	35	32	35				
9th	174	30	17	52	30	57	33	64	37				
10th	183	49	27	64	35	66	36						
11th	170	43	25	58	34								
12th	161	34	21										
	2,311	515		687		666		624					
Averages (%)			22		32		34		35				

% OF FACTS
SOLD FIRST YEAR

% SOLD BY
END OF FOURTH YEAR

This Agent took 314 Facts (Confidential Questionnaires) in his first year. That resulted in sixty-nine New Clients, or 22 percent of the Facts. By year two the Agent had sold 100 or 32 percent of the Facts, and through year three 104 New Clients had been obtained. The bottom totals for this Agent show that he converted an average of 22 percent of the Facts into Clients in year one, 32 percent through year two, and 34 percent through year three.

Step Three – Coding the Cases Opened

During each month as cases were opened, they were coded by the Agent as New (3) or Repeat (1). If the case was opened on an existing client then a "1" was recorded in the Category column of the *Success Manual* (see the following illustration). Those "1s" would become Repeat Sales. If the case was opened on a new prospective client who had never previously purchased from either the Agent or the company, then a "3" was placed in the Category column. The results for one Agent are shown next.

In this partial illustration of Cases Opened note that the balance of cases that this Agent opened on "1s" (old Clients) is too heavy. That is, this Agent is living off Repeat Sales from established Clients. If more cases on new Prospects aren't opened, the Agent will eventually run out of good, active Clients and his sales and income will decline. Remember, personal freedom comes through Client Building. Even established Financial Services Professionals with many old Clients ("1s") should strive to open twelve to fifteen cases per month on prospective New Clients ("3s").

Cases Opened Codes

1 - Repeat sale to existing Client

2 - A Client new to you but not new to the company

3 - A Client new to you and the company

4 - An ancillary sale (spouse, dependant, other)

Cases Opened illustration

MONTHLY RECORD OF NEW CASES OPENED

	DATE	NAME	ACTION DATE	CATEGORY	NEW FACTS?	ILLUSTRATION	AMOUNT	SOLD, A, DF
	1	WRAY	7	1	U	EP	25000	25
	1	ALLISON	—	1	U	EP	117000	A
	2	URENA	—	1	U	L	25000	25
	2	WELCH	—	3	Y	EP	113000	25
	3	RYAN J.	3	3	Y	EP	8900	
	4	ARONSON	5	1	U	EP	25000	
	14	SCHULTZ	10	1	U	BUS	100000	
	14	HEYMEYER	—	1	Y	EP	193000	80
	14	WELLS	—	1	N	EST	92000	92
	16	DUNN, T.	4	3	Y	L	22000	I II $ 10
	17	ZINKLE	—	1	U	EP	13000	11.3
	17	MYRON	—	1	N	INS	600 MO	600 M

CATEGORY 1

CASES OPENED ON EXISTING POLICY OWNERS

CATEGORY 3

CASES OPENED ON NEW CLIENTS

Notice that in almost every case, the column headed New Facts shows that this Agent did a good job by either obtaining complete new Facts (code letter "Y") or updating the old ones (code letter "U").

Step Four – Tracking the Cases Opened

The fourth and final step in the tabulation process involved transferring the results for both New and Repeat Cases Opened to an annual summary table like the one shown next. You can accomplish this same process with your own results by using the table provided in the back of your *Success Manual/Productivity Planner.*

Annual Review illustration

NEW CASES OPENED

REPEAT BUSINESS CASES OPENED

ANNUAL REVIEW OF CASES OPENED BY THE MONTH AND THEIR ULTIMATE DISPOSITION										
	C.O.'S NEW CLIENTS	NO. AND AMT. SOLD	AUTO	DEAD FILED	STILL OPEN	C.O.'S OTHERS	NO. AND AMT. SOLD	AUTO	DEAD FILED	STILL OPEN
JANUARY	7	3-80	2	2	—	22	17-533	5	—	—
FEBRUARY	4	1-25	2	1	—	12	8-125	3	1	—
MARCH	10	3-197	3	4	—	20	13-218	7	—	—
APRIL	6	1-10	5	—	—	22	15-359	6	1	—
MAY	10	2-55	6	1	1	19	9-157	10	—	—
JUNE	13	7-125	4	2	—	8	4-77	3	1	—
JULY	7	4-124	2	1	—	13	8-115	4	1	—
AUGUST	13	6-270	5	2	—	14	10-404	4	—	—
SEPTEMBER	12	6-300	4	2	—	14	11-250	1	2	—
OCTOBER	14	4-138	6	3	1	21	10-300	6	5	—
NOVEMBER	13	2-40	3	2	6	21	10-260	10	1	—
DECEMBER	8		1	1	6	10	3-80	2	1	4
	117	39-1,364	43	21	14	196	118-2,878	61	13	4

SUMMARY	TOTAL	SOLD	PERCENT-AGE	VOLUME	PREMIUM	AV. VOL.	AV. PREM.		
NEW CLIENTS	117	39	33%	1,364	20,664	34,974	15.15		
OTHERS	196	118	60%	2,878	62,500	24,389	22.10		
TOTAL									

CASES OPENED

Do not let too many cases with old policyowners or Clients produce a false sense of superior production or a higher closing ratio

When evaluating selling efficiency at the end of the year, it is important to be able to separate New Sales from Repeat Sales. If all sales to both new and old Clients are lumped together, a deceptive picture will result. An established Financial Services Professional focusing on old policyowners or Clients appears to be a superior producer of sales with a higher closing ratio. That is because it's easier to pick up repeat business from satisfied old Clients!

On the other hand, if the Cases Opened on Repeat Sales, spouses and children (ancillary sales) are extracted and evaluated separately, as shown in the previous example, a much more meaningful picture emerges.

Notice in the Annual Review summary table the Agent opened a total of 313 cases (117 on New Clients plus 196 repeat or ancillary sales); he ultimately sold 157 cases (lives). That resulted in an overall closing ratio (cases sold divided by cases opened) of 50 percent. A closer examination, however, revealed that the closing ratio for *sales to existing Clients is 60 percent* (low for an experienced Financial Services Professional) while the closing ratio for *sales to New Clients is 33 percent* (about average).

A critical distinction between the closing ratio for sales to existing Clients and the closing ratio for sales to New Clients

The Research Results

The basic concepts of *Building a Financial Services Clientele* began with a process of sifting and winnowing from which certain basic truths and relationships were ultimately developed. After twenty-five years of sifting, winnowing and research, what results are known? Let's take each of the ten research questions one at a time.

> **Question 1:** Given a known number of Qualified Suspects, how many of this original group will eventually buy and become Clients?

> **Answer:** The results show that of the 150,000 Suspects tracked, approximately *15,000 or 10 percent* went on to become Clients. The following illustration shows the basic conversion ratios between Qualified Suspects, Facts, and New Clients.

Continual Sifting and Winnowing

Sifting	*Winnowing*	
150,000 Suspects	**45,000 Facts**	**15,000 + Clients**
	Inverview Forms Completed	

Question 2: When, if ever, is the individual finally sold?

Answer: The results indicate that from a given group of Qualified Suspects, *about 6 percent of them were sold in the first year. Approximately 3 percent more were sold in the second year, and 1 percent more in year three.* The sales from the first three years totaled about 10 percent of the Suspects. As can be seen from the results of Question One, this 10 percent is approximately the total number of Suspects who can be expected to become Clients even over a longer period of time. That takes us to question three.

Question 3: How long will it take to completely process or digest a given group of Suspects? That is, how long before all of the Suspects who are going to become Clients, finally do so?

Answer: On average, all of the New Clients who can be expected from a given block of Suspects will buy within the first *three to four years.* In essence, all of the New Client potential from a block of Suspects will be used up within three to four years. That, of course, does not take into account the future repeat sales to those Clients or their subsequent referrals.

Question 4: How many of the Suspects will ultimately become Prospects by divulging Facts?

Answer: The results show that out of the 150,000 Suspects, approximately *45,000 or 30 percent* granted Facts and became Prospects.

Question 5: What happens to the Suspects who do not give Facts? How many agree to keep in touch and how many will be discarded or dead filed?

Answer: When Suspects were recorded in the *Success Manual,* a code was entered that told what happened during the first exposure to the Suspect. Using that code researchers found that 30 percent of the Suspects granted Facts, 35 percent agreed to keep in touch and 35 percent showed no potential for that Agent and were dead filed.

Question 6: Given a known number of Prospects, how many will become Clients?

Answer: On average, about 33 percent of a given block of Prospects will eventually be sold and become Clients.

Question 7: When, if ever, is the Prospect finally sold?

Answer: About 20 percent of a given block of Prospects will be sold and become Clients in the first year. Approximately 10 percent will be sold in year two and an additional 3 percent in year three, for a total of 33 percent.

Question 8: How long will it take to completely process or digest a given number of Prospects? That is, how long before all of the Prospects who are going to become Clients finally do so?

Answer: The results indicate that almost all of the Prospects who are going to buy the first time and become Clients do so within *three to four* years.

Question 9: What is the closing ratio (cases sold divided by cases opened) when selling to New Clients versus repeat sales to existing Clients?

Answer: Agents selling to New Clients *experienced a Closing Ratio of approximately 33 percent.* Agents selling to existing Clients *averaged better than 60 percent.*

No matter how experienced an Agent is, the closing ratio on prospective New Clients tends to be much less favorable than on repeat sales. Whether the Agent is young or old, experienced or relatively inexperienced, a 33 percent overall success ratio on Cases Opened on New Clients has seemed to be about par, whereas 60 percent or better is common on Cases Opened on others. It is important to point out that there is no reason to expect a different result for Financial Services Professionals selling financial products other than life insurance.

The key is to keep records so you can differentiate your effectiveness between selling new versus existing Clients. This allows you to implement corrections as needed to improve your success.

This evaluation of Cases Opened proved to be of such significance that it deserves special emphasis:

When all cases are recorded together – potential New Clients along with repeat sales, spouses, and children – a deceiving picture emerges that nearly always makes the experienced Financial Services Professional look as if they have the closing ratios of superstars. In reality, however, they are often only living off their own fat!

Furthermore, it is often discovered that the more experienced Agents have a poorer closing ratio on their Cases Opened with New Clients than the newer salesperson! With a hefty backlog of renewals and easy pickups on old Clients, these seasoned Financial Services Professionalss may not have the motivation to give it their all with tougher prospective New Clients.

Question 10: What is the average number of sales that can be expected from each New Client over time?

Answer: The statistics from this study revealed that, on average, each New Client would buy *four to six* times from the Financial Services Professional. It was found that a yearly block of 50 New Clients would ultimately account for between 200 to 300 annual sales over the Financial Services Professional's career. Some recent research has suggested that with the development of a wider variety of products, the ultimate number of purchases by one New Client is now between five and seven times.

Let's look at that result more carefully in light of the recent changes in the financial services industry. The Agents in the Granum Agency were almost exclusively selling life insurance during the research period. They did sell some annuities and disability insurance, but long-term care insurance, equities, and other financial products weren't available or weren't emphasized.

*The results showed that the more experienced Financial Professionals often had a poorer closing ratio on their Cases Opened **with New Clients** than the newer salesperson!*

Given the dramatic increase in the number of products Financial Services Professionals can now provide to their Clients, it seems reasonable to believe that the number of potential sales to a good Client could climb into the twenties or higher! Can you see why a long-term relationship based upon trust and regular contact is so critical to your success? In essence, the expansion of the potential role of the new financial services professional has made the practice of client building more valuable than ever!

The expansion of the potential role of the new financial services professional has made the practice of client building more valuable than ever.

What Do the Results Mean to You?

10–3–1

Perhaps the most important understanding to emerge from that data is the famous 10 - 3 - 1 ratio. Stated simply, it means that for every New Client you expect to add to your client base you will have to acquire and process ten Qualified Suspects and do three Fact Finding Interviews. The next graphic characterizes this famous relationship.

The Statistics of Client Acquisition

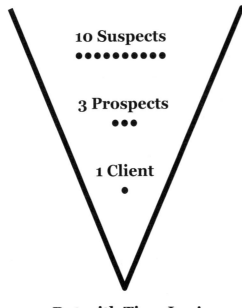

10 Suspects
●●●●●●●●●●

3 Prospects
●●●

1 Client
●

But with Time Lag!

Note there is a time lag!

The 10 - 3 - 1 ratio appears to be fairly straight-forward, but it is important to note there is a time lag in completing New Client Acquisition. All of the Qualified Suspects obtained in a given year who will ultimately become Prospects do not do so in the first year. The conversion from Prospect to Client has a time lag built in as well. Remember from the research that some of those who divulge Facts, and ultimately become Clients, do not buy immediately.

Time Lag From Year One to Year Five

Year One	Year Two	Year Three	Year Four	Year Five
100 Suspects				
30 Fact Finders				
6 → + *3* → + *1*			= *10* Clients	

Time Lag from Facts to Client

Statistics indicate that 40% of the Prospects who will ultimately become Clients will defer their initial purchase until the second or third year. If you fail to keep in touch, all 40% will be lost!

The results clearly measure a time lag between taking Facts (Confidential Questionnaire) and the Prospects agreeing to the first purchase. Facts interviews should result in the acquisition of New Clients at a rate of about 20 percent the first year, an additional 10 percent from the original group the second year, and a final 3 percent in the third and subsequent years. That will generate an eventual total of ten New Clients from each thirty new Facts taken.

A key point to note is that only 20 percent, or six of the thirty Prospects, will agree to buy in the first year. The other four Prospects will defer their purchase until years two or three. That means 40 percent of the Prospects who will ultimately become Clients will defer their initial purchase. Without a system to stay in touch with them, their business is lost! OCS provides this organized system that will guide your activities so you keep in touch and bring in this deferred business.

Are The Results Applicable to Financial Services Professionals other than Life Insurance Agents?

We suspect the findings regarding New Client Acquisition are also true for Financial Services Professionals other than life insurance Agents. It is hard to be sure because no one has done the longitudinal research on the various groups and markets. It seems fair to say that if other financial services professionals are using a comparable consultative sales process, the results should be similar.

Long Term Communication Is Difficult but Necessary

In order to accommodate the three-year purchase time lag, you must keep in touch with your Prospects for at least three years even though they haven't bought anything yet!

Not only must you stay in contact, but you must also keep records on those Prospects or you will never know how many would have ultimately become Clients. In short, without the OCS to keep you on track you would never realize you were missing out on 40 percent of your business simply because you failed to stay in touch.

This is even more important with the abundance of financial products you represent today. Now that you have more products to sell, it seems logical that a New Client is even more valuable than ever. How many ways can we emphasize the importance of understanding your New Client Acquisition statistics?

Given the Time Lag, How Many Suspects and Facts Do You Need to Achieve a Fast Start?

Consider this: If you are processing 500 (100 percent) Suspects a year, you can expect a flow of 150 (30 percent) Facts and fifty (10 percent) New Clients a year. But since there is no flow of New Clients in the early years from previously taken Facts, you should set a goal of acquiring more than 150 new Facts in order to get off to a fast start.

Based on recent experience with successful fast starters, we recommend acquiring 300 new Facts in your first year, 250 the second year, 200 the third, and 150 new Facts every year thereafter. If the pace of 300 the first year is a bit too rapid, approximately the same results will eventually be enjoyed if you obtain 250 new Facts for *each* of the first three years before dropping to the continuous 150 rate. Generating 150 Facts per year will ensure a constant influx of fifty New Clients, which research shows will guarantee increasing sales and income year after year.

What Happens to the Qualified Suspects Who Do Not Immediately Become Prospects?

The previous graphic illustrates that, on average, for every 100 Qualified Suspects processed you will obtain thirty Fact Finding Interviews. What happens to the other 70 percent of the Suspects who don't initially grant Facts? The research revealed that in the first full year approximately 35 percent of the Qualified Suspects processed were dead filed (never contacted again) and another 35 percent agreed to let the Financial Services Professional stay in touch. These Suspects are retained in the system to be contacted again with the goal that they ultimately grant Facts (Confidential Questionnaire) interviews, become Prospects, and, possibly, Clients.

The Importance of Fifty New Clients a Year

Without a backlog of Qualified Suspects and previously taken Facts to turn into New Clients, a new Financial Professional must generate a sizeable number of new Facts quickly

If a new Financial Services Professional were to take only 150 Facts a year in the early years, it would take close to four years to build to the rate of fifty New Clients per year. *That is much too long.* Without a backlog of renewals, or Repeat Sales from established Clients, the resultant slow sales pace would likely not generate the level of income desired by the new producer. The recommended rate and anticipated results are shown next.

New Client Acquisition Over First Ten Years

Years	Facts	(20%) 1	(10%) 2	(3%) 3	4	5	6	7	8	9	10
				of Facts from a given year						
1	300	60	30	9							
2	250		50	25	8						
3	200			40	20	6					
4	150				30	15	5				
5	150					30	15	5			
6	150						30	15	5		
7	150							30	15	5	
8	150								30	15	5
9	150									30	15
10	150										30
New Clients		60	80	74	58	51	50	50	50	50	50
Ancillary Sales 50%*		30	40	37	29	25	25	25	25	25	25
New Sales Made		90	120	111	87	76	75	75	75	75	75
Repeat Sales 1/5th**		0	18	42	64	82	97	112	127	142	157
Total Sales for Year		90	138	153	151	158	172	187	202	217	232
Cumulative Client Total Over Years		60	140	214	272	323	373	423	473	523	573

> * "Ancillary Sales" are sales to spouses, children, other dependents, business partners or key persons. It is estimated that you will sell about 50% of your new client total.

> ** The Repeat Sale number in each box assumes you will sell 1/5th of your cumulative client base and then add 50% more lives for the additional ancillary sales (Year 4 had a client base of 272. This means that in year 5 you would sell 20% of 272, or 54 lives, plus another 50% of the 54 for a total of 82 repeat sales).

New Clients

The table illustrates that a given group of Facts should generate New Clients at the rate of 20 percent the first year, 10 percent the second, and about 3 percent the third year. By generating 300 Facts the first year, you could expect sixty New Clients in year one, thirty more the second year, and nine the third year. Obtaining the recommended number of Facts each year can generate New Clients at the rate of sixty the first year, eighty the second, seventy-four the third, fifty-eight the fourth, and then leveling off at about fifty per year thereafter. As mentioned previously, if the 300 initial Facts pace seems too swift, similar results can be gained by taking 250 Facts a year (about twenty-one per month) for the first three years.

Ancillary Sales

In at least half (50 percent) of the cases when New Clients are acquired it should be possible to pick up additional sales from the same New Client. This can be accomplished by insuring the spouse, one or more of the children or other dependents. In a business case it may come in the form of insuring a business partner or a key employee. The additional sales also could come from equities, annuities, or other products. These additional sales are called Ancillary Sales and are shown on the table.

New Sales Made

This row illustrates the total number of New Sales Made per year, as attained through New Clients and Ancillary Sales. These totals, of course, do not include any Repeat Sales. Note that 100 sales are still within reach the first year.

Repeat Sales

In the second and subsequent years, about 20 percent of the previously sold clients can be expected to repeat. Another way of looking at this same result is to *assume that you will sell 1/5th (20 percent) of your client base in any given year*. When you add the Ancillary Sales that will accompany these you will reach your total Repeat Sales figure. For example, notice that Year 4 produced a base of 272 Clients. Assuming that you sold 1/5th of them in Year 5 you would have a Repeat Sales total of 272 divided by five, or fifty-four sales. When you consider the 50 percent Ancillary Sales that would result from these fifty-four, you add twenty-seven more Repeat Sales. This yields the Year 5 total of eighty-two Repeat Sales.

It is safe to assume that you will sell 1/5th (20%) of your client base in any given year

Total Sales for Year

This row shows the Total Sales each year. With a fast start you can be making over 200 sales in your eighth year!

Cumulative Client Total Over Years

This final sequence shows the cumulative total of Clients in your practice. Notice that 573 Clients can be obtained by the end of the 10th year. The table, however, assumes no attrition in Clients. We know, of course, that some Clients will drop out of our client base. Some will move, some will divorce, some will change advisors, some lapse their policies, and some will die. A rule of thumb suggests an attrition rate of between 9 and 10 percent in the first ten years of a practice. This would still result in a Fast Start Financial Services Professional obtaining over 500 Clients in the first ten years.

The Value of a New Client

Why New Clients Are So Important

Obviously, New Clients are important because they are the basis of your career development. But, consider these three specific reasons why they are so important to you:

1. They make life easier.

2. They offer great economic rewards.

3. They offer psychological rewards.

How Do New Clients Make Life Easier?

You only need to *sell* Prospects once. After that, they *buy* from you. Also, repeat sales take far less time than initial sales. The first sale is the toughest because you really must make three sales:

1. The sale of yourself.

2. The sale of your company.

3. The sale of your idea.

After this you only need to make one sale – the sale of a new idea or the continuation of an old one. This is much easier!

Repeat Sales Are up to Ten Times Faster

Granum's research revealed that it takes about twenty hours of hard work to acquire a new Client. Think about it. You have to get a referral; book an appointment; do your approach and take a Fact Finder; put the case together; present it; close it; if necessary get it underwritten and finally delivered. That takes about twenty hours. The research shows, however, that subsequent sales to the same Client only take between two to four hours. Most of the hard work has already been done and the critical trust has already been created.

If you use the OCS to maintain regular contact with your Clients and sustain and nurture these relationships, you will enjoy relatively effortless Repeat Sales to them and to their dependents. The combination of good service and a professional, caring relationship brings great rewards. They will buy everything from you. They will keep what they buy. And, they will refer you to their valued friends.

The Economic Value of New Clients

The economic value of a new Client can be estimated as illustrated in this conservative example.

The Economic Value of a New Client

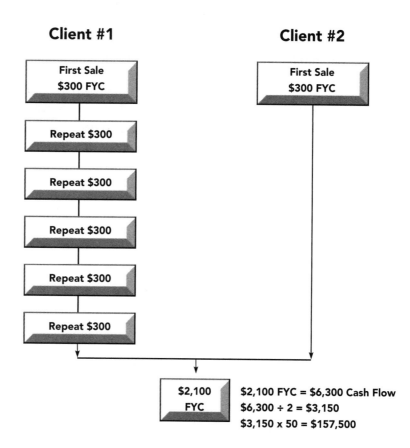

Consider a Financial Services Professional who closes an initial sale on Client #1 and Client #2. Each sale has a First Year Commission (FYC) of $300. Even if half of these New Clients (Client #2) never buy again, the total sales to these two New Clients will produce $2,100 in FYC. The assumption is that Client #1 will follow the industry average and make between five to seven core product (life or disability insurance only) purchases over time. That ultimately generates – including renewals, service fees, and company benefits – about $6,300 in cash flow, or an average of $3,150 per Client. Fifty New Clients per year can ultimately generate $157,500 ($3,150 x 50) in annual cash flow – on core products alone.

Of course, with the expanded range of products available to Financial Services Professionals today, the number of total sales and subsequent revenue should soar. Also, this formula does not account for any increase in average case size over the five Repeat Sales to Client #1. Experience shows that the last few sales tend to be significantly larger than the initial sale. Combine this with the prospective value of all of the business that flows from referrals from these two Clients, and you get a clear idea of just how valuable a New Client can be!

The Psychological Value of New Clients

Next we'll consider the psychological satisfaction that comes from developing an adequate number of New Clients. The bottom line shows the number of New Clients a Fast Start Financial Services Professional acquired during his first ten years in the business. The top line shows the total number of sales each year over that same period.

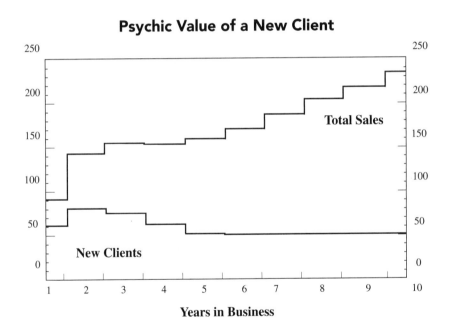

Psychic Value of a New Client

The top line, representing Total Sales, is fairly close to the bottom line in year one. Over time, however, the Total Sales line really takes off and continues at a very high level as long as it is supported by the annual input of fifty New Clients. As a matter of fact, the New Clients line could be reduced in later years and the Total Sales line would still continue – temporarily – at a high level. Eventually, though, the Financial Services Professional would plateau, decline, and lose the opportunity to achieve the desired personal freedom.

Increased sales and positive reinforcement

The psychological value here is twofold. The first is shown by the chart. It feels good to see your sales steadily climb over the years. The second involves the psychological concept of *positive reinforcement*. Behavior that is followed by positive reinforcement (some sort of reward) tends to increase.

Most Financial Services Professionals agree that it is exponentially beneficial to increase their activity to a level that will support New Client acquisition at the recommended rate of fifty per year. But this is difficult to do. The problem is that the day-to-day business world is filled with disappointments and setbacks that can be discouraging.

Unfortunately, such disappointments often lead to reductions in activity instead of to increases. Generally, most of us need a steady flow of positive reinforcement to overcome the negative forces and sustain high levels of productive activity. Obtaining a New Client adds significant positive reinforcement not only because of the economic value, but also because each resulting Repeat Sale provides a psychological lift. The continual sales that accompany fifty New Clients serve as constant *reinforcers* and make it much easier to maintain a good attitude and sustain our desired high activity levels.

Data Supports the Importance of a Fast Start

Many reading this book will be new Financial Services Professionals in their first year in the financial services business. This section is especially important for you – or for any Financial Sales Professional who wants to jump start a stalled career. A previous illustration showed the desired rate of New Client Acquisition during the first ten years in the business. The same illustration is reproduced here and clearly shows the power of obtaining 300 Facts in the first year.

New Client Acquisition Over First Ten Years

		(20%)	(10%)	(3%)	of Facts from a given year						
Years	Facts	1	2	3	4	5	6	7	8	9	10
1	300	60	30	9							
2	250		50	25	8						
3	200			40	20	6					
4	150				30	15	5				
5	150					30	15	5			
6	150						30	15	5		
7	150							30	15	5	
8	150								30	15	5
9	150									30	15
10	150										30
New Clients		60	80	74	58	51	50	50	50	50	50
Ancillary Sales 50%*		30	40	37	29	25	25	25	25	25	25
New Sales Sold		90	120	111	87	76	75	75	75	75	75
Repeat Sales 1/5th**		0	18	42	64	82	97	112	127	142	157
Total Sales for Year		90	138	153	151	158	172	187	202	217	232
Cumulative Client Total Over Years		60	140	214	272	323	373	423	473	523	573

Now let's compare this chart with an almost identical table with the only exception being that the new Financial Services Professional was able to obtain a steady flow of just 150 Facts during the first ten years.

New Client Acquisition With Only 150 Facts per Year

		(20%)	(10%)	(3%)	of Facts from a given year						
Years	Facts	1	2	3	4	5	6	7	8	9	10
1	150	30	15	5							
2	150		30	15	5						
3	150			30	15	5					
4	150				30	15	5				
5	150					30	15	5			
6	150						30	15	5		
7	150							30	15	5	
8	150								30	15	5
9	150									30	15
10	150										30
New Clients		30	45	50	50	50	50	50	50	50	50
Ancillary Sales 50%*		15	22	25	25	25	25	25	25	25	25
New Sales Sold		45	67	75	75	75	75	75	75	75	75
Repeat Sales 1/5th**		0	9	22	37	52	67	82	97	112	127
Total Sales for Year		45	76	97	112	127	142	157	172	187	202
Cumulative Client Total Over Years		30	75	125	175	225	275	325	375	425	475

First Year Commission Earned

Year	1	2	3	4	5	6	7	8	9	10
Ave. Case Size in First Year Commission	Earnings in Thousands of Dollars ($1,000's) Using a Fast Start of 300 Facts In Year One									
$300	27	41.4	45.9	45.4	47.3	51.5	56	60.5	65	69.5
$500	45	69	76.5	75.6	78.8	85.9	93.4	101	108	116
$700	63	96.6	107	106	110	120	131	141	152	162
	Earnings in Thousands of Dollars ($1,000's) Using Only 150 Facts Each Year									
$300	13.5	22.8	29.1	33.6	38.1	42.6	47.1	51.6	56.1	60.6
$500	22.5	38	48.5	56	63.5	71	78.5	86	93.5	101
$700	31.5	53.2	67.9	78.4	88.9	99.4	110	120	131	141

Notice that the New Clients growth does not reach fifty until the third year. Additionally, Total Sales for Year does not approximate 100 until year three. With the fast start the new Financial Services Professional makes almost 100 sales and obtains sixty New Clients in the first year!

Activity translates into FYC

You might ask, "So what?" The reason can be found in the First Year Commission earnings of these two Financial Services Professionals. Using a case size of $300 FYC, the Fast Start Financial Services Professional earns $27,000 in FYC in year one and $41,400 in year two. The 150 Facts Financial Services Professional earns only $13,500 in FYC in the first year and $22,800 in the second, *if there is a second year.*

Over time, the 150 Facts Financial Services Professional will grow and will do very well. Eventually, the renewals, the Repeat Sales, and the company bonuses will build nicely. The problem is that for many new Financial Services Professionals *there isn't time to wait.* They have financial requirements now and they must become profitable in their first year. The best way to guarantee longevity is to be certain to obtain between 250 to 300 Facts (Confidential Questionnaire) in your first year. That gets you off the launching pad. Put another way – *Under no circumstances allow yourself to fall below 150 Facts in your first three years* or you will be courting disaster. Twelve Facts per month is the absolute bottom number you can have and expect to survive.

Activity and Efficiency Points

How Much Activity Is Needed?

The science of the business shows us what we must do in order to succeed. We have learned that a new Financial Services Professional needs to process enough Qualified Suspects in his first year to generate between 250 and 300 Facts. This can be achieved by identifying 800 to 1,000 Qualified Suspects.

An experienced Financial Services Professional needs to process about 500 Qualified Suspects to generate 150 Facts in order to attain the desired fifty New Clients. The exact numbers will, of course, depend upon the Financial Services Professional's skills, natural markets, and the power of the referred lead nominators.

Using a Point System

The One Card System is unique in that it provides a built-in scorekeeping mechanism with which to judge your activity and efficiency levels. That scorecard is the "Activity and Efficiency Points" section of the *Success Manual* or *Productivity Planner*. This is where you record a daily point count that reflects your activity.

Your scorecard of activity and efficiency points

The points are called Activity and Efficiency Points because they not only track your daily business activity, but they give you a measure of your business efficiency for the month. Earning 100 points in a month is like operating at 100 percent efficiency. Sixty points a month suggests a business operating at 60 percent efficiency. It's something akin to grades in school. A grade of 90 to 100 points is clearly an "A"; 80 to 90 points is a "B"; 70 to 80 points is a "C"; and so forth.

Points are assigned for each type of significant activity in the client building process. In the previous discussion on what a new Financial Services Professional had to accomplish in order to become successful, several key activities were identified. All of these earn activity and efficiency points:

- Obtaining Qualified Suspects;

- Securing Fact Finding Interviews;

- Opening cases; and

- Conducting Closing Interviews.

The *Success Manual* also awards points for one further activity – Lunches (business meals of all types).

You earn points on the following basis:

- Each Qualified Suspect   1/2 point

- Each Lunch (or meal)   1 point

- Each Fact Finding Interview   1 point

- Each Case Opened   1 point

- Each Closing Interview   1 point

What Do Points Accomplish?

The daily and monthly points indicate whether or not you are giving yourself enough of a chance to succeed. That is, are you getting enough exposure in the market? Within reason, the higher the point count the greater the exposure and the better the opportunity to succeed. The point count is tallied every working day in the business. The *CAM® System* (discussed subsequently in this book) automatically calculates your average points earned per day, per month, and per kept appointment. It also calculates the average dollar value of each point in earned first year commission.

Points Keep You Focused

The point count is a very valuable tool for staying focused. The bane of most Financial Services Professionals is that they get sidetracked. They lose focus and before they know it several weeks or months have passed by and their momentum is gone. Recording your point count on a daily basis constantly exposes you to exactly what you have accomplished that day. Points do not measure hours spent in the business, but what actually was achieved. Hence, they are both activity *and efficiency* points.

Points Are Positive Reinforcements

A challenge in the financial services business is that many rewards are delayed or deferred. When a sale is made, the Financial Services Professional often doesn't get paid until the case goes through underwriting and is placed in force. Sometimes trusts, buy-sell agreements, or other legal matters must be completed before a sale can be finalized. The length of time between the initial referral and collecting the FYC check from the company can be weeks, months, or even years. If getting paid on a case is the positive reinforcer, it might come too late to have any immediate impact on the Financial Services Professional's activity or mood.

Psychology tells us that the real power of positive reinforcement isn't in the amount or size of the reward, but in its timing. A small reward delivered immediately can be much more powerful than a large award delivered much later. Activity and efficiency points can be powerful, positive reinforcements for Financial Services Professional activity because they are delivered *immediately* upon completion of the activity or accomplishment.

Points Measure Your Client Building Pace

Al Granum's twenty-eight years of actual management experience revealed some basic truths about the point system and success. A general guideline is that 1,400 points in the first year, 1,300 in the second year and 1,200 in the third and subsequent years are suggested for a fast start in the business. Naturally, these are approximate point counts. The exact points required are impacted by your selling skills, market, and ability to prospect for high quality referred leads.

- 1,400 points the first year
- 1,300 points the second year
- 1,200 points the third and subsequent years

Points Help You Earn Money

An interesting finding about the point system is that the dollar value of each point goes up dramatically with each incremental increase. In other words, the dollar value of the additional points over 100 per month is much greater than those of the points below 100. It is similar to a manufacturing business. Once you have passed your break-even point, all additional production is that much more profitable. The additional points above 100 earn you much more money. When you fully understand that idea you will find those additional points to be extremely motivating. To visually dramatize the principle, the next graph illustrates the dollar value of points calculated on a group of average first year Life Insurance Agents.

The Dollar Value of Points

Total Cash in Hand Over the First Year

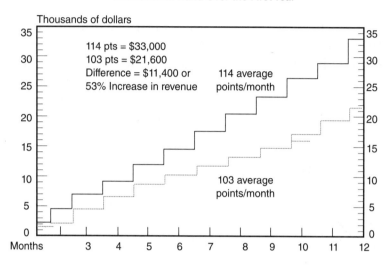

Note that the group represented by the lower line averaged 103 points per month for a year; the top group averaged 114 points per month for the same time period. The difference between the groups was eleven points per month, or about a 10 percent difference in points earned. The 114 point group, however, earned $33,000 while the 103 point group earned $21,600 for the year. Although the 114 point group only earned 10 percent more points, they earned over 50 percent more money! Marginal increments in earned points produce disproportionate increases in compensation.

Benefits of the Science to You

Predictable Relationships

Knowledge of what the record has been and of what par is makes the future more predictable. This lends excitement to the quest for improvement and offers a buffer against the anxiety that distracts so many otherwise talented Financial Services Professionals. The One Card System gives you the tools to understand the science of <u>your</u> business.

Chapter 3

Understanding the Original System

Why It's Important to Learn the Original Approach

It may strike you as funny to think about writing information on cards and filing them in a box. But it works. And many of today's most successful Financial Services Professionals and Managers continue to utilize the system as it was originally designed. This is why we still offer these products today even though they may appear outdated. It's also the reason many experienced Financial Services Professionals recommend that you use the system as originally designed for the first 90-180 days. This will enable you to understand the underlying philosophy of this business administration system as well as the organizational skills and professional habits it was designed to create.

In the second part of this book we will explain more modern methods for using the system. However, it's critical that you understand how the original system was designed and used in order to succeed with an automated approach today. Unfortunately, this isn't hit-or-miss. It's a proven process and it's important that you understand all aspects before transitioning to an automated approach.

So, continue reading... even if you don't plan to use the cards in your practice. You'll have the foundation needed for long-term success.

Managing Time and Relationships

The process of building a large clientele is really the process of building relationships. It has been said many times that "sales people are selling products, but customers are buying relationships." This is certainly true in the financial services profession. Relationships are built and maintained over time. Two primary keys to building solid, lasting relationships are:

1. You must earn your Clients' trust and respect by following through on your commitments. Simply put, you must do what you say you are going to do.

2. You must stay in touch on a regular basis.

At first glance, these goals may seem simple. The problem is that you must build and maintain relationships with hundreds and hundreds of people. As we've already discussed, a tremendous number of Qualified Suspects and Prospects must be processed in order to obtain enough Clients. During the first five years of your career, for example, over 3,000 Qualified Suspects must be processed in order to get off to a fast start. Without a system to record and manage all of those contacts you could not possibly keep track of them all. It would be difficult to keep all of the balls in the air. You may become overwhelmed and begin to forget commitments, thereby losing regular touch with Suspects, Prospects, and Clients. When that happens, relationships suffer. The One Card System will help ensure that doesn't happen.

Components of the Original System

The One Card System is much more than a card box. It is an integrated system of distinct components that work together to allow you to maximize your efficiency and effectiveness. The components of the original system include:

- Card File box;

- OCS *Control Booklet;*

- Prospect File Folder with Case History Notes;

- *One Thousand Clients* book;

- Confidential Questionnaire (Facts) form; and

- *Success Manual.*

The first four components will be discussed in detail throughout this section. Since the use of the *Success Manual* is central to the successful implementation of the system, an entire section has been devoted to it later in this book.

The *OCS Planner* is also available for those who prefer an annual appointment book rather than twelve monthly booklets. The *OCS Planner* combines the business functions of the monthly *OCS Control Booklets* and *Success Manual* in one comprehensive planning, appointment, and activity tracking calendar. An entire chapter has been devoted to the *OCS Productivity Planner* in the second section of this book. This chapter will focus on the coordinated use of the original OCS components.

Supplies

To properly understand the original version of the OCS, it is helpful to have at least a starter supply of the following materials (available in the *OCS Starter Kit*):

1. OCS Card File box, including the following:

   - Alphabetical, Monthly, and 1-31 index tabs;

   - Additions, Reject (Dead File), and Inactive (Quiet File) index tabs;

   - Yellow 3" x 5" Suspect cards;

   - White 3" x 5" Prospect cards;

   - OCS Control Card.

2. *OCS Control Booklets* (at least twelve) or an *OCS Productivity Planner/Calendar*

3. Prospect File Folders

   - Standard 9" x 12" lightweight manila file folders;

   - Case History sheets

4. One Thousand Clients book

5. Success Manual

6. Confidential Questionnaire (Facts) forms

The Distinction between a Qualified Suspect and Prospect

The OCS Card File, combined with the *OCS Control Booklet* and Case History, interact to guide your daily contacts. Before examining the implementation of these important tools, it is essential to review the differences between a Qualified Suspect and a Prospect.

> **Qualified Suspect** – A Qualified Suspect is an individual (or entity) about whom you have enough information to <u>suspect</u> you would like to have it as a Client. A Suspect is considered to be *qualified* when you know the name, occupation, approximate age and income, and the business address and telephone number.

> **Prospect** – A Prospect is a Qualified Suspect for whom a Fact Finding Interview has been conducted. It is not until the completion of a Fact Finding Interview that you will truly know enough about the Suspect to determine whether he, she, or it will be eligible to become a Client.

Keep in mind this is different from the conventional use of the word Prospect. In conventional sales language, the term Prospect is used to refer to any name or lead. In the OCS, a qualified lead is called a Qualified Suspect and only *after* a Fact Finding Interview is conducted will the individual become known as a Prospect.

With those two important distinctions in mind, let's return to the mechanics of the One Card System and learn the proper use of its components.

Setting up the Card File

A properly arranged OCS Card File will position the 1-31 index tabs first in the box, followed by the Monthly and the Alphabetical tabs. The index tabs labeled Additions, Reject, and Inactive should follow the Alphabetical tabs. The OCS Control Card should be placed in the very back of the box.

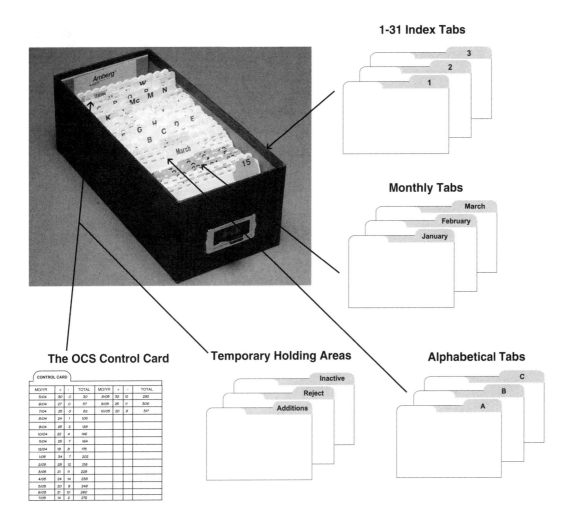

1-31 Index Tabs

Monthly Tabs

The OCS Control Card

Temporary Holding Areas

Alphabetical Tabs

The Daily 1-31 and Monthly Tabs:
For Qualified Suspects Only

Processing New Qualified Suspects

A Qualified Suspect, once again, is an individual about whom you have enough information to *suspect* you would like to have him or her as a Client. The individual may be someone you know, someone you have recently met, or a complete stranger to whom you have been introduced by a nominator. The first step is to prepare a yellow Suspect card when the individual is first qualified. Use a pencil or erasable pen to record the information since corrections are usually necessary.

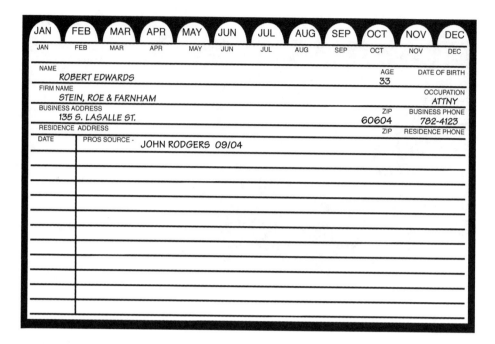

The yellow Suspect card will contain all known information about a Suspect, including a record of all conversations, until a Fact Finding Interview is conducted and a permanent file folder is created for the individual. At that point, the yellow Suspect card will then be taped to the first page of the Case History in the permanent file, where future contacts and conversations will be documented.

Where is the New Yellow Suspect Card Filed?

Once the information about the Suspect has been entered on the yellow Suspect card it is placed in the 1-31 section of the Card File. The index tabs are numbered 1-31 to correspond to the actual dates of the current month. The yellow Suspect card is placed behind the numerical tab corresponding to the date that the Qualified Suspect is to be called for an appointment.

The Next Step – Calling the Suspect

When the Suspect is called, the results and details of the conversation are recorded on the yellow Suspect card and it is moved forward through the 1-31 or Monthly tabs, or it is dead filed. We will next consider the four possible outcomes for this initial call: schedule an appointment; unable to schedule appointment but permitted to stay in contact; decide to discontinue contact based on findings of original call; or unable to reach the suspect.

What Happens to the Yellow Suspect Card?

Suppose a nominator gives you qualifying information about a Suspect on March 21 and agrees to introduce you by email, phone call, or some other method on March 22. Based on this, you determine you will call the Suspect on March 25 and place the yellow Suspect card behind the 25 tab of the 1-31 section in the Card File. When you call the Suspect on March 25, there will be four possible results:

1. The first and most desirable possibility is that you will schedule an appointment with the Suspect. In this case, the yellow Suspect card is moved to the 1-31 tab corresponding to the date of the appointment. Therefore, if the appointment is scheduled for April 2, the yellow Suspect card is placed behind the 2 tab.

2. The second possible outcome is that you are unable to secure an appointment but obtain permission to stay in touch with the Suspect. You may wish to ask for the Suspect's date of birth and record it on the yellow card. The card is then either moved forward to the month of the Suspect's birthday or an arbitrary six months ahead. The benefit of the former is that it allows you to arrange your follow up call near the Suspect's birthday to enhance relationship building opportunities with congratulatory wishes. Either way, the Suspect will be contacted at that future time when the Suspect card shows up again.

3. The third possibility is that you may decide, based on your conversation with the Suspect, to discontinue any future contact. The decision to dead file a Suspect is an important part of keeping the One Card System lean with good quality leads. When you dead file a Suspect, the yellow card is simply torn up and thrown away.

4. The final possibility is that you are unable to reach the Suspect within 30 days of acquiring the name and qualifying information. It is important that all Qualified Suspects be contacted within the first thirty days if the Card File is to remain lean with high quality leads. If you are unable to contact the Suspect within thirty days, the yellow Suspect card should either be destroyed or placed in the nominator's file for re-qualification. This is known as the Thirty-Day Rule.

The Research Results Concerning Your First Contact

While the objective in calling Qualified Suspects is to secure an interview, we know this will not always happen. OCS research has found that, on average, during the first contact:

- Thirty percent will grant an interview;

- Thirty-five percent will permit you to stay in touch and will have their yellow Suspect card moved ahead in the 1-31 or Monthly tabs; and

- Thirty-five percent will be dead filed.

Therefore, it is important to eliminate or dead file those Suspects who have no interest or inclination toward your services by calling *all* Suspects within thirty days. In so doing, the yellow Suspect cards remaining in your system will be those of either individuals who are very receptive – having agreed to an interview – or are known to be relatively receptive by granting permission to stay in touch.

The Section for Incomplete Yellow Cards

An informal but very important section of your OCS Card File is the section immediately in front of the 1-31 index tabs. This area holds yellow Suspect cards with the names of all individuals of interest for which you are missing some of the information required to turn them into Qualified Suspects.

Cards should never stay in the informal holding area for more than just a few days. You must either qualify them or eliminate them. There is no good reason for accumulating names that are not *live* or being actively processed through your OCS system.

The Alphabetical Tabs: For Prospects Only

The new White Prospect Card is filed behind the Additions Tab until the Monthly Planning Session.

Qualified Suspects Become Prospects

You will recall that a Qualified Suspect becomes an OCS Prospect upon completion of a Fact Finding Interview. At that time a white Prospect card, a Prospect File Folder, and a Case History sheet are created. If you are not able to obtain New Facts, then the Suspect's yellow card is simply moved to the next appropriate index tab or destroyed.

Preparing the White Prospect Card

The white Prospect card should include only the Prospect's name, date of birth, and the source of the Prospect. Summaries of all conversations with the Prospect are now to be recorded on the Case History sheet in the Prospect's File folder, not on the white Prospect card.

To properly prepare a white Prospect card, remove all of the monthly tabs from the top of the card except for the one indicating the Prospect's month of birth. The card is then filed behind the Additions tab where it will be temporarily held until your monthly planning session (conducted at the end of the third week of each month) for inventory tabulation purposes. *At that time*, the card will be moved to the Alphabetical section of the OCS Card File for Automatic contact twice a year. As will be explained in more detail later, one automatic contact will occur on or shortly before a birthday and the other contact about six months later. These twice yearly contacts are referred to as *Automatics*.

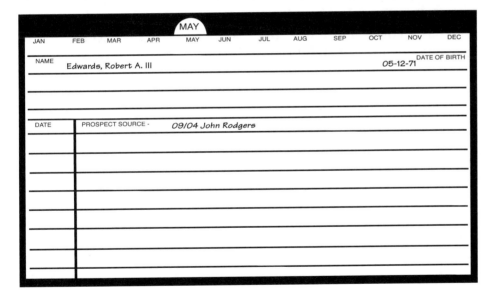

Temporary Holding Sections

There are a few special index tabs that are placed in the back of the OCS Card File box, immediately behind the A-Z section, and signify holding areas for white Prospect cards before they are processed:

1. Additions;

2. Reject (sometimes labeled Dead File); and

3. Inactive (sometimes labeled Quiet File).

These areas help keep the Alphabetical section of your Card File box as lean as possible. Only the white cards of the highest quality Prospects and active Clients should reside in the system.

Additions Tab

As we have just discussed, when a new white Prospect card is prepared it will ultimately be added to the Alphabetical section of the OCS Card File. Initially, however, the new Prospect card is placed behind the Additions tab and is temporarily held there for your inventory count during your monthly planning session. After the Control Card is updated, these new white cards will be filed in the Alphabetical section for automatic twice yearly follow-up.

Reject (Dead File) Tab for Rejected Prospects

Keep in mind that the white cards in your Card File should represent *active* Prospects and Clients. There will be situations in which some of your Prospects do not initially act on your recommendations. As previously covered, the Granum research found that 40 percent of individuals who ultimately become Clients defer their initial purchases to the second or subsequent years. Consequently, if a Prospect does not purchase a product initially, you must decide whether or not to stay in touch through the automatic, twice yearly contact schedule of the OCS.

Some of the Prospects with whom you keep in touch will eventually act on your recommendations and will, therefore, become Clients. Others will continue to procrastinate after repeated contacts or give other reasons not to act on your recommendations. In those situations you may determine that further contact is unwarranted and will decide to remove those Prospect cards from your OCS Card File. The Reject (Dead File) tab holds the white cards of Prospects you wish to discard from your OCS until your monthly planning session.

Inactive (Quiet File) Tab for Inactive Clients

As your practice matures there will be Clients who have either purchased all they are going to purchase, or who no longer meet your minimum specifications for an Active Client. In either case, you will need to remove them – their white card – from your active OCS.

If, however, you simply remove their card, your OCS Control Card won't have an accurate inventory count. In order to be prepared for the monthly planning session, use the Inactive tab to temporarily hold the white cards of the Clients you wish to remove.

The OCS Control Card

An Inventory of Relationships

As you build and maintain your OCS, you will track your progress by maintaining a record of the number of active white cards in your system. This record is maintained on a simple index card called the OCS Control Card that is located in the very back of the Card File. The OCS Control Card represents an inventory of your active business relationships.

CONTROL CARD							
MO/YR	+	-	TOTAL	MO/YR	+	-	TOTAL
5/04	30	0	30	8/05	32	12	292
6/04	27	0	57	9/05	25	11	306
7/04	25	0	82	10/05	20	9	317
8/04	24	1	105				
9/04	25	2	128				
10/04	22	4	146				
11/04	25	7	164				
12/04	19	8	175				
1/05	34	7	202				
2/05	28	12	218				
3/05	21	11	228				
4/05	24	14	238				
5/05	20	9	249				
6/05	21	10	260				
7/05	14	2	272				

During your monthly planning session you will tally the number of white cards being added to your system from the Additions tab, along with the total number of deletions from the Rejects and Inactive tabs. The net result of this tally will be recorded on the OCS Control Card, allowing you to keep track of your monthly progress. Your objective is to build to the level of 500 white Prospect cards within your first three years, without compromising quality.

How Many Additions and Deletions Can You Expect?

As you build the number of white Prospect cards to your goal of 500, you will probably find that your additions and deletions will average from twenty to twenty-five names per month. Even in a well-seasoned card file, the turnover is quite rapid, which you will discover if you do your job properly. Notice in the OCS Control Card illustration that the Prospect cards grew fairly rapidly in the early months. Once the representative started calling the Automatics, however, deletions began and the net gain slowed significantly.

Keep an eye on this continuous record. A drop-off in either input or output is a serious warning sign that can indicate inadequate prospecting or lack of attention to the elimination of deadwood. Those who are either rejected or quiet filed must be replaced if stagnation is to be avoided.

Only the Best Get In and Stay In

Remember that any card in the 1-31, Monthly or Alphabetical sections of the OCS Card File box is considered to be a Qualified Suspect, an active Prospect, or an Active Client. The Suspects (yellow cards) go behind the 1-31 or Monthly tabs. The Prospects and Clients (white cards) are filed behind an Alphabetical tab. All Prospects and Clients filed in this Alphabetical section must be contacted twice each year. If you don't contact them all at least twice a year, a process called anti-selection will begin to occur.

What Is Anti-Selection?

Think about it. If you don't contact all of the Suspects, Prospects, and Clients when the system signals you to do so, you will probably begin to contact only those you feel good about. Who, then, will you continue to sell? Obviously, you will sell the people you continue to contact. Those people will eventually become satisfied and saturated and will no longer be considered active. At that point, you will remove them from the system and quiet file them.

What does this mean to your business? Over time, the majority of the cards remaining in the Card File will represent Suspects and Prospects that you do not feel like calling. Anti-selection means you are slowly reducing your OCS to *only those people you do not want to call*. Soon the idea of using the OCS becomes aversive and you stop benefitting from it all together.

We all have a tendency to have preconceived notions about our Suspects and Prospects. The OCS prevents us from acting upon those pre-judgments. Don't let anti-selection happen to you. Call them all.

The Prospect File Folder

When a Qualified Suspect becomes a Prospect, you will prepare a Prospect File Folder in addition to the white card. The Case History is an exceedingly important part of the file as it will contain all records of contacts or conversations with the Prospect or Client.

The Benefits of Keeping a Case History

An updated Case History will benefit you in several ways:

- It shows Prospects and Clients that you care about them because you will be able to pick up threads of previous business and personal conversations.

- It will help you eliminate Prospects that seem *live* but aren't. If Prospects procrastinate, you will record their reasons. After that happens several times, you will review their prior reasons with them and together determine if further contact is warranted.

- A careful record of Client contact helps protect you in cases of potential litigation. A written record of contacts and conversation summaries is very important and is part of the documentation of your professional conduct.

- The Case History will also indicate when no additional business is anticipated from a Client who has been saturated and satisfied. They would then be placed on an inactive status and quiet filed. While you will still service inactive Clients through periodic statements or correspondence, you will no longer proactively contact those Clients on a twice yearly basis.

Setting up the Prospect File

Using a standard 9" x 12" manila file folder, add the individual's full name (last name first for alphabetical filing) and date of birth on the tab. The folder itself should contain the following information along with any other materials required by your company.

- The Facts form or Confidential Questionnaire. This should be kept on top for ease of reference to telephone numbers, spouse or children's names, and other pertinent information you may need when contacting them.

- Case History Notes. This is a chronological record of your contacts and conversations with each Prospect. These sheets should be paper clipped together with the most recent page on top.

- Copies of correspondence, proposals, applications, and any other information necessary to round out the file. These documents are all filed after the Confidential Questionnaire or Facts form and Case History with the latest material on top.

CASE HISTORY SHEET FOR: PHONE:

DATE	TIME	COMMENTS

JAN FEB MAR APR MAY JUN JUL AUG SEP OCT NOV DEC
JAN FEB MAR APR MAY JUN JUL AUG SEP OCT NOV DEC

NAME	EDWARDS, ROBERT A. II	AGE 33	DATE OF BIRTH
FIRM NAME	STEIN, ROE & FARNHAM		OCCUPATION Attny
BUSINESS ADDRESS	135 S. LASALLE ST.	ZIP 60604	BUSINESS PHONE 782-4123
RESIDENCE ADDRESS			RESIDENCE PHONE

DATE	PROS SOURCE - JOHN RODGERS 09/04
9/4	P.A. letter mailed
9/7	Phoned – not in; Phoned, ✓ 9/10 his office 1:00
9/10	Stood-up, lunch-big client; asst. resch'd ✓
	to 9/17 @ 11:30 his office
9/17	✓ Rush approach but was impressed.
	Next ✓ my office 9/24 @ 10:30 for Facts.

DATE	TIME	COMMENTS
9/24	10:30-12:00	My office. Good conditions, Took Facts. Wants
		"finer things" for family. Sincere – high
		character. Priorities: 1.) Family Protection
		2.) College Funding 3.) Retirement Planning
		Next appt. he & wife here @ 4:00 on 9/30.
		RL: - Brother – Frank E. – Attny also – NL.

The Control Booklet

A Key Component

The *OCS Control Booklet* was developed to be more than an appointment book or pocket planner – it is a key component for building your clientele. It works with the other tools of the One Card System to coordinate and implement your monthly work plan. Together, they form an integrated system that permits you to plan and control your daily activities.

Always With You

Your *OCS Control Booklet* should always be with you. You should also maintain a one year supply of *Control Booklet*s in your desk so that notations can be made for future months' activities.

Nine Sections

The *OCS Control Booklet* is divided into nine sections. Of course, today you can set up a similar function on your iPhone, Droid, or tablet to include these sections:

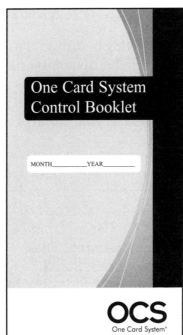

1. Instructions

2. Birthday Automatics

3. Review Automatics

4. Non-Automatics

5. Daily Pages

6. Month at a Glance Calendar

7. Appointment Spread Sheet

8. Unfinished Priority Work

9. New Suspects

Instructions Page

Instructions for the abbreviations used to record your daily activities and accomplishments are outlined on the first page. Included is the valuable Dot and Check Mark system for recording your phone activity.

The Automatics Pages

The next three sections of the *Control Booklet* are called Automatics pages because they are used to record Prospect and Suspect contacts that are automatically prompted either by the white cards or by the producer. As previously mentioned, all active Prospects and Clients must be contacted twice per year – once on or near their birthday and again six months later. Birthday contacts are called Birthday Automatics. The contacts scheduled for six months later are called Review Automatics. Contacts that are scheduled for other reasons are called Non-Automatics. The *Control Booklet* works together with the Card File box to prompt these automatic contacts. It is the regular nature of those contacts that continues to build the quality and trust of these relationships.

Birthday Automatics

Birthday Automatics are scheduled contacts with a Prospect or Client whose birthday will occur in the month associated with the Control Booklet. The purpose of the automatic is to trigger a phone call and, perhaps, a birthday lunch. That lunch meeting provides an excellent opportunity for Referred Lead Prospecting or other marketing efforts.

During the monthly planning session, you will prepare your work plan for the upcoming month. Your work plan includes identifying and listing all of the Prospects and Clients that you intend to contact that month. You will identify your upcoming Birthday Automatics and list them in your *Control Booklet* on the Birthday Automatics pages.

The first step is to identify the Prospects and Clients whose birthdays will occur in the month you are planning. You will recall that when the white cards were created all of the monthly tabs were removed except for the month of the Prospect's birth. Simply go to the A-Z section of your OCS Card File and run your finger along the tabs of the month you are planning. These are the individuals who will have birthdays in that month. Pull these cards up, not out, and record the name and date of the birthday on the Birthday Automatics pages.

For example, if your monthly planning session is on May 19, you will be looking for June tabs. The following illustration shows a properly completed Birthday Automatics page.

June Birthdays

No.	Birthday	Name	Result
1	9	Allen, C.	
2	26	Bergstrom, J.	
3	2	Carter, K.	
4	6	Gonzalez, T.	
5	28	Kohler, A.	
6	23	Lowenthal, L.	
7	6	Mills, H.	
8	14	Nolan, C.	
9	7	Parker, E.	
10	19	Rawlston, P.	
11	21	Sorenson, T.	
12	15	Tabor, W.	
13	5	Wallace, D.	
14	30	Williams, B.	
15	11	Young, D.	
16	16	Zeder, F.	

When you have completed this task you will notice that the names are listed in alphabetical order. This allows you to quickly update the Results of contacts or appointments and evaluate your effectiveness during these excellent prospecting opportunities.

You will then transfer the names to the top of the Daily Page representing the day you wish to place the birthday call. When a birthday lunch is desired, schedule the contact at least one week prior to the birthday. If the call is simply to provide congratulatory greetings, schedule the contact either the day of the birthday, or the business day before the birthday. Appropriate language for Birthday Automatic phone calls can be found in the Pre-Approach, Telephoning, and Approach chapter of this book. Birthday Automatic phone scripts for assistants can be found in the chapter on Self-Management.

Review Automatics

Review Automatics represent your second scheduled contact with Prospects and Clients each year. For clients, the purpose is to trigger a telephone call six months after their birthday for the purpose of offering to conduct a review of their financial and insurance program. Prospects who have not acted on your previous recommendations are also contacted at this time for the purpose of scheduling an appointment to review the discussions that took place during the Fact Finding and Closing Interviews. Your objective is to determine if the previous recommendations are still appropriate and to encourage the Prospect to act on them!

In order to identify Review Automatics for the month you are planning you must go through the Alphabetical section of the OCS Card File box again, just as you did when identifying Birthday Automatics. This time, however, you will be looking for the exposed tabs that are *six months prior to the month you are planning*.

Again, using a May 19 planning date, you will be identifying the Review Automatic calls that you will make in the month of June. Therefore, you will be looking for the cards that have a birthday tab that is six months prior to June which, in this case, would be the December tabs. Pull the cards up, not out, and record the names on the Review Automatics page in your *Control Booklet*. An example is shown below.

Review Automatics (December Birthdays)

No.	Birthday	Name	Result
1		Abbott, S.	
2		Chen, P.	
3		Donovan, K.	
4		Ellis, G.	
5		Ivorsen, K.	
6		Martinez, A.	
7		Matthews, J.	
8		O'Niel, B.	
9		Rollins, S.	
10		Tanaka, N.	
11		Taylor, C.	
12		Ungstaad, L.	
13		Vanelli, E.	
14		Warren, P.	

The names of these individuals should then be transferred to the top of the *first ten* Daily Pages of the *OCS Control Booklet*. You want to call Review Automatics as early in the month as possible in order for the review to be scheduled in the same month.

Again, a Results column is provided on the Review Automatics pages to allow you to quickly assess your effectiveness during these business-producing appointments. Scripts for your Review Automatics phone calls can be found in the Pre-Approach, Telephoning and Approach chapter of this textbook. Recommended language for assistants can be found in the Self-Management chapter.

Do Not Prejudge the Selections

When you list the Birthday and Review Automatics, do not attempt to prejudge the strength of any given Prospect or Client. Do not make any personal selections. If a card is in the OCS Card File box, you must enter the name on the appropriate page of the *Control Booklet*.

Do not attempt to evaluate OCS Prospects in a vacuum! Eliminate cards only on the basis of repeated negative reactions to your automatic contacts. If you contact only those you think have the best potential, you will soon find yourself a victim of the anti-selection we explained earlier. Again, since you would be eliminating names chosen only from those whom you feel would be apt to buy, your poorer Prospects would remain in your system as expensive, nonmotivating dead wood.

Non-Automatics

The next section is for listing Non-Automatics. These are OCS Prospects or Clients who will be called during the upcoming month for some special reason, even though they are between Birthday and Review Automatic dates. These calls are not triggered by Prospect cards but by you. That is, if you have some special reason you want to contact a Prospect or Client in the upcoming month, then record the name in the Non-Automatics section of that month's *Control Booklet*.

Recording Future Non-Automatic Contacts

You should always have twelve *Control Booklets* for the upcoming months in your desk drawer. When a Prospect makes a legitimate request for a future call back at a time other than one of the Automatics, you simply enter the name on the Non-Automatic page in the front of the appropriate *Control Booklet*. This Non-Automatic list should never be long. Unless there is a very special reason for the Non-Automatic time, simply permit the name to come up on the next regular Automatic. If there is any doubt, ask the Prospect. You might try the following:

"I'll be happy to give you a call in February if you'd like to get together then. However, my records indicate we're due for a call in April. Would that work or do you have a more immediate need?"

Chances are the Prospect will agree and you can forego the additional contact because he or she will turn up automatically the following April. This is an example of how the automatic operation of the system can keep you from falling into a pattern of demoralizing callbacks.

The Daily Pages

The top section of your *Control Booklet* Daily Page is for transferring the names from the Birthday, Review, and Non-Automatics lists. Simply record those at the top of the Daily Page corresponding to the date that you want to make the call. Each day *pull the file folders* for the list of names at the top of that Daily Page. The complete file should be kept in front of you so you can review previous conversations for valuable background information and then make appropriate notations during the actual call. If you fail to reach someone whose name has been listed, draw a wavy line through the name and move that name forward to the next working day. If you do reach the person and dispose of the name, cross it off by drawing a straight line through it.

Check Your Plan versus Your Results

The center section of each Daily Page will be used to plan your activity and appointments for the day and record your accomplishments as they occur.

Note that the results of appointment and phone activity are recorded in the accomplishments section. As you dial, record your activity and results using the following codes. These codes are also explained on the Instructions page of the *Control Booklet*.

- Use a dot every time a dial is made.

- Change the dot to a check mark if the individual is reached and spoken with.

- Cross the check mark with a slash mark when no appointment is obtained but the Suspect grants permission to stay in touch.

- Cross the check mark with a double slash if an appointment is agreed upon.

At the end of the day, accomplishments are posted to the *Success Manual*, which will be explained in detail in the next chapter. Any activities that were not accomplished are moved forward to the next business day and the entire page is X-ed out.

BIRTHDAY		Telephoning	Telephoning	Telephoning	Night Telephoning
~~Gonzalez~~	6	~~Tanaka~~			
~~Parker~~	7	~~Taylor~~			
~~Tabor~~ ∧∧	15	~~Ungstadd~~			
		~~Rollins~~			

Hour	ACTIVITY	ACCOMPLISHMENT
7:30	Prepare for day	
8:00	Case Prep	Ivorsen
9:00	Telephoning	⨯ ... ⨯ ⨯ ... ✓ . ⨯ ...
		.. ⨯ . ✓ ... ⨯ .. ⨯ .
10:30	Collins, A-CL	(⨯) VA pres.; decision ⨯ 6/9
11:30	Mills, H-BL	(⨯) 4QS
2:00	Tollefson, B.-AP	(⨯) FF, CO - Life
4:00	Mackey, P-AP	Resch'd to 6/8 (.. ✓ .. ⨯ .)
5:00	Admin	
	↓	
6:30	Abbott, S-CL	(⨯) Bot. LTC, 2QS

OFFICE WORK:

   Case Prep: ~~Ivorsen~~

    (Dialing Totals: 36-11-6)

OUTSIDE ACTIVITIES:

EXPENSES:

   Business Meal $9.50; Parking $3

Month at a Glance Calendar

This section contains a monthly calendar to help you identify your available selling time. Record all firm or office meetings, training classes, conferences, holidays or other nonselling commitments. Then calculate the amount of time you have available for field appointments or phone calls, drawing your attention to the amount of selling versus non-selling time available in the month. Divide the number of field days available into your monthly OCS Activity and Efficiency point goal (100 OCS points per month for experienced representatives) to determine your *daily* point goal for the month.

Month at a Glance

Month ___June___   Year ___2006___

MON	TUE	WED	THU	FRI	SAT/SUN
			1	2 — 10:30 Client Builder 12:30 Meeting	3 Study ChFC / 4
5	6	7	8	9	10 Fly to San Diego / 11 MDRT
12	13	14	15	16	17 Study ChFC / 18
	← MDRT ANNUAL MTG. →				
19	20	21	22	23	24 Study ChFC / 25
26	27	28	29	30 — 1:00 ChFC ↓ Exam	

Appointment Spread Sheet

The Appointment Spread Sheet offers you an overall view of your month's appointment schedule. Transfer any non-selling commitments, such as training sessions or firm meetings, to the appropriate time slots on your Appointment Spread Sheet. Then, highlight all available appointment time periods and strive to fill them all!

While calling for appointments, which should be done at a scheduled time each day, have your Appointment Spread Sheet open before you. Many Financial Services Professionals schedule phone calls every day from 9:00 a.m. until 10:00 a.m. Attempt to fill every appointment hour without too much regard to the geographical location of the OCS Prospect or Suspect.

Normally, from one third to one half of your scheduled appointments will be postponed or canceled so that even a day that starts out fully booked will probably provide adequate flexibility. If it does not and you find yourself running short of time, you can always call ahead and reschedule the next appointment yourself. Create a schedule with set appointment time slots. Doctors, lawyers, and hair stylists have set appointment times, and so should you. Avoid changing the hours shown. Professional business people do not and neither should you! A sample of a typical Appointment Spread Sheet is shown for your reference.

Appointment Spread Sheet

#	Day	7:30	9:00	10:30	11:30	1:00	2:00	3:00	4:00	5:00	6:30	#
1	THURS	Prep.	Telephone	Torrelli, M.		York, M.	Jacobs, T.		Kraus, M.			1
2	FRI	Prep.	Telephone	CLIENT	BLDR. MTG.	Carter, K.		Collins, A.		Abbott, S.		2
3	SAT	Study	Telephone	←	STUDY	ChFC →						3
4	SUN		Telephone									4
5	MON	Prep.	Telephone	Fredricks, N.		Wallace, D.		Ivorsen, K.		Kraus, M.		5
6	TUES	Prep.	Telephone	Collins, A.	Mills, H.		Tollefson, B.		Mackey, P.		Abbott, S.	6
7	WED	Prep.	Telephone	Jacobs, T.	Martinez, A.	Harris, D.		York, M.				7
8	THURS	Prep.	Telephone	Lake, P.	Donovan, K.	Stuart, C.	Torrelli, M.		Mackey, P.			8
9	FRI	Prep.	Telephone	Ivorsen, K.	Young, D.	Harris, D.		Collins, A.		Fredricks, N.		9
10	SAT		Telephone				MDRT					10
11	SUN		Telephone									11
12	MON		Telephone									12
13	TUES		Telephone									13
14	WED		Telephone									14
15	THURS	Prep.	Telephone	Jacobs, T.	Tabor, W.		Torrelli, M.		Stuart, C.	Donovan, K.		15
16	FRI	Prep.	Telephone	Mackey, P.	O'Niel, B.	Zeder, F.		Harris, D.	Tollefson, B.	Adams, E.		16
17	SAT	Study	Telephone	←	STUDY	ChFC →						17
18	SUN		Telephone									18
19			Telephone									19
20			Telephone									20
21			Telephone									21
22			Telephone									22
23			Telephone									23
24			Telephone									24
25			Telephone									25
26			Telephone									26
27			Telephone									27
28			Telephone									28
29			Telephone									29
30			Telephone									30
31			Telephone									31
	Day	7:30	9:00	10:30	11:30	1:00	2:00	3:00	4:00	5:00		

Unfinished Priority Work

This section is used to list unfinished priority tasks. Routine case preparation and proposals should be prepared immediately and never entered here. However, work related to reviews, deliveries, service, elaborate estate planning, business insurance, and joint-work proposals may be listed here and crossed off when completed.

New Suspects

This is simply a sheet upon which to list potential new Suspects, should you not have yellow Suspect cards on hand when you identify a name and qualifying information.

Final Comments

This completes the nine sections of the *OCS Control Booklet*. The point needs to be stressed that the *Control Booklet* is specifically designed for the activities of the financial services professional. It works hand in hand with the OCS Card File, Prospect File folders, and the *Success Manual*. When you add the *One Thousand Clients* book you have a complete and integrated system for administering your client building process.

In the upcoming chapter on the *OCS Productivity Planner* you will see that the planner provides all of the same functions as twelve *OCS Control Booklets* and includes a complete *Success Manual*.

The One Thousand Clients Book

Premature Retrogression

The motivation for creating the One Card System came in part from the following observation by Al Granum:

> "By far the most important lesson I've learned in almost forty years in the industry is that many career agents who devote their lifetime to our business *prematurely retrogress*. That is, they begin to drift off of the client building mission and the health and vigor of their practice begins to slowly wind down. Often this occurs without the agent even being fully aware of what is happening. This is primarily because he pays insufficient attention to *the quantity and the quality* of his active clientele."

You can avoid this tragedy by using the *One Thousand Clients* book. As previously explained, clients are paying entities – checkbooks or accounts – and an Active Client is one you believe is likely to need additional products or services and likely to buy from you again. Obtain more than 1,000 if you wish, fewer if you want, but in any event, it is imperative that you know the truth and that you watch your trend.

Attention to client building is necessary because of the curve (curse) of *premature retrogression*, which is illustrated below. The dotted curve represents typical premature retrogression. What does this mean? It means that the successful financial representative – one who regularly qualifies for the MDRT – tends to plateau in FYC production. Income climbs as renewals and fees pile up, but actual productivity – as measured by new FYC production – plateaus and retrogresses.

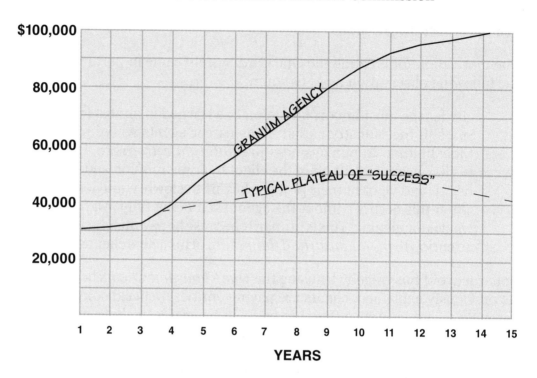

Annualized Core Product First Year Commission

The *One Thousand Clients* book has been designed to help you stay focused on the quantity and quality of your clientele. It measures your progress toward the *Magnificent Obsession* of obtaining 1,000 paying entities in your career. It keeps you focused on the client building mission.

If you are new to the financial services profession, you will want to start keeping records with your very first New Client. Experienced producers may begin by listing only currently Active Clients who have good potential for additional sales. A portion of a new producer's first year entries might look something like this:

NEW CLIENTS								
Consecutive New Client Number	Month / Year	Active Client Number	Name	Age	Occupation	Income	FYC Premium	Future FYC* Premium
1	1 / 199-	1	Jones, Tom/Eliz.	28/26	Med. Intern/R.N.	24/45	820	6,000?
2	1 / 199-	2	Smith, William	30	Elec. Engr.	51	820	1500
3	1 / 199-	3	Fox, Gordon/Susan	28/28	Systems Anlst./ Teacher	65/42	760	1500
4	1 / 199-	✗	Townsend, Barbara	34	CPA	42	1100	Transfrd.
5	2 / 199-	5	Swenson, Robert	45	Sales Mgr.	60	1800	1000
	/							
70	5 / 199-	69	Andrews, Sam	31	Architect	75	750	2000
71	5 / 199-	70	Parker Industries	Inc. 1989	Building Supplies	–	3500	5000
72	5 / 199-	71	Nordell, Debra/Jim	35/36	Orthodontist/ M.D.-Gen.Pract.	200/120	2800	6000+
73	/							
74	/							
75	/							

*Make Future FYC/Premium column entries in pencil until the client dies or is positively deactivated.

The One Card System research revealed that Clients who were well served over the years purchased an average of five to seven core products (more when you consider equity sales). So, in addition to demographic information, the *One Thousand Clients* book asks the representative to estimate the future first year commission that is probable, based on his or her knowledge of the facts and circumstances of the Client. This is a more accurate representation of the economic value of a Client than first year commission alone.

Composite Client Evaluation

At the end of each year, after X-ing those who are no longer active and reestimating future FYC for those who remain, the one year summary line should be completed on the Composite Client Evaluation page as shown below.

	COMPOSITE CLIENT EVALUATION							
YEAR	Year-to-Date			Current Year Only				FUTURE POTENTIAL FYC Premium
	Clients			Average			FYC Premium	
	Plus	Minus	Total	Age	Income	FYC Premium	Income	
1997	12	0	12	28.0	32,581	490	1.50	14,600
1998	80	5	87	29.7	36,206	532	1.47	83,600
1999	61	8	140	32.1	38,750	589	1.52	142,960

The process of formulating the Composite Client Evaluation allows you to track the average age, income, and first sale FYC of the New Clients you are adding each year. It also allows you to track the total number of Active Clients in your client base, along with their total future first year commission potential. Many financial services professionals consider this number to be part of the goodwill value of their practice. That is, future potential first year commission represents the value of the relationships they have developed, excluding referrals, *if they stay in touch* with their Clients and serve them well.

Least Acceptable Suspects

To a large extent, the level of success that you will reach in your career is dependent on the economic potential of your clientele. Of course, this is a function of the initial screening of the new Suspects that are added to your One Card System. Therefore, the Least Acceptable New Suspects page of the *One Thousand Clients* book is provided for you to record the minimum acceptable profile (age, income, and occupation) of the new Suspects you will knowingly allow into your OCS each year.

Annualized Core Product First Year Commission

Use this chart to graph your annualized core product first year commissions for each year of your career. The chart provides a visual representation of your actual achievements and will help you avoid the trap of premature retrogression we spoke of earlier.

The Client Acquisition Process:
A Graphic Summary

Let's take a moment to review a graphic summary of the New Client Acquisition process. What are the sequences of events and OCS components you will use to obtain a New Client?

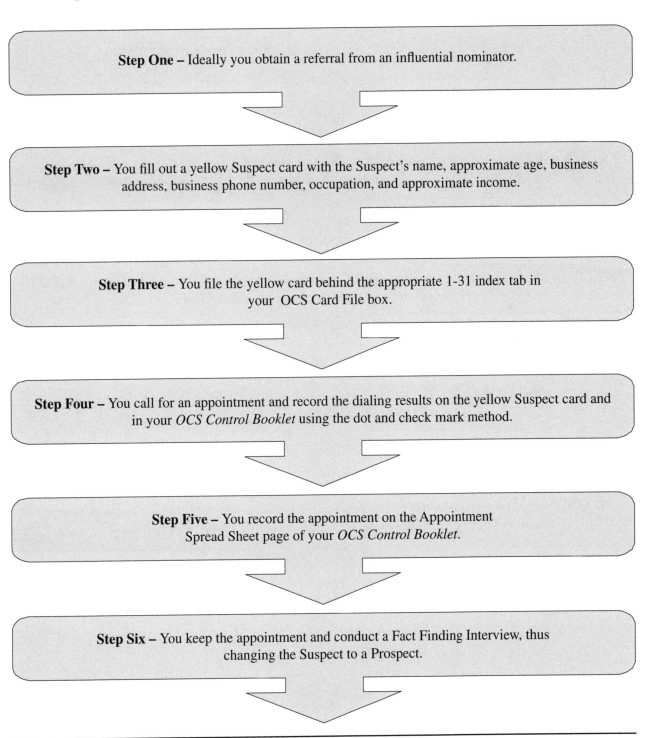

Step One – Ideally you obtain a referral from an influential nominator.

Step Two – You fill out a yellow Suspect card with the Suspect's name, approximate age, business address, business phone number, occupation, and approximate income.

Step Three – You file the yellow card behind the appropriate 1-31 index tab in your OCS Card File box.

Step Four – You call for an appointment and record the dialing results on the yellow Suspect card and in your *OCS Control Booklet* using the dot and check mark method.

Step Five – You record the appointment on the Appointment Spread Sheet page of your *OCS Control Booklet*.

Step Six – You keep the appointment and conduct a Fact Finding Interview, thus changing the Suspect to a Prospect.

Step Seven – You create a Prospect File folder and begin the Case History Notes.

Step Eight – You create a white Prospect card and clip off all tabs but the birth month.

Step Nine – You file the white card behind the Additions tab and during the monthly planning session use it to update your OCS Control card. You then file the white card alphabetically.

Step Ten – You meet with your Prospect, present your proposal and make the sale! You update the Case History Notes and celebrate obtaining a New Client.

Step Eleven – You use the white card to signal Birthday and Review meetings, always updating the Case History Notes.

Step Twelve – You sustain contact and meet regularly, thus strengthening your relationship, making more and more repeat sales and increasing your ability to obtain more referrals!

Chapter 4

The Success Manual

Introduction

The *Success Manual* is critical to the system. Without it, you're flying blind. It is your record of business activity and production that tracks the month to month health of your business. It is unique because it uses Suspect and case names to provide a *visual picture* of your monthly activity. It is your professional activity management system.

Each month starts fresh with a new blank slate. As activity is recorded at the end of each day, you can quickly identify your accomplishments and what remains to be done. The data allows an objective analysis of your business strengths, your activity patterns, your Sales Cycle conversion ratios, inventory, average case size, mix of business, markets, and more. Perhaps the most important function is that it *keeps you focused* on what is truly important: the activities that drive the client building process.

Organization of the *Success Manual*

The *Success Manual* is divided into four sections:

1. Personal Income Planning;

2. Annual Production Records;

3. Monthly Summaries of Business Activity; and

4. Annual Review and Planning.

Personal Income Planning

The first page is a summary of your personal income needs for the year. It helps you stay focused on the Bottom Line. It allows you to zero in on the amount of business you must produce each and every week in order to meet your financial objectives.

Annual Production Records

The next five pages are your production records for the year. Here you record production on both a company credit basis as well as for MDRT purposes. There is an important Left to Go column on three of the production record pages that constantly reminds you of where you are in relationship to your annual production goals.

Monthly Summaries of Business Activity

The center section of the *Success Manual* consists of Monthly Summary of Business Activity pages. There are two pages for each month of the year. At the end of each day you record all activity and production in the appropriate columns. The recording and analysis of the Monthly Summary pages will be discussed thoroughly in the next few pages of this chapter.

The Columns Are Scaled

The columns are scaled to represent the approximate amount of each activity required for an experienced producer to succeed. For example, there are forty-nine rows available for Qualified Suspects, but only eighteen for New Facts. If you are new to the business, you will need many more Qualified Suspects and New Facts or Confidential Questionnaires. In order to have enough space to record these you will need to photocopy the left page and add it to the month's summary page.

No Entries Are Carried Forward from Previous Months

Every month's summary page starts clean. As the month progresses, the number of entries in each column provides an immediate visual impression of what has been accomplished, as well as the work yet to be done. Pages with previous months' activities are reviewed, updated, and reviewed again until all items of unfinished business have been accounted for. Since there are no "let's kid ourselves entries" carried forward, it is painfully obvious when the page is turned to the new month that we start fresh all over again. Each month brings renewed focus to the activity that has to be done in *every* important area in order to sustain the client building effort.

There are two psychological advantages of beginning fresh each month. One is the confidence that comes with knowing that we are dealing with an unadorned reality and aren't fooling ourselves. The second is that, if you were to carry forward and post previous months' activity, you would *see* all of the unfinished tasks on your agenda. This often feels overwhelming and creates a negative motivation that prevents one from adding to the burden by attempting further new activity. The constant addition of new activity is essential if you are to maintain your momentum in the client building process.

Activity and Efficiency Points

Each activity is assigned a point value to represent its relative importance in the client building process. Additionally, a point is awarded for Business Meals to recognize the efficient use of those particularly valuable times. Hours put in do not count. What you do during those hours does. Thus, the Activity and Efficiency Points column allows you to assess whether or not you are doing enough of the right activities. The point system quickly tells you whether or not you are giving yourself a fair chance to succeed.

Annual Review and Planning

The final pages of the *Success Manual* are for Annual Review and Planning. There are three tables provided to allow you to record the cumulative total of Qualified Suspects, New Fact Finding Interviews, and Cases Opened and sold for the current and previous years. These results are obtained by scanning the actual names in current and previous years' *Success Manuals* and counting the number of people who ultimately became Clients. With these charts you can track your own 10-3-1 ratio for the purpose of preparing and personalizing your business plan. Refer back to Chapter 2, "The Goal: Building a Lifelong Supply of Clients", for a detailed analysis of the Annual Review tables.

Using the Monthly Summary Pages

Qualified Suspects

The first section on each monthly page of the *Success Manual* is the record of Qualified Suspects.

DATE	NAME	NOMIN.'S INITIALS	WHERE SECURED	HOW TO BE PROMOTED	AGE	INCOME	OCCUPATION	CO,A,DF, 31
2	Harris, D.	KC	BL	NL	38	100	Bus. Own.	(CO)
↓	Vaughn, T.	↓	↓	↓	36	75	Elec. Eng.	DF
5	Fulton, T.	DW	BL	NL	30	45	Asst. Prof	DF
	Ericks, W.				39	100	Prof.	31
↓	Harvey, B.	↓	↓	↓	40	100	Prof.	(DF)
5	Hoffman, J.	MK	CL	NL	42	150	Lawyer	31
↓	Colter, M.	↓	↓	↓	35	60	Paralegal	DF
6	Aperlee, D.	HM	BL	NL	58	200	Vet	31
	Aperlee, D. Jr				32	100	Vet	31
	Zimmer, H				62	–	Ret. Vet	DF
↓	Franklin, T	↓	↓	↓	55	200	Bus. Own	(31)

QUALIFIED SUSPECTS

A Suspect is considered to be Qualified when you know the following information:

1. Name and age;

2. Business telephone number and address;

3. Occupation/Title; and

4. Approximate income.

This information may have been obtained through your own personal investigation or it may have been secured through a referral from a trusted nominator.

Nominator's Initials

The nominator's initials should be recorded in the third column. When you personally find the Qualified Suspect, write the word *Self* in the same column. Other codes may be used and tailored to other methods of suspecting that you may be using.

By scanning down this column you will be able to see the number and percentage of your Suspects who are coming from Referred Lead Prospecting efforts. This is the most efficient and effective method of identifying potential Clients of high quality.

Where Secured

In the Where Secured column, a code is used to indicate the circumstances surrounding the situation that existed when the Qualified Suspect's name was obtained. Codes for this column are:

S   Is the code for a special suspecting session excluding business meals.

L   Represents suspecting that took place at a luncheon or breakfast other than a BL.

BL   Indicates a birthday luncheon.

AP   Stands for suspecting that was done at the conclusion of an approach (New Seen) call.

FF   Is for suspecting at the end of a Fact Finding Interview.

CL   Signifies suspecting following a Closing Interview.

D   Identifies suspecting at the conclusion of a Delivery Interview.

TEL   Is the code for suspecting accomplished on the telephone.

R   Indicates Suspecting following a Client Review.

Periodically scan down this column as the month progresses. You should be suspecting throughout the Sales Cycle and in a variety of settings. If you are, you should see a sufficient number of Suspects coming into your system throughout the month.

How to Be Promoted

It is not enough to only acquire names in your Referred Lead Prospecting effort. You also want to find out as much qualifying information as possible, and then turn those names into *introductions* by borrowing the influence and prestige of your nominator. The How to Be Promoted column allows you to record the degree of strength of the introduction the nominator agrees to give you. Codes to be used for this purpose are:

> **L** Indicates a preapproach email and attachment or letter and brochure with no mention of the nominator's name.

> **DL** Indicates a direct email and attachment or letter and brochure in which the nominator permits the use of his name but does not add a personal note of introduction.

> **NL** Is the code used when the nominator adds a personal introductory note to the preapproach email, letter, or brochure.

Obviously, the NL code indicates the strongest degree of introduction. You will be introduced to a proven method of obtaining handwritten introductions from your nominators in a later chapter.

Age, Income, and Occupation

The next three columns headed Age, Income, and Occupation are self-explanatory and are to be filled in on the basis of information received from the nominator, not information received later. Again, in a subsequent chapter, you will learn time-tested language for obtaining this information in a professional manner. These qualifications should meet or exceed the minimum specifications you have listed on the Least Acceptable New Suspect page of your *One Thousand Clients* book.

DATE	NAME	NOMIN.'S INITIALS	WHERE SECURED	HOW TO BE PROMOTED	AGE	INCOME	OCCUPATION	CO,A,DF, 31
	QUALIFIED SUSPECTS							
2	Harris, D.	KC	BL	NL	38	100	Bus. Own.	(CO)
↓	Vaughn, T.	↓	↓	↓	36	75	Elec. Eng.	DF
5	Fulton, T.	DW	BL	NL	30	45	Asst. Prof	DF
|	Ericks, W.	|	|	|	39	100	Prof.	31
↓	Harvey, B.	↓	↓	↓	40	100	Prof.	(DF)
5	Hoffman, J.	MK	CL	NL	42	150	Lawyer	31
↓	Colter, M.	↓	↓	↓	35	60	Paralegal	DF
6	Aperlee, D.	HM	BL	NL	58	200	Vet	31
|	Aperlee, D. Jr	|	|	|	32	100	Vet	31
|	Zimmer, H	|	|	|	62	–	Ret. Vet	DF
↓	Franklin, T	↓	↓	↓	55	200	Bus. Own	(31)

CO, A, DF, and 31

The final column is used to show the outcome of your contacts with Qualified Suspects. The absence of an entry in this column shows that the Suspect has not yet been processed. The objective is to follow through promptly in all cases.

An entry *must* appear in this column within thirty days of when the name was recorded. This is known as the Thirty-Day Rule. If no contact is made within thirty days and you still feel the Suspect has potential, then the column is marked DF and the yellow card is placed in the front of the nominator's file folder to remind you to discuss the Suspect again with the nominator.

A circle around a code always means the Suspect was seen *and a Fact Finder or Confidential Questionnaire was taken.* The code inside the circle indicates the outcome of the Fact Finding Interview.

CO Indicates the Suspect was seen and a single need case was opened. (A complete Confidential Questionnaire did not occur.)

(**CO**) Means a Confidential Questionnaire was taken and a case was opened.

(**A**) Stands for Automatic. Although a Confidential Questionnaire was secured, no case was opened. The white card will be placed in the alphabetical section of the OCS Card File for Automatic twice yearly contact.

31 Identifies Qualified Suspects who were reached by phone or seen in person and from whom you verified the basic information. A Confidential Questionnaire has not yet been taken, but you either have an appointment scheduled or have received permission to stay in touch. The yellow Suspect card is simply moved forward in the 1-31 or Monthly index tabs.

(**DF**) Signifies Dead Filed even though Facts were taken and everything was discarded.

( ) Again, note that the symbol recorded in the last column must always be circled if a Fact Finding Interview was completed.

When a Suspect is eventually sold, whether immediately or several years later, the name is circled in red and the date and amount of the first sale are shown in the circle. Over a period of time, these notations of sales provide the data upon which to project future results and to measure improvements in effectiveness.

Since the Qualified Suspects section of the *Success Manual* will be reviewed regularly for years to come, you are urged to be particularly neat in your original entry and to make it in ink.

New Facts

Building a permanent clientele is a richly rewarding experience. Build to 500 Active Clients and replace those who fall by the wayside. Spend a personally satisfying and profitable life working with these hand-picked Clients and their dependents. The building of a permanent clientele hinges upon your first securing a complete Fact Finder or Confidential Questionnaire.

When a Confidential Questionnaire is obtained for the first time, enter the last name and first initial of the individual in one of the boxes in this column. Updates and reviews of previously taken Confidential Questionnaires are never recorded here. When a Prospect is sold for the first time, box their New Facts box in red and write in the face amount of the sale.

Strive to fill 300 boxes your first year, 250 your second year, 200 your third, and at least 150 every year thereafter. As mentioned earlier, newer producers will need to photocopy the left page of the Monthly Summary to allow room to record the increased number of entries required in early months.

Cases Opened

When a case is opened, either on a new situation resulting from a new Confidential Questionnaire or where previously obtained Confidential Questionnaires are being reviewed and updated, an entry is made on a line in this section. A case is defined as having been opened on a premium paying entity when these three conditions have been met:

1. All of the information necessary to complete a specific recommendation or illustration has been obtained;

2. The illustration has, in fact, been prepared or ordered; and

3. You expect to be able to present the illustration to your Prospect within two weeks and believe that business should result within six weeks.

NEW FACTS
Torrelli, M.
Jacobs, T.
Collins, A.
Fredricks, N.
Tollefson, B.
Mackey, P.
Harris, D.

CASES OPENED							
DATE	NAME	ACT. DATE	CATEGORY	NEW FACTS?	ILLUSTRATION	AMOUNT	SOLD, A, DF
1	Torrelli, M.	✠ 6/15	3	Y	EP	450 L 2700 DI	
1	Jacobs, T.	✠ 6/15	3	N	EQ	IRA ROLLOVER	
1	Kraus, M.	–	4	U	L	2 Juv 100 Kea.	I $
2	Collins, A.	–	3	Y	VA	125K SPDA	I
2	Abbott, S.	–	1	U	LTC	4K/MO	I $
5	Fredricks Industries	✠ 6/19	3	Y	BUS	401(K)	
5	Ivorsen, K.	–	TC	U	L	250VL	
6	Tollefson, B.	✠ 6/16	3	Y	L	500L	I $
7	Martinez, A.	✠ 6/19	1	U	EQ	Mut. Fd.	

Action Date

The third column is used to record the next action date on an open case. If the next action is an appointment, the date of the appointment is shown along with a check mark with two slash marks ✠. If the action intended is just a phone call, only the date is shown without the check mark. Once all action called for has been completed, write only a (—). Since the information recorded in this column will change, it should be written lightly in pencil so that it can be easily erased and updated.

The Action Date column should also be inspected every day. The entries show whether or not you are on top of every case and will alert you to undue delay that could be creeping into your operation. You should have appointments scheduled with at least 80 percent of those cases still presumed open at any given time. If you don't, you are either kidding yourself or not doing a sufficient job of controlling the sales process.

Category

The next column headed Category is coded to indicate the source of the case being opened. The following codes should be used:

1   Stands for a case opened on an existing Client.

2   Indicates a case opened on a potential Client who is new to you, but has already purchased a product from your company. (This is sometimes referred to as an orphan.)

3   Represents a case opened on a potential Client who is both new to you *and* to the company.

4   Signifies a case opened on a spouse, children, or other ancillary lives such as business partners or key persons.

TC Indicates a term conversion case.

The information recorded in this column is vital to the evaluation of the results of cases opened with *New Clients* in contrast to the results of cases opened with the easier repeat sale and dependents categories. This column measures the Nitty Gritty of the client building effort!

New Facts?

This column uses the following codes to indicate the type of fact finding discussion that resulted in the opening of the case:

Y   Indicates that a new Confidential Questionnaire was completed for the *very first time.*

U   Means a previously completed Confidential Questionnaire was reviewed and updated.

N   Means that no complete Confidential Questionnaire, old or new, was used.

DATE	NAME	ACT. DATE	CATEGORY	NEW FACTS?	ILLUSTRATION	AMOUNT	SOLD, A, DF
		CASES OPENED					
1	Torrelli, M.	6/15 #	3	Y	EP	450 L 2700 DI	
1	Jacobs, T.	6/15 #	3	N	EQ	IRA ROLLOVER	
1	Kraus, M.	–	4	U	L	2 Juv 100 Kea.	I $
2	Collins, A.	–	3	Y	VA	125K SPDA	I
2	Abbott, S.	–	1	U	LTC	4K/MO	I $
5	Fredricks Industries	6/19 #	3	Y	BUS	401(K)	
5	Ivorsen, K.	–	TC	U	L	250VL	
6	Tollefson, B.	6/16 #	3	Y	L	500L	I $
7	Martinez, A.	6/19 #	1	U	EQ	Mut. Fd.	

Illustration

The Illustration column is used to show the type of illustration or case being prepared. The following codes, along with others tailored to the needs and markets of the producer, may be used here:

EP   An electronically prepared complete needs analysis program

L   A life insurance case

DI   Disability income insurance case

LTC   Long Term Care

EQ   Equities case

BUS   Business insurance case

EST   Estate planning case

AN   Annuity case

VA   Variable Annuity

G   Group insurance case

M   Major Medical case

Amount

The exact amount (death benefit or volume) called for by the proposal is shown in the column headed Amount.

Sold, A, DF

The last column under the Cases Opened section indicates the ultimate disposition of the case. When business is in the works the notations in this column should be made in pencil to indicate what has been done. For example:

I   Indicates that Part I of the application has been taken.

II   Means that the medical examination, which is Part II of the application, has been taken.

$ Shows it is prepaid.

Once issued and placed in force, these symbols will be erased and replaced with the amount sold circled in red.

When the case is not sold the following codes are used:

A   Stands for Automatic. You believe the Prospect still has the potential to become a Client so the white card is kept in the OCS for Automatic twice yearly contact.

DF   Means the individual has been dead filed.

The last column in the Cases Opened section (Sold, A, DF) should be inspected daily. The records of cases opened in previous months must be periodically reviewed until there is a final entry for every case.

Closing Interviews

This section is used to record the names and dates of Closing Interviews with individuals (cases). A Closing Interview is defined as a face-to-face (not telephone) conversation during which the Prospect is asked to take some affirmative action such as signing an application, agreeing to take a medical examination, or paying the first premium.

Attempt # \ Time Lag

In the column headed Attempt # \ Time Lag a notation is made as to the number of the Closing Interview (e.g., the 1st closing interview, the 2nd closing interview, etc.). Multiple closes may indicate a lack of diligence and dedication at the time of the first close or a skill deficit in the Fact Finding Interview. On the other hand, a lack of multiple closes may be a sign of giving up too easily.

The Time Lag should be shown in days going all the way back to the date the case was originally opened. For example, if the case was opened on the first of the month and a first closing interview was held on the 11th, the time lag shown at the time of that close would be 10. If a second closing interview was conducted a week later on the same case, the closing interview would be recorded again for 18th. However, the attempt number would be 2 and the time lag would be 17. The percentage of successful closes can be materially increased if this time lag is held to a minimum.

CLOSING INTERVIEWS			
DATE	NAME	ATTEMPT # / TIME LAG	TYPE CASE
5	Kraus, M.	5 / 1	L
6	Collins, A.	4 / 1	VA
6	Abbott, S.	6 / 1	LTC
7	York, M.	10 / 2	DI
8	Torrelli, M.	7 / 1	EP
9	Ivorsen, K.	4 / 1	L

Type of Case

Finally, the last column is used to note the type of case. The same codes used for Type of Illustration column in the Cases Opened section may be used in this column. For example, the letters EP stand for an electronically prepared complete program, L means a life insurance presentation, EQ stands for the presentation of an equities solution, and so on. Other codes may be used to fit your special needs or markets.

Analyzing the Closing Section Data

As was true of the three sections previously discussed (Qualified Suspects, New Facts, and Cases Opened), the length of the column in this section and the number of available spaces in it is intended to be a guide as to the amount of closing activity for which a superior producer should strive every month. New producers should average at least 20 Closing Interviews per month.

Each month starts with a clean sheet, and by the end of the month it is expected that all columns have been substantially filled. Balanced activity, coupled with a sense of urgency, should result in superior performance. If they do not, then the basic sales skills should be analyzed. There is, however, little use in analyzing techniques if the quantity of activity is insufficient or if the time lag between steps of the sales process is excessive.

Business

This section of the *Success Manual* is divided into two parts. The top of the section is used to record pertinent information on applications being sent to the Home Office. The lower portion is used when a case has been approved or issued, the premium paid, and the contract placed in force.

BUSINESS					
SENT TO THE HOME OFFICE					
DATE	NAME	CATEGORY	AMOUNT (000)	TYPE	ANNUALIZED FYC
6	Kraus, P.	4	100	WL	300
6	Kraus, A.	4	100	WL	320
7	Abbott, S.	1	3	LTC	1500
8	York, M.	3	2.5	DI	730
9	Ivorsen, K.	TC	250	VL	1400
9	Collins, A.	3	100	VA	2500

Date and Name

Record the date the application was submitted (or placed in force) and the name of the applicant.

Category

Use the fourth column to code the types of cases being submitted or placed. The codes used here are the same as those used to describe Category of business in the Cases Opened section:

1 Stands for a Repeat Sale to an existing Client.

2 Indicates a sale to a Client that is new to you but not to the company. (This is sometimes referred to as an orphan.)

3 Is a sale to a true, new Client. That is, the Client is both new to you and to the company.

4 Signifies a sale on a spouse, children, or other ancillary lives such as business partners or key persons.

TC Indicates a term conversion case.

Amount

Record the face amount or volume of the product being sent to the company or placed in force in the third column.

Type

Indicate the type of product applied for or placed in force.

Annualized First Year Commission

The fifth column is for a record of First Year Commission. The amount required to meet one's budget should be kept in mind since this figure is one of the most significant measures of individual accomplishment. The first page of the *Success Manual* provides for personal income planning, and the bottom portion of that sheet is designed to remind you to relate your requirements to your results at all times.

Activity and Efficiency Points

The final columns in the monthly section of the *Success Manual* allow you to summarize the important client building activities you conducted on each day of the month. Activity and Efficiency Points are awarded for certain types of business activities. Points measure whether or not you are getting enough exposure in the market. That is, are you giving yourself enough of a chance to succeed?

One efficiency point is credited for:

- A *business meal* with a nominator, Prospect, Client, or Suspect.

- A *new Fact Finding—Confidential Questionnaire—Interview* completed.

- A *new Case Opened*, either from a new Fact Finding Interview, by updating a previously taken Confidential Questionnaire, or on a package sale basis.

- A *Closing Interview*.

One-half efficiency point is credited for:

- Each Qualified Suspect obtained and recorded.

A single interview should result in several points by accomplishing a combination of the five items. Your objective should be to *strive to earn at least two points per kept appointment*. For example, business luncheons should result in at least two points in addition to the business meal point. To illustrate, a business luncheon with a nominator, during which six new Qualified Suspects were obtained, would earn four Activity and Efficiency Points: one for the lunch, and three for the Qualified Suspects.

At the end of each day you will record your total number of activities for the day in the *row* next to the appropriate date. You should continually monitor the point count for the appropriate quantity and balance of activity. The data entered here is transcribed *each evening* from your *OCS Control Booklet*'s Daily Pages.

Date of the Month	Appts. Scheduled	Appts. Kept	PHONING FOR APPOINTMENTS			1 pt MEALS		.5 pts			Approaches	1 pt New Facts	1 pt Cases Opened	1 pt Closing Interviews	Points
			Dialed	Reached	Appts.	Name	Results	Qualified Suspects	Referrals Attempts	Referrals Obtained					
1	4	3	28	6	3	—		0	0	0	2	2	3	0	5
2	3	3	26	7	4	Carter (BL) 2 QS		2	1	2	1	1	2	0	5
3	STUDY CHFC														
4	7	6	54	13	7	1		2	1	2	3	3	5	0	10
5	4	4	25	9	4	Wallace (BL) 3 QS		5	2	5	1	1	2	1	8.5
6	5	4	36	11	5	Mills (BL) 4 QS		6	2	6	1	1	1	2	8
7	5	3	30	11	5	Martinez (R) U, CO		3	1	3	1	0	1	1	4.5
8	5	5	30	8	4	Donovan (R) U, CO		5	2	5	2	1	2	1	7.5
9	4	4	28	9	5	Young (BL) 4QS		8	3	8	0	1	1	2	9
10	MDRT														
11	23/30	20/26	149/203	49/61	23/30	5/6		27/29	10/11	27/29	5/8	4/7	7/12	7/7	36.5/46.5
12															

ACTIVITY AND EFFICIENCY POINTS

Date

The Date column simply lists the calendar number of that day of the month.

Appointments Made

In order to obtain the required Activity and Efficiency Points, you must have an adequate number of interviews. The Appointments Made column is used to record the number of appointments you had scheduled (written in your *OCS Control Book*) that day. These appointments are for business purposes. That is, they can be for prospecting, approaching, fact finding, closing, delivery, or reviews.

Appointments Kept

This column is used to record the number of kept appointments during the day. In most cases, six or seven appointments per day must be scheduled in order to average four kept.

Phoning for Appointments

The next three columns are devoted to a record of telephoning activity. Since the sales sequence starts with telephoning for appointments, everything else falls into place if this is done consistently. The columns are used to record the number of dials made for the purpose of securing an appointment, the number of people actually reached, and the appointments that resulted. These totals are transferred each evening from the *OCS Control Book*'s Daily Pages.

- **Dialed**—This is the number of dials made each day. These are only dials to secure business appointments with Suspects, Prospects or Active Clients.

- **Reached**—An entry is recorded for the number of times when you speak personally to the decision maker (not a secretary unless they can book the appointment for their boss). This column is for recording the number of reaches for that day.

- **Appts.**—This column is used to record the number of appointments secured from those individuals you reached that day.

The original One Card System research revealed that, on average, three people were dialed to reach one. Two people were reached in order to make one appointment. Finally, about two appointments needed to be secured in order to have one actually kept. (This, of course, depends upon your market, skills, and the influence of the nominator.) In general, however, it took an average of at least six dials to make an appointment. Furthermore, it took about twelve dials to secure two appointments and consequently have one kept.

Current OCS statistics indicate that, in many geographical areas, it may take five to six dials to reach the one Qualified Suspect. Of those reached, however, appointments continue to result 50 percent of the time. Therefore, at least one uninterrupted hour must be scheduled daily for these phone calls. If you have all the cards and files ready and you remain brief, it should be possible to make from twenty-five to thirty-six dials in an hour. If your records reveal that additional dials are needed to achieve the required number of reaches and appointments, then schedule additional daily time for your calls.

| Date of the Month | Appts. Scheduled | Appts. Kept | PHONING FOR APPOINTMENTS | | | 1 pt MEALS | | | .5 pts | | | | 1 pt | 1 pt | 1 pt | |
			Dialed	Reached	Appts.	Name		Results	Qualified Suspects	Referrals Attempts	Referrals Obtained	Approaches	New Facts	Cases Opened	Closing Interviews	Points
1	4	3	28	6	3	—			0	0	0	2	2	3	0	5
2	3	3	26	7	4	Carter (BL) 2 QS			2	1	2	1	1	2	0	5
3	STUDY CHFC															
4	7	6	54	13	7	1			2	1	2	3	3	5	0	10
5	4	4	25	9	4	Wallace (BL) 3 QS			5	2	5	1	1	2	1	8.5
6	5	4	36	11	5	Mills (BL) 4 QS			6	2	6	1	1	1	2	8
7	5	3	30	11	5	Martinez (R) U, CO			3	1	3	1	0	1	1	4.5
8	5	5	30	8	4	Donovan (R) U, CO			5	2	5	2	1	2	1	7.5
9	4	4	28	9	5	Young (BL) 4QS			8	3	8	0	1	1	2	9
10	MDRT															
11	23/30	20/26	149/203	49/61	23/30	5/6			27/29	10/11	27/29	5/8	4/7	7/12	7/7	36.5/46.5
12																

Table title: **ACTIVITY AND EFFICIENCY POINTS**

Business Meals

Business lunches and breakfasts provide an excellent opportunity to meet with busy executives, business owners, or professionals. They also provide an opportunity to build relationships in a more relaxed setting.

Since business meals are an investment of your time and business capital, it is important to achieve a return on that investment. That return can best be measured by the Activity and Efficiency Points earned during the meeting. Therefore, *strive to earn an average of least two points in addition to the business meal point.*

- **Name**—When a business meal is held, the name of the individual is recorded and the results of the meeting are shown. A most important luncheon objective is to obtain names of, and introductions to, well-qualified Suspects. Most birthday lunches should be used for that purpose. Lunches may also be used to take new Facts Forms or Confidential Questionnaires, review old ones, open cases, close them, and conduct Delivery Interviews.

- **Results**—This column is used to record the business results that came from the meeting. Here, again, simple codes are used. *This column is not used to record points, but results.*

  S Is used for Suspect(s).

  FF Denotes a Fact Finder or Confidential Questionnaire was taken.

  CO Is used for Case Opened.

  CL Signifies a Closing Interview.

  D Means a Delivery took place.

  R Indicates a Client Review.

Qualified Suspects

Record the total number of Qualified Suspects obtained that day.

Referral Attempts

Record the number of meetings during the day in which you attempted to obtain referrals.

Referrals Obtained

This column is used to record the total number of referrals obtained during that day.

Approaches (Also Called *New Seens*)

Record the number of initial appointments that were held with Qualified Suspects for the purpose of explaining your services and proceeding to fact finding.

New Facts

Indicate the number of _new_ Fact Finding Interviews completed that day. Updates of previous Fact Finders or Confidential Questionnaires are not included.

Cases Opened

The number of Cases Opened for that day is recorded here.

Closing Interviews

The number of Closing Interviews for the day is recorded here.

Points

This column is used to record the total number of points earned that day. Again, Activity and Efficiency Points are credited at the rate of one point each for every business meal, new Fact Finding Interview, Case Opened, and Closing Interview. One-half point is allowed for each Qualified Suspect.

The key is to be sure to obtain at least five or six balanced points each day. It is the _daily focus_ that keeps you on track toward success.

Point Goals

Strive for at least twenty points in each category with a total of well over 100 in every full month. A competent producer should have sufficient activity to earn a total of at least 1,200 points a year. However, for a new Financial Services Professional, the target must be 1,400 points the first year, 1,300 the second, and 1,200 thereafter. In order to hit those point totals, the new person must interview an average of three-and-a-half to four people per day. The cumulative total should be monitored on a weekly and monthly basis so that insufficient activity can be corrected before time runs out.

Activity and Efficiency Points as a Planning Tool

Take a few minutes prior to scheduled appointments to consider all the point count possibilities for that appointment. Clearly identify your primary objective for the appointment, and then consider how additional points can be earned at the same meeting. This can pay big dividends. Preplanning makes it possible for an effective Financial Services Professional to average over two points per kept appointment. Experience shows that agents who do not preplan average only one point per interview.

For example, though the primary objective of a Birthday Lunch with a Client may be to obtain Qualified Suspects, it may be possible to do much more with proper advance preparation and planning. You could also open a simple case and conduct a quick package close after the suspecting job has been done. This would earn two additional points. A Delivery Interview is one of the strongest opportunities for suspecting, but it may also present a chance to open and close a simple case. Look for opportunities to add ancillary sales for dependents or business needs. In other words, regardless of the primary objective, planning and preparation can easily double your sales efficiency per interview.

Think ahead and *be prepared*.

Chapter 5

Putting it All Together

Up to this point, we have discussed the various components of the One Card System independently. Now we will examine how the components work together to help you plan and administer the activities of your practice. This section will be divided into the following eight parts:

1. The OCS as a self-management tool,

2. Progressive expectations,

3. Goal setting,

4. The monthly planning session,

5. The OCS in action,

6. Utilizing an assistant,

7. Monthly Client Builder Meetings, and

8. The annual review.

The OCS as a Self-Management Tool

The individuals who are attracted to this career tend to have entrepreneurial spirits. They are seeking the independence that comes from establishing a substantial clientele. However, entrepreneurial enterprises are not without risk and many fail. According to Michael Gerber, author of *The E-Myth*, the reason that many entrepreneurs fail is that they spend all of their time working *in* their businesses and not enough time working *on* them.

The One Card System provides the tools and the business structure that allow you to step out of the day-to-day hectic pace of making the calls and seeing the people to objectively work *on* your business. As will be explained in this section, the proper use of the OCS includes business rituals that help you to establish a work plan and then check and evaluate your progress on a daily basis.

Early in your career, your trainer or manager can play a key role in ensuring that you understand and properly implement the system. This includes firmly establishing the habits and skills that are required to succeed. Good management also requires minimizing the numerous distractions that can cause you to get off track. Ultimately, however, this is a self-management business. Proper use of the One Card System will allow you to successfully and intelligently supervise yourself and continue to move in the direction of your business goals.

Progressive Expectations

If you are new to the career, you will want to know relatively early whether or not a career in the sale of financial services is right for you. We only have one life to lead and it would certainly be a great tragedy to become too heavily involved in a career in which we did not have a fighting chance to succeed.

Since it is impossible to measure or predict early success or failure from sales results, Progressive Expectations have been developed based on the actual activity records of the past. They are designed to help the new associate understand the activity requirements for early success in the career. Progressive Expectations make it possible for you to determine, relatively quickly, whether or not you are on the right track. They are as follows:

The First Twenty-five Days

The expectations of the first twenty-five field days are:

- 150 Activity and Efficiency Points; and

- Eighty Kept Appointments (an average of 3.75 per day).

If you miss these expectations in the first twenty-five field days, consider this a yellow alert. Try again in earnest for another twenty-five field days. If you still cannot reach these activity levels, then this should be considered a red alert. If you choose to try again for yet another twenty-five field days and still cannot hit the mark, it is an indication that this career may be very difficult for you – both emotionally and financially.

If, on the other hand, you successfully reach the benchmark of the first twenty-five days, then proceed to the next level of Progressive Expectations.

The Next Six Months

The expectations of the next six calendar months are:

- Interview eighteen people weekly (kept appointments);

- Earn an average of 117 Activity and Efficiency Points monthly (700 by the end of the sixth month); and

- Meet financial needs with at least twenty-six applications.

Once again, give yourself a maximum of three attempts to meet the above expectations, following the same yellow alert and red alert guidelines. If you are successful in reaching or exceeding the second level of expectations, you are well on your way!

First Full Calendar Year

The expectations during your first full calendar year are:

- Qualify as a Provisional Applicant for the Million Dollar Round Table (MDRT); and

- Pass one course leading to an industry recognized professional designation.

By meeting this level of expectation, you can be relatively confident that you are on track for a satisfying and rewarding career!

First Fifteen Years

Your personal career expectations over the next fifteen years should be to qualify for the MDRT annually (at a minimum) and to pass a minimum of one industry course leading to a designation per year until the designation has been obtained. You may proceed at a faster pace if you wish and earn more than one designation, but the minimum is one course per year.

Expectations for Office Occupancy

Although this expectation may not concern you initially, you should be aware that most firms have production requirements for different offices, ranging from cubicles to private offices. While each firm will differ slightly in its own requirements, there is a general guideline of which you should be aware. To qualify for a private office, most firms require active qualification for the MDRT from the commissions shown on the associate's commission statement. So, there are many reasons to target MDRT production levels annually!

Goal Setting

Good self-management begins with setting goals and establishing a work plan. The top portion of the Personal Income Planning page, found in the *Success Manual,* is provided to help you establish your income goals for the year. You will also find a Personal Financial Planning page in the *OCS Productivity Planner.*

As you keep activity and production records in your *Success Manual,* you will eventually be able to determine your own activity-to-sales conversion ratios. This knowledge will allow you to convert your income goals into meaningful activity plans that are based on your own markets and skills. Space is provided on the lower portion of the page for you to record other business goals, such as monthly activity goals, your annual objective for New Client accounts, and continuing education plans.

The Monthly Planning Session

An important business ritual found in the OCS is the monthly planning session. It occurs at the end of the third week of each month, during non-selling time. It is during this time that you will establish your work plan for the coming month. All of the components of the One Card System will be used to help you evaluate your progress toward your annual goals and organize your business operation for the month ahead. The following is a summary of the steps of the monthly planning session that will be explained in more detail in the pages that follow.

It is recommended that you follow the original manual approach for the first three to six months to build a strong foundation of understanding of the system. After this you can take advantage of automated tools – such as the *Career Activity Management (CAM) System* – to succeed in today's financial services profession.

You will need the following components:

- Your OCS Card File,

- The *OCS Control Booklet* for the upcoming month or your *OCS Productivity Planner,*

- Your *Success Manual,* and

- Your *One Thousand Clients* book.

1. **Prepare the OCS Card File**

   - Update OCS Control Card

   - Clear out temporary holding tabs:

     Additions to A-Z Section

     Rejects discarded

     Inactives placed in Client file folders (Quiet Files)

   - Move yellow cards from Monthly to 1-31 tabs

2. **Prepare the *OCS Control Booklet* or your *OCS Productivity Planner* for the next month**

   - Prepare Month at a Glance pages:

     Mark out non-selling times

     Identify the number of selling days and daily OCS point goal

   - Prepare Appointment Spread Sheet of the *OCS Control Booklet* or the weekly appointment pages of your *OCS Productivity Planner*:

     Record previously committed non-selling times

- Complete Automatic Pages:

  Transfer names to appropriate Daily Pages in the *Control Booklet* or to the top of the appropriate day in the *OCS Productivity Planner*.

3. **Update *Success Manual***

- Production Record:

  Calculate MDRT status

- Production Graph:

  Calculate progress toward year-to-date income goals

4. **Update *One Thousand Clients* Book**

- Cross out Client accounts that have become inactive

- Record New Clients

- Update estimates of future potential from reviews conducted during the previous month

Monthly Planning in Detail

1. Prepare Your OCS Card File

A. Update the OCS Control Card

- Record the total number of white cards being *added* to your OCS (temporarily being held behind the Additions tab) in the plus (+) column of the OCS Control card.

- Then record the total number of white cards being *deleted* from your system (temporarily being held behind the Reject and Inactive tabs) in the minus (-) column of the OCS Control card.

- Calculate the net total of white cards in your OCS Card File and record that number in the Total column.

MO/YR	+	-	TOTAL	MO/YR	+	-	TOTAL
5/04	30	0	30	8/05	32	12	292
6/04	27	0	57	9/05	25	11	306
7/04	25	0	82	10/05	20	9	317
8/04	24	1	105				
9/04	25	2	128				
10/04	22	4	146				
11/04	25	7	164				
12/04	19	8	175				
1/05	34	7	202				
2/05	28	12	218				
3/05	21	11	228				
4/05	24	14	238				
5/05	20	9	249				
6/05	21	10	260				
7/05	14	2	272				

CONTROL CARD

An inventory of relationships

Remember, the OCS Control Card maintains an inventory of the number of Active Prospect and Client cards that you have in your OCS. Many Financial Services Professionals feel this is their *inventory of business relationships*. Think about it. White cards represent individuals with whom you have conducted a Fact Finding Interview. Many of these individuals will be Active Clients and all will be Prospects. Either way, you will have had an *in-depth discussion* with each one of them.

Once again, your objective is to build your OCS Card File to a level of at least 500 active white cards. This makes the career so much easier! Each decision maker represented by a white card *must* be contacted twice per year. These 500 cards translate to 1,000 conversations per year, or approximately eighty-three per month, with individuals with whom you have a relationship! Some of the Prospects will act on your recommendations and become Clients; some of the Active Clients will buy additional products, and many of these individuals will continue to refer you to others.

B. Clear out Temporary Holding Tabs

   •   Additions Tab—File the white cards that have been temporarily held behind the Additions tab behind the appropriate A-Z tabs of the Alphabetical section. These individuals or accounts are considered active and will be contacted twice per year.

- Reject Tab—The Reject tab has temporarily held the white cards of *Prospects* who, after repeated contacts and procrastinations, you have decided to remove from your system. These cards may be discarded. The corresponding files and their contents may either be discarded or placed in a Rejected Prospects file drawer, depending on your company's compliance regulations.

- Inactive Tab—This section will have temporarily held the white cards of the *Clients* whom you believe are saturated based on their Case History records and offer no additional business potential. After updating the OCS Control Card, you may remove these cards and place them into the Client's File folder. The file folder is then placed into an Inactive Clients (Quiet Files) file drawer.

C.   Move the Yellow Suspect Cards from the Monthly to 1-31 Tabs

- The Monthly tabs hold the yellow Suspect cards of the Qualified Suspects who have given you permission to stay in touch. Simply move the yellow cards filed behind the next month's tab to the appropriate 1-31 tab corresponding to the date you plan to make the call.

2. Prepare Next Month's *OCS Control Booklet* or the Upcoming Month in Your *OCS Productivity Planner*

A.   Prepare the Month at a Glance pages

Record any non-selling commitments such as firm or office meetings, training classes, industry meetings, holidays, etc. Estimate how many hours or days these commitments will take from your available selling time. Then calculate the total number of days that are available for selling. Divide that number into your monthly OCS Activity and Efficiency Point goal to determine how many OCS points you must earn each field day in order to achieve the necessary exposure in the marketplace.

MON	**TUE**	**WED**	**THU**	**FRI**	**SAT/SUN**

Month at a Glance

Month ___Feb.___   Year ___200-___

MON	TUE	WED	THU	FRI	SAT/SUN
	1	2	3	4 7:00-9:00 Firm Mtg.	5 / 6
7	8	9	10	11	12 / 13
14	15	16 8:00 Estate Planning Seminar 3:00 (6hrs. C.E.)	17	18 7:00-8:00 Monthly Planning	19 / 20
21	22	23	24	25	26 / 27
28					

B. Prepare the Appointment Spread Sheet in the *Control Booklet*

If you are using the *OCS Control Booklet* version of the system, this is the master appointment sheet from which you will be scheduling appointments while on the phone or in the field. Transfer any non-selling commitments that have been recorded on your Month at a Glance pages to avoid scheduling appointments during time periods that you already have committed. Identify the times that are available for selling appointments with a highlighter and then endeavor to fill them all!

| | | | | | | **Appointment Spread Sheet** | | |
	Day	7:30	9:00	10:30	11:30	1:00	2:00	3:00
1	Tues.		Samuels, K.			Dalton, P.		
2	Wed.						Thompson, A	
3	Thurs.							
4	Fri.	Firm Mtg.						
5	Sat.							
6	Sun.							
7	Mon.							
8	Tues.					CLIENT BLDR. MTG.		
9	Wed.							
10	Thurs.							
11	Fri.							
12	Sat.							

If you are using the *OCS Productivity Planner,* simply transfer any non-selling commitments to the appropriate weekly pages.

C.   Complete the Automatic Pages

You will recall that the One Card System prompts you to automatically contact all Active Clients and Prospects twice per year. One contact will occur just before the individual's birthday and the other will occur six months later.

To prepare the Automatics pages in the front of the next month's *OCS Control Book* or the Automatic Contacts page of your *OCS Productivity Planner,* you will need to refer to the Alphabetical section of your OCS Card File box. Remember that when you prepared your white cards, all of the monthly tabs were removed from the top of the card except the one corresponding to the birth month.

Birthday Automatics

You may now easily identify – from the exposed monthly tabs – all of the individuals who will have birthdays in the upcoming month. Simply pull the appropriate cards up – not out – from the box and then alphabetically enter the names and birthdays on the Birthday Automatics page. By listing the names alphabetically, it will be easier to locate a name when updating the Results column throughout the month.

Birthday Automatics

No.	Birthday	Name	Result
1	9	Allen, C.	
2	26	Bergstrom, J.	
3	2	Carter, K.	
4	6	Gonzalez, T.	
5	28	Kohler, A.	
6	23	Lowenthal, L.	
7	6	Mills, H.	
8	14	Nolan, C.	
9	7	Parker, E.	
10	19	Rawlston, P.	
11	21	Sorenson, T.	
12	15	Tabor, W.	
13	5	Wallace, D.	
14	30	Williams, B.	
15	11	Young, D.	
16	16	Zeder, F.	

Review Automatics

In order to identify Review Automatics for the next month you need to go through the Alphabetical section of the OCS Card File box again, just as you did when identifying Birthday Automatics. This time, however, you won't be looking for people whose birthday is coming up next month, but rather for cards with exposed birth month tabs that are six months prior to the upcoming month.

Using a January 23 planning date, for example, you will be identifying the Review Automatic calls to be made in the month of February. Pull up the cards that have a birthday tab that is six months prior to February. In this case, that would be the August tabs. Pull up – not out – the cards with August birthday tabs and record the name and birthday on the Review Automatics page in your *OCS Control Book* or Automatic Contacts page in your *OCS Productivity Planner*.

Review Automatics

No.	Birthday	Name	Result
1		Abbott, S.	
2		Chen, P.	
3		Donovan, K.	
4		Ellis, G.	
5		Ivorsen, K.	
6		Martinez, A.	
7		Matthews, J.	
8		O'Niel, B.	
9		Rollins, S.	
10		Tanaka, N.	
11		Taylor, C.	
12		Ungstaad, L.	
13		Vanelli, E.	
14		Warren, P.	
15			
16			
17			
18			
19			

D.   Transfer the Names to the Appropriate Daily Pages

The final step of preparing the *OCS Control Booklet* is to transfer the names of the individuals listed on the Automatic pages to the top of the appropriate Daily Pages, or to the top of the appropriate day of the *OCS Productivity Planner*. When you wish to schedule a lunch, Birthday Automatics should be called one week prior to the birthday. All Review Automatics should be called within the first ten days of the month so that the review can be scheduled during the same month.

3. Update *Success Manual* Tables and Graphs

A.   Update Production Records

This table is designed to keep you clearly focused on the goal of achieving MDRT qualifying status. Record all applications that have been approved and placed in force since the last monthly planning session. Then, calculate the amount of production still required to achieve MDRT qualifying status.

PRODUCTION RECORD							
INSURED OR ACCOUNT OWNER	POLICY OR ACCOUNT NUMBER	LIFE OR CASE CR.	EFFECTIVE DATE	COMPANY PRODUCTION CREDIT	PLAN	MDRT CREDIT	LEFT TO GO
1							
2							
3							
4							
5							
6							
7							
8							
9							
10							
11							
12							
13							
14							
15							
16							

B.   Update Production Graph

The Production Graph helps to keep you focused on your progress toward your annual income goals. The graph allows you to chart your cumulative year-to-date income goal in black ink at the beginning of the year. The Y axis values have been left blank so you can personalize the income values.

During each monthly planning session, plot your year-to-date income in red to give yourself a visual record of your progress. The table at the bottom of the graph is designed to help you numerically determine where you stand in relation to your goals.

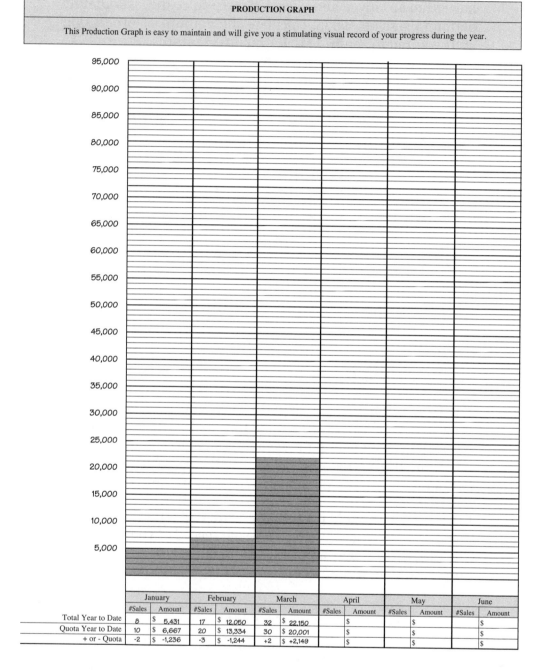

PRODUCTION GRAPH

This Production Graph is easy to maintain and will give you a stimulating visual record of your progress during the year.

	January		February		March		April		May		June	
	#Sales	Amount	#Sales	Amount	#Sales	Amount	#Sales	Amount	#Sales	Amount	#Sales	Amount
Total Year to Date	8	$ 5,431	17	$ 12,050	32	$ 22,150		$		$		$
Quota Year to Date	10	$ 6,667	20	$ 13,334	30	$ 20,001		$		$		$
+ or - Quota	-2	$ -1,236	-3	$ -1,244	+2	$ +2,149		$		$		$

4. Update Your *One Thousand Clients* Book

The final step of the monthly planning session is to update your *One Thousand Clients* book.

- Begin by crossing out the Active Client number of any Client accounts that were placed on Inactive (Quiet File) status during the previous month.

- Then add the New Client accounts that were added since the last monthly planning session. (By crossing out the inactive Clients first, it will be easier to record the Active Client number of the new accounts you are adding.)

- Finally, for those Client accounts on whom you conducted reviews since the previous session, go back and update your estimated future first year commission potential for each Client account.

By updating your *One Thousand Clients* book in this manner each month, you will be able to track your progress toward your New Client account goal for the year. Additionally, you will keep your finger on the pulse of your practice – the Quantity and Quality of your active clientele.

			NEW CLIENTS					
Consecutive New Client Number	Month / Year	Active Client Number	Name	Age	Occupation	Income	FYC Premium	Future FYC* Premium
1	1 / 199-	1	Jones, Tom/Eliz.	28/26	Med. Intern/R.N.	24/45	820	6,000?
2	1 / 199-	2	Smith, William	30	Elec. Engr.	51	820	1500
3	1 / 199-	3	Fox, Gordon/Susan	28/28	Systems Anlst./ Teacher	65/42	760	1500
4	1 / 199-	4	Townsend, Barbara	34	CPA	42	1100	Transfrd.
5	2 / 199-	5	Swenson, Robert	45	Sales Mgr.	60	1800	1000
	/							
70	5 / 199-	69	Andrews, Sam	31	Architect	75	750	2000
71	5 / 199-	70	Parker Industries	Inc. 1989	Building Supplies	–	3500	5000
72	5 / 199-	71	Nordell, Debra/Jim	35/36	Orthodontist/ M.D.-Gen.Pract.	200/120	2800	6000+
73	/							
74	/							
75	/							

*Make Future FYC/Premium column entries in pencil until the client dies or is positively deactivated.

The One Card System in Action

By now you are probably beginning to see that the One Card System is more than just a tickler card system. The cards and the OCS Card File, while important, are only *components* of the One Card System; they are *not* the whole system. It is the relationship among *all* of the components – the synergy that comes from all of the tools and procedures working together – that produces a result far greater than the sum total of the separate parts.

Now that you have an understanding of the monthly planning session, let's examine how the system can help you smoothly implement your monthly work plan.

A Word about Assistants

Initially, you can easily handle all clerical details on your own. As your production approaches Million Dollar Round Table levels, however, a part-time assistant may be useful. When reaching 100 applications per year with MDRT level production, a full-time assistant becomes desirable for further growth.

The following description of the OCS Daily Steps will walk you through a typical day of the newer associate without an assistant. Later in the book, we will discuss the use of the OCS with a full-time assistant.

The OCS Daily Steps

Work a Structured Day

It is necessary to understand the fundamentals of the Structured Day Model before we discuss the daily steps of the OCS. The daily tasks of this career can be overwhelming, causing the mind to jump from one unfinished task to another. The resulting chaos not only produces anxiety but can also lead to an entire day going by with little of significance being fully accomplished.

The Structured Day Model of the One Card System segments the day into time periods to which various tasks or activities are assigned. This helps you stay focused throughout the day and feel more confident from being in control of your business. It also increases the likelihood that the important activities of client building will be accomplished.

The Structured Day starts by arriving for work at a regular time each day. Start earlier than is customary in your community if you can. We recommend starting at 7:30 a.m. to avoid the commuter and traffic rush and to get a jump on everyone else. Then, organize your day in the following manner.

7:30 a.m. to 9:00 a.m. – Preparing for the Day

- Complete any Posting and Planning that was not accomplished the previous evening. (More about Posting and Planning later.)

- Refer to the current Daily Page of your *OCS Control Booklet* (or *OCS Productivity Planner*) and pull all file folders of any Prospects or Clients who are listed for that day's phone calls. Place the file folders on your desk together with the day's 1-31 yellow Suspect cards. Ensure that you have a combination of at least 36 file folders and/or yellow cards to call.

- Next pull the file folders of the individuals to be seen that day and check them to be sure everything is ready.

- Look at the schedule for the day and estimate its potential total Activity and Efficiency Point count. Consider ways to make each appointment pay off to the maximum.

- Having completed the above tasks, you may use this preparation time to complete tasks for future appointments.

- Prior to the phone call hour, refile folders not used for your planned phone calls, including those on which office work is to be done that day. In a smoothly running office, no other files should be out at this point. File folders should be back in their proper places in the file drawers except when they are actually being used. This helps you avoid the distractions of clutter.

9:00 a.m. to 10:00 a.m. – Phone Calls

It is recommended that you reserve from 9:00 a.m. until 10:00 a.m. each morning for phone calls. This should be considered sacred time that no one violates – not your Clients, your manager, or you. Additional afternoon or evening phone time may be necessary, depending on your results. Remember that the entire sales process starts here, but 25 percent to 50 percent of all appointments made will probably be postponed or canceled. Therefore, adequate daily phone activity is a must!

- Begin by first dialing your Prospects or Clients to warm up. Quickly scan the Case History before dialing to pick up the threads of prior conversations. Then call the Qualified Suspects from your yellow cards.

- Record all telephoning activity on the Daily Page of your *OCS Control Booklet* or *OCS Productivity Planner* as you dial. (Use the dot and check method previously described.)

- Record all appointments scheduled on the Appointment Spread Sheet page of the *OCS Control Booklet,* or on the weekly pages of your *OCS Productivity Planner.*

- At the end of your phone session, keep yellow cards of the individuals who you were unable with you throughout the day. This way, you can call again between appointments or in the event an appointment is postponed.

10:30 a.m. to 5:00 p.m. – Rule #1: Time

Rule #1 applies *at least* three business days per week. Simply put, it means that between the hours of 10:30 a.m. and 5:00 p.m. you should *do nothing other than see people or work to see people.* Appointments with Suspects, Prospects, and Clients should be scheduled during this time period. If an appointment cancels or reschedules, then get on the phone to schedule more appointments.

You may allow a little more flexibility the other two days of the week for case preparation, but you should also have some appointments on those days as well. By practicing Rule #1 *at least* three days per week, following the time periods on your Appointment Spread Sheet, you should be able to keep between fifteen and eighteen appointments per week.

5:00 p.m. to 6:00 p.m. – Administrative Time

Until you have an assistant, use this time to handle other administrative items such as creating new Prospect File folders, updating Case History Notes for the day, or ordering medical requirements. Open and respond to mail and e-mail at the end of each day to avoid distractions during important phone and appointment time periods.

A Word about Evening Appointments

Throughout this text we have emphasized the importance of daytime activity. Remember that you teach your Prospects and Clients how to do business with you. As soon as possible, teach them to come to your office, or at least to meet with you during business hours at their offices.

However, we also recognize there will be times when evening appointments will be necessary. In these instances, try to schedule the appointment for 6:30 p.m., suggesting a half hour for your Prospects to have a quick meal before you arrive. This will allow them – and you – to have the rest of the evening for your families.

Post and Plan Each Evening

Posting and Planning is one of the most important business activities of the day! It is the process of first posting the current day's activity and accomplishments, and then planning the day (and days) ahead. If you had no evening appointment, then Post and Plan before you leave the office. If not, take a few minutes in the evening to do so at home.

You will need your *OCS Control Booklet* and *Success Manual* (or your *OCS Productivity Planner*) for Posting and Planning. The steps of the Posting process are:

- Working from your *OCS Control Booklet*, post your phone activity in the Activity and Efficiency Points section of your *Success Manual*. Also post your activity totals for all other areas in this section. Calculate and evaluate your point total for the day.

  If you are using the *OCS Productivity Planner,* you have the option of recording activity totals in the lower portion of the weekly pages. However, this is not a substitute for updating the *Success Manual* in the back of the *Planner.* Remember, the *Success Manual* records <u>the names</u> of the Suspects, Prospects and Clients you work with. If you neglect updating the *Success Manual* you lose the up-to-date overview snapshot of your practice.

- Enter the names of all new Qualified Suspects in the *Success Manual.* Complete new yellow cards for these individuals if you have not already done so.

- Complete the New Facts, Cases Opened, Closing Interviews, and Business Submitted/Placed sections with the names and corresponding information according to the activity of the day.

- Scan and update previous *Success Manual* recordings by turning to the oldest page that still has unprocessed Qualified Suspects or unprocessed Cases Opened.

- Scan the list of unprocessed Qualified Suspects to see if any have been processed. If so, complete the disposition column of the

Qualified Suspect section with one of the following codes. Circle the code if a Fact Finding Interview has occurred.

CO Case Opened

A Automatic

DF Dead File

31 Move Ahead

- Scan the New Facts column for sales. Enter the date and amount of the sale and box the square in red. Cross through the squares of any Prospects that have been dead filed.

- Scan the Action Dates in the Cases Opened section to be certain that every item is current and that every name appears on its proper page of the *OCS Control Booklet* or *OCS Productivity Planner*.

- Scan the submitted cases that have not been issued and paid for to be sure that action is scheduled. Do the same for every page up through the current month.

- Record today's business expenditures, for income tax purposes, on the current Daily Page of the *OCS Control Booklet*. (Monthly business expense pages are also provided in the back of the *OCS Productivity Planner*.)

- Transfer the names of all unprocessed phone calls (Automatics) to the next appropriate new page of the *OCS Control Booklet*, or the next appropriate day of the *Productivity Planner*.

- Examine items listed for Office Work. Cross off the items that were completed. Transfer unfinished office work to an appropriate day. Then cross out the page when every item has been accounted for.

- Examine listings of Birthday Automatics, Review Automatics, and Non-Automatics on the front pages of the *OCS Control Booklet*, or monthly planning section of your *Productivity Planner*, to record the results to date.

Now shift your attention to *planning* the day (and days) ahead.

- Schedule the case preparation work for any new Fact Finding Interviews completed that day. Do not fall victim to waiting until the last day before the Closing Interview to analyze the case. Allow yourself ample time should additional questions arise. Likewise, schedule time to prepare for any reviews that may be coming up.

- Look at the next day's schedule and estimate its potential efficiency point count. Consider ways of maximizing the point earning opportunities of each appointment.

- Look at the Appointment Spread Sheet to examine the number of appointments you have scheduled ahead for this week and the next. If the quantity of appointments is insufficient, schedule additional phone time over the next few days.

The Posting and Planning process is the time you spend at the end of each day to objectively work *on* your business. The entire process should only take five to ten minutes per day. Yet, if you do it daily and follow the Structured Day Model, you will find yourself much more relaxed, efficient, and in control of your business.

Client Builder Meetings

What Is a Client Builder Meeting?

A Client Builder is a monthly Financial Services Professionals peer group meeting designed for the purpose of enhancing your career. The idea originally was based on the case study method of the Harvard Business School. Over the years, the model has evolved so that it is currently built around the concept of a board of directors meeting.

In a Client Builder Meeting, you are viewed as a business owner who has assembled your board of directors for a monthly report. When it is your turn to present, you present all of your activity and production data for the month just concluded. This data comes directly out of your *Success Manual* and often includes an analysis generated by a software program such as the *CAM© Report*. You then give a report to your peers about your perception of the state of your business during the past month. This includes the highs, the lows, the successes and the frustrations. You try to summarize where you currently see your business going, and what will be your primary focus for the upcoming month. You might discuss what you see as the immediate and long-term challenges.

Your peers, in turn, give you honest feedback. Their job is to share their best thoughts, suggestions and analyses as both a member of the board and a caring associate.

The Seven Purposes of a Client Builder Meeting

1. To help career development by focusing on the building of your client base rather than just sales.

2. To choose long and short-term goals for your career development.

3. To measure and evaluate progress toward those goals.

4. To provide a monthly snapshot of your professional and career development.

5. To improve Sales Cycle understanding and skills.

6. To provide an atmosphere for support and celebration.

7. To foster the ongoing process of being your best.

The Meeting Format

Approximately eight to ten members constitute an ideal group. The group meets on the same day once a month and meetings usually take about two to three hours. Groups are usually formed on the basis of experience or production levels.

Member Expectations

As an active group member, the expectation is that you will attend all meetings and will be prepared for your presentation. This includes a tabulation of all of your activity and production results for the month as well as the contents of your personal report to the group. You are expected to be on time, stay for the entire meeting and not take phone calls or focus on emails through your smart phone.

The Member Presentation Format

Generally, a report and discussion take approximately fifteen to twenty minutes. You begin your report by presenting your activity and production data for the month. This can be done with a laptop and LCD projector or by handing out hard copies. Your presentation usually lasts about seven to ten minutes as you present your perspective on what has occurred in the past month. As you present your report, your board members should be taking notes so they can remember the important points of your presentations during the year.

Following your report, you should listen carefully to the board members discuss what has taken place during the month as they give their views about the strengths, weaknesses and important opportunities they see. During this discussion period you should remain silent and not respond – just listen. You should, however, answer direct questions from the group members.

Following this five to ten minute period, you are given an opportunity to summarize what you heard as the most important points. In addition, you can clarify any points that you are unclear about or feel need further elaboration. This is not a time to defend yourself, but to listen and reflect.

Finally, you conclude your presentation time by committing to a goal for the month. This should be what you feel will be *the most important thing you can do in the next thirty days to make a positive difference in your business*. This goal is recorded by other group members and there is an expectation of accountability to the group on this commitment. Generally, the goal involves controllable activity rather than sales results.

Accountability and Support

As Al Granum has so eloquently said: "Human nature being what it is, the probability that we will do what we know we should do, what we know we need to do, and what we really want to do, goes up significantly when we make a commitment to our peers." A good Client Builder Meeting is built around honesty and caring accountability. In essence, there is an understanding and trust that provides the heart and soul of a successful group. The understanding is this: If you will tell me the honest truth about *your* business, I will tell you the honest truth about my business, and then we will both make every effort to help one another succeed.

Facilitation of the Meeting

The agency manager may attend the meeting and either the manager, a Financial Services Professional from another group, or an outside professional can function in the role of the moderator or facilitator. Generally, it is best if the agency manager does not function as the moderator because this is not a management meeting. It is a peer Financial Services Professional meeting and it is often too difficult for the manager to keep his or her mouth shut. Sometimes, however, there isn't anyone else qualified to moderate so it has to be the manager.

The facilitator's role is to encourage interaction between the Financial Services Professionals, not to dominate the conversation. Additionally, the goal of the facilitator is to try to avoid lengthy off track discussions and keep the group on time. Ideally, the total group time is divided equally amongst the participating Financial Services Professionals.

In Conclusion

In a successful Client Builder Meeting, the members will begin to identify skill, focus, and motivational strengths and deficits in one another as they continue to listen to the monthly reports. This, in turn, leads to better feedback, a clearer career perspective, and the establishment of meaningful monthly goals. As members spend time together and confide in each other, a sense of trust and camaraderie develops. Soon, the feedback flows from a feeling of genuine caring about one another. This concern and support is the true foundation of a great Client Builder Meeting.

The Annual Review

The key to your planning process is the Annual Review. Your Annual Review involves a careful analysis of the data you have collected and tabulated in the back of your *Success Manual.* You will be using the same forms for your own analysis that were used in the Granum Agency research. You will be able to directly compare your results with those of the study. *You can determine your own 10-3-1 ratio.*

The Research Record

Historical averages from the twenty-five-year study tell us that:

- Approximately 10 percent of a representative's Suspects were eventually sold.

- Approximately 33 percent of representative's new Confidential Questionnaires (fact finding interviews) ultimately resulted in New Clients.

- The percentage of New Clients acquired from Confidential Questionnaires was about 33 percent while the percentage of sales to Cases Opened by updating Confidential Questionnaires on Old Clients was about 66 percent.

These statistical results are important and interesting as points of departure, but *an individual's own record is far more meaningful.* This record is established by accurate maintenance and intelligent evaluation of the data provided by the *Success Manual.*

Preparing for Your Annual Review

In preparation for each annual review, the permanent record of Qualified Suspects and new Confidential Questionnaires obtained for the current and previous years (going back four or five years) should be brought up-to-date to show the first year commission, volume, and date of all first sales. Results are then tabulated on the pages designed for this purpose in the back of your *Success Manual.*

The next portion of the annual review (Annual Review of Cases Opened by the Month and Their Ultimate Disposition) shows what eventually happened to all cases opened during the current year. Again, this form is found in the back of your *Success Manual. It is important to pay attention to the breakdown between Cases Opened on prospective New Clients and all other cases.*

Examples from One Successful Financial Services Professional

On this and the following pages are reproductions of actual annual review records of a successful Financial Services Professional. After you study and tabulate your personal results, you should summarize observations and conclusions on the inside back cover of your *Success Manual.* Your Personal Goals should be clearly set forth. Here you also record your assessment of your business as your funding vehicle.

A Financial Services Professional's Sales to Qualified Suspects

This table summarizes all of this Financial Services Professional's sales to Qualified Suspects.

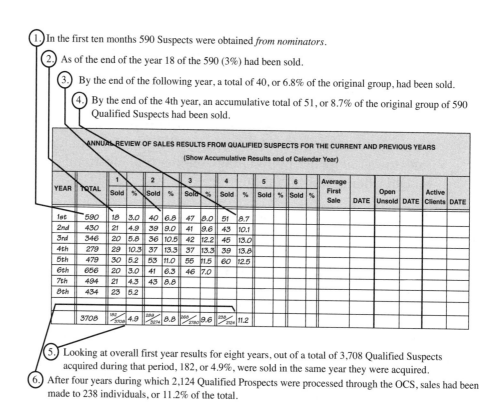

1. In the first ten months 590 Suspects were obtained *from nominators*.

2. As of the end of the year 18 of the 590 (3%) had been sold.

3. By the end of the following year, a total of 40, or 6.8% of the original group, had been sold.

4. By the end of the 4th year, an accumulative total of 51, or 8.7% of the original group of 590 Qualified Suspects had been sold.

ANNUAL REVIEW OF SALES RESULTS FROM QUALIFIED SUSPECTS FOR THE CURRENT AND PREVIOUS YEARS

(Show Accumulative Results end of Calendar Year)

YEAR	TOTAL	1 Sold	%	2 Sold	%	3 Sold	%	4 Sold	%	5 Sold	%	6 Sold	%	Average First Sale	DATE	Open Unsold	DATE	Active Clients	DATE
1st	590	18	3.0	40	6.8	47	8.0	51	8.7										
2nd	430	21	4.9	39	9.0	41	9.6	43	10.1										
3rd	346	20	5.8	36	10.5	42	12.2	45	13.0										
4th	279	29	10.3	37	13.3	37	13.3	39	13.8										
5th	479	30	5.2	53	11.0	55	11.5	60	12.5										
6th	656	20	3.0	41	6.3	46	7.0												
7th	494	21	4.3	43	8.8														
8th	434	23	5.2																
	3708	182/3708	4.9	289/3274	8.8	268/2780	9.6	238/2124	11.2										

5. Looking at overall first year results for eight years, out of a total of 3,708 Qualified Suspects acquired during that period, 182, or 4.9%, were sold in the same year they were acquired.

6. After four years during which 2,124 Qualified Prospects were processed through the OCS, sales had been made to 238 individuals, or 11.2% of the total.

Study the Results of the Qualified Suspects

In reviewing these figures, notice the far reaching effect the processing of Suspects has on the results of future years. With these facts in mind, if this Financial Services Professional would like to consistently acquire fifty or more New Clients each and every year, it would seem that (unless efficiency can be improved) the Financial Services Professional must organize to process about 446 new Suspects every year (11.2% x 446 = 50).

It's a Long Career

Before going on, take another look at this Financial Services Professional's actual accumulative percentage success ratios. Study the third year results when the accumulative success percentage started at 8 percent, rose to 9.6 percent, to 12.2 percent and peaked at 13.3 percent where it looked as if this Financial Services Professional was going to be able to rewrite the book. But the next year dropped to 11.5 percent and then to 7 percent, so that overall the six-year accumulative total was 9.6 percent. In other words, though one year may be up a little, another year is apt to be down a bit, so each individual's results need to be constantly monitored. *You must avoid the complacency that can come with one or two good years.*

Sales to Prospects

The table you have just studied summarizes all of this Financial Services Professional's sales to Qualified Suspects. The next table summarizes all of the sales made to Prospects upon whom Confidential Questionnaires had been obtained.

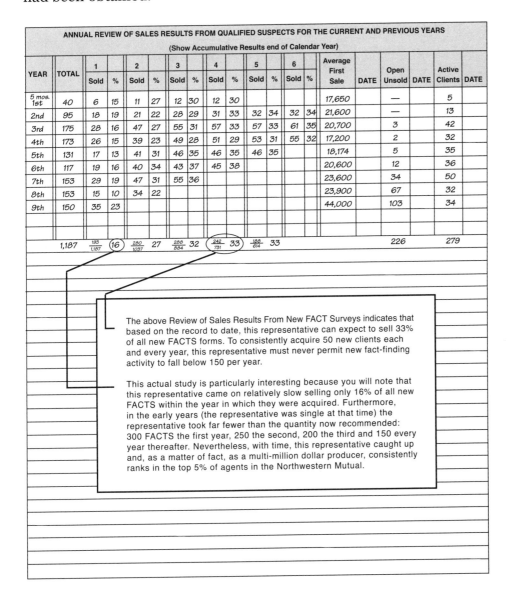

		1		2		3		4		5		6		Average First Sale	DATE	Open Unsold	DATE	Active Clients	DATE
YEAR	TOTAL	Sold	%	Sold	%	Sold	%	Sold	%	Sold	%	Sold	%						
5 mos. 1st	40	6	15	11	27	12	30	12	30					17,650		—		5	
2nd	95	18	19	21	22	28	29	31	33	32	34	32	34	21,600		—		13	
3rd	175	28	16	47	27	55	31	57	33	57	33	61	35	20,700		3		42	
4th	173	26	15	39	23	49	28	51	29	53	31	55	32	17,200		2		32	
5th	131	17	13	41	31	46	35	46	35	46	35			18,174		5		35	
6th	117	19	16	40	34	43	37	45	38					20,600		12		36	
7th	153	29	19	47	31	55	36							23,600		34		50	
8th	153	15	10	34	22									23,900		67		32	
9th	150	35	23											44,000		103		34	
	1,187	193/1,187	(16)	280/1037	27	288/884	32	242/731	33	188/614	33					226		279	

ANNUAL REVIEW OF SALES RESULTS FROM QUALIFIED SUSPECTS FOR THE CURRENT AND PREVIOUS YEARS
(Show Accumulative Results end of Calendar Year)

The above Review of Sales Results From New FACT Surveys indicates that based on the record to date, this representative can expect to sell 33% of all new FACTS forms. To consistently acquire 50 new clients each and every year, this representative must never permit new fact-finding activity to fall below 150 per year.

This actual study is particularly interesting because you will note that this representative came on relatively slow selling only 16% of all new FACTS within the year in which they were acquired. Furthermore, in the early years (the representative was single at that time) the representative took far fewer than the quantity now recommended: 300 FACTS the first year, 250 the second, 200 the third and 150 every year thereafter. Nevertheless, with time, this representative caught up and, as a matter of fact, as a multi-million dollar producer, consistently ranks in the top 5% of agents in the Northwestern Mutual.

Sales from Cases Opened

The third important table included in this Financial Services Professional's Annual Review is reproduced next. It shows what happened to all of the Cases Opened during the year and makes the very, very important distinction between Cases Opened on prospective *New Clients* and Cases Opened on all *others*.

ANNUAL REVIEW OF CASES OPENED BY THE MONTH AND THEIR ULTIMATE DISPOSITION

	C.O.'S NEW CLIENTS	# & AMT. SOLD	AUTO	DEAD FILED	STILL OPEN	C.O.'S OTHERS	# & AMT. SOLD	AUTO	DEAD FILED	STILL OPEN
JANUARY	12	8-300	3	1	0	7	4-40	3	0	0
FEBRUARY	23	14-565	5	4	0	7	3-114	2	2	0
MARCH	11	5-280	1	4	1	6	4-142	2	0	0
APRIL	16	5-235	11	0	0	8	6-104	2	0	0
MAY	13	6-335	4	3	0	6	4-51	2	0	0
JUNE		(one month vacation)								
JULY	15	5-177	9	0	1	5	3-33	2	0	0
AUGUST	9	3-90	6	0	0	8	3-68	3	1	1
SEPTEMBER	8	3-125	4	1	0	7	4-88	2	0	1
OCTOBER	10	1-100	8	0	1	12	8-195	4	0	0
NOVEMBER	14	3-60	6	0	5	9	5-151	1	0	3
DECEMBER	7	2-98	0	0	5	2	1-40	0	0	1
	138	55-2,365	57	13	13	77	45-1,041	23	3	6

SUMMARY	TOTAL	SOLD	PERCENT-AGE	VOLUME	PREMIUM	AV. VOL.	AV. PREM.
NEW CLIENTS	138	55	40	2,365		43,000	
OTHERS	78	46	60	1,041		22,600	
TOTAL	216	101	46	3,406		33,700	

COMMENTS: *The 40% success ratio with new clients is unusually high. Don't plan on this high a percentage until it is proven over a number of years!*

PROJECTIONS: *In view of the above try to open at least 150 cases on prospective new clients!*

Summary of the Annual Review

The purpose of the Annual Review is for you to take an objective (scientific) look at your business and career. It is also an opportunity to re-evaluate your progress toward your personal goals. Since the career is the funding vehicle for your other goals it is important to record your activity and production data and thoroughly analyze it at least once a year to see how you are doing. Using this analysis you can then lay out a valid plan for your next year.

A thorough Annual Review requires tabulating your *Success Manual* data and then studying the results. Study, again, the results for the Financial Services Professional used as an example in this text. Then compare how your personal results compare to both the example Financial Services Professional and the twenty-five-year research findings. It has been said that it is critical to *know the truth of your situation and take appropriate action*. The Annual Review is the process that allows you to do just that!

Utilizing a Sales Assistant

It has been said that the essence of business is leverage. For the financial services professional, your primary leverage can come through the services of a *sales* assistant. Notice the emphasis on *sales*. The purpose of having an assistant is to transfer both administrative and certain Sales Cycle duties (telephoning, underwriting, follow-up, and routine case preparation) to free up your time for increased prospecting, fact finding, and closing activities. In other words, the goal of your assistant should be to keep you *in the field* performing the $200+ an hour work.

Duties of a Sales Assistant

Before hiring a sales assistant, it is important to clearly define their duties and activities. This will allow you to identify the skills you will look for when interviewing a prospective assistant. The following is a list of recommended duties for a sales assistant.

* The Preapproach phase of the Sales Cycle, including:

    * Preparing and tracking all yellow Suspect cards,

    * Sending all preapproach communications,

    * Making phone calls for *all* appointments (initial appointments as well as Birthday and Review Automatics), and

    * Preparing Prompting Lists for prospecting appointments.

* The running of the OCS to include:

    * Creating and tracking white OCS Prospect cards,

- Preparation of Birthday and Review Automatics lists in the *Control Booklet or Productivity Planner*,

- Preparation of Client birthday cards, if appropriate,

- Keeping the Appointment Spread Sheet of the *OCS Control Booklet* up to date or maintaining the weekly appointment pages of the *Productivity Planner*),

- Recording each day's activity in the *Success Manual*,

- Maintaining the Case History and the file folder, and

- Updating the *One Thousand Clients* book.

- Preparation of all routine proposals and illustrations.

- Ordering medical exams, Attending Physician's Statements (APS) and other underwriting requirements.

- Follow-up and servicing of applications in underwriting.

- Handling incoming service calls.

- Routine filing and other clerical responsibilities.

Skills of a Sales Assistant

It is important to keep in mind that the number one job of sales assistants is *calling for appointments*. Therefore, these individuals must have good communication skills. They must be professional and upbeat on the phone. Additionally, they cannot be afraid to make calls, and they must be disciplined enough to make all required calls, each and every day.

Organization skills are also important. The OCS will go a long way toward giving assistants an organizational structure. They must learn it and follow it to the T.

Computer skills and dictation transcription skills are a must. Your assistant must be able to quickly master your company's computer illustration systems and must be adept at using basic programs such as Microsoft® Office. Mastery of graphics and spreadsheet programs, such as Microsoft® PowerPoint and Microsoft® Excel is equally important for proposal preparation purposes. Additionally, if your assistant will be transcribing your dictated letters and Case History Notes for you, transcription skills are a must. Many Financial Services Professionals today are using commercial transcriptions services that send back results via email. If you are using such a system, your assistant must be capable of formatting email text for your proposals and reports.

Chapter 10 will discuss the use of Prompting Lists as a way of increasing referrals. Since the preparation of these lists is the job of your assistant, they will need to be familiar with internet search programs such as Google. You can readily see that a wide range of computer skills are very important in an assistant.

Finally, your sales assistant must be a self-starter. You will be meeting with your assistant each morning to provide instruction and guidance, to update all of the cases in progress and in underwriting, and for recording your activity and production results from the prior day. Beyond that, if you are doing your job of prospecting, and the assistant is doing his or her job on the phone, you will be in the field for the majority of the day. Your sales assistant must be the type of individual who can work independently and resolve problems in your absence.

Daily Supervision and Delegation

As mentioned, you will meet with your assistant each morning for supervision and delegation purposes. Strive to meet as early as possible each morning to review and assign all work for the day, and then avoid interruptions throughout the day. The following is a list of suggested items to be discussed each morning.

1. Items your sales assistant is to bring daily:

   - *Success Manual,*

   - File folders for all appointments for the day, with proposals, illustrations, etc., prepared and ready to go,

   - Notes from incoming calls from previous day (including the corresponding file folders),

   - Incoming mail, including e-mail, previously opened and prioritized,

   - Underwriting status reports,

   - Questions file (a list of tasks that the assistant is unable to accomplish without your direction), and

   - Note pad and pencil.

2. Items you are to bring:

    - *OCS Control Booklet* or *Productivity Planner*,

    - Prospect or Client File Folders from the previous day with Case History Notes, follow-up letters, case preparation instructions, and miscellaneous follow-up instructions for all files,

    - Names, addresses, daytime phone numbers, and qualifying information for all new Qualified Suspects that have been obtained, and

    - Notes for special assignments, such as business travel arrangements, etc.

3. Items to be reviewed and discussed daily:

    - Post all activities from the previous day in the *Success Manual*.

    - List new Qualified Suspects, New Facts (Confidential Questionnaires), Cases Opened, Closing Interviews, and Business Submitted or placed.

    - Record assistant's (and Financial Services Professional's) phone call activity and results. Analyze the quantity of calls and the appointments scheduled.

    - Calculate Activity and Efficiency Points.

    - Scan the Cases Opened section of the *Success Manual*. Discuss the status of cases that are still in progress, update action dates, and assign follow-up activities as needed.

    - Scan the disposition column of the Qualified Suspects section from current and previous months. Are there any Suspects who have yet to be contacted?

    - Review the status of cases in underwriting. What do you need to follow-up on? What can your assistant follow-up on?

    - Review the *OCS Control Booklet* or your *Productivity Planner* to coordinate and update your appointment schedule.

    - Review office work items from the previous day. Cross off items that have been completed. Move forward those to be completed today or on a future date. Delegate all possible items to your assistant.

- Give your assistant information regarding all new Qualified Suspects obtained the previous day for yellow card preparation and follow-up.

- Give your assistant the file folders for all appointments from the previous day and any associated notes or dictation that includes Case History Notes, case preparation instructions, follow-up letters, and assignments for each.

- Review incoming calls and incoming mail from the previous day. Are there any tasks to be added to the daily office items list?

- Review the progress on the preparation of required Prompting Lists.

- Review the file folders for today's appointments that your assistant has brought to the meeting. Is everything in order?

Work to Be Done by the Assistant Alone

1. Finish the preparation of yellow Suspect cards. Also prepare the corresponding pre-approach letters with appropriate accompanying material.

2. Handle dictation to prepare the Case History notes, letters, and special instructions from the previous day's work. Check for instructions regarding the needed creation of Prompting Lists.

3. As early as possible, reconfirm the Financial Services Professional's appointments for the day. As some postpone, try to reschedule another time.

4. Start calling for new appointments as soon as you have reconfirmed those originally scheduled for the day. Stay with it until everyone requested has been reached. Follow up during the balance of the day to contact hard-to-reach people.

5. Maintain an organized work station and file all case folders before leaving for lunch or for the day.

6. Open and prioritize incoming mail and email, and pull all associated file folders. Match up all correspondence with the applicable files before working on any item. Finally, examine each file and its

related correspondence and take appropriate action. Save your questions for the following day's morning planning session on any item that requires direction.

7. Handle all incoming phone calls. If an issue cannot be solved alone, include it with questions for the next morning planning session. Avoid interruptions!

8. At the end of the third week of each month, prepare the OCS for the next month as described in the section about the monthly planning process.

9. Other than the morning planning session and an occasional late afternoon emergency discussion, do not interrupt the Financial Services Professional during the day. (Likewise, the representative should eliminate all conversation with the assistant after the planning session in order to focus on their own work!)

Training and Daily Activity of the Assistant

Since Job One of your assistant is to call for appointments, it is suggested that you train new assistants on this important skill *first*. Suggested phone language for the assistant can be found in Chapter 11. Or, you can modify whatever effective scripts you are currently using for use by your assistant. Be sure to model the use of the basic language to demonstrate to your new assistant that the language does work – on a law of averages basis.

Use the first few weeks of your assistant's employment to carefully evaluate phone activity and results. If your new assistant cannot adequately master this very important skill, then replace the person immediately, before you have spent the time to teach him or her the business.

Beyond phone skill training, it is very important that your assistant master the OCS. The *Building a Financial Services Clientele* book should be used as your training tool in this area. Also, utilize company training manuals and your firm's training classes for new associates. These provide excellent resources to help leverage your time in the training of an assistant.

Create a Procedures Manual

Each time your assistant brings you a procedural question which he or she cannot resolve alone, take the time during your morning supervision session to explain the appropriate course of action. Have your assistant take careful notes, and then ask him or her to write up a procedure report for future reference. Review the report for accuracy during the next morning's supervision session. Then, have your assistant create a manual for all such reports. This manual will serve as a valuable resource for future reference or for the training of a temporary or a new assistant.

Sales Assistant Compensation

It is suggested that the sales assistant's compensation be a combination of hourly wage and activity incentive. The hourly wage must be competitive with wages in your area. The activity incentive piece that is outlined below is an added bonus that is designed to drive your assistant's behavior toward the activities that will lead to the desired result; that is, increasing *your* field activities.

To focus the attention of an assistant where it belongs you, the Financial Services Professional, should first decide what's a reasonable accomplishment each month in the areas of new Suspects, new Facts, new Cases Opened and telephoning for appointments.

Assistant's incentive bonus chart

Labels (left): Monthly Goal; Cumulative Monthly Goals; Actual Monthly Activity; Actual Total Activity For Year

	QUALIFIED SUSPECTS	NEW FACTS	CASES OPENED ON NEW CLIENTS	SECRETARY PHONES FOR APPOINTMENTS
JAN	(42) / 44 $25	13 / 12	13 / 15 $25	100 / 75
FEB	84 / 60 $25 / 140	26 / 13 $25 / 25	26 / 12 $25 / 27	200 / 130 ($50) / 206
MAR	(126) / 25 $25 / 129	39 / 15 $50 / 40	39 / 13 $25 / 40	300 / 100 $25 / 305
APR	168 / (30) / 39	52 / 10 / 50	52 / 18 / 58	400 / 50 / 355
MAY	210 / 45 $25 / (204)	65 / 13 $25 / 63	65 / 10 $25 / 68	500 / 150 $50 / 505
	252	78	78	600

(Note at right of FEB row: Missed Bonus In January—Made It Up In February)

In the example of the assistant's incentive bonus chart, the figure in the upper left hand corner of each square is the monthly goal shown cumulatively. Figures in the center of the square represent actual monthly activity and cumulative activity for the year.

For example, in the Qualified Suspects column, the monthly goal is forty-two. By the end of March, new Qualified Suspects should total 126 (3 x 42). Actual activity in March produced only twenty-five, but activity for the year to date has produced a total of 129 (44 + 60 + 25) for an excess of three over the cumulative goal to date.

For each category in which the *monthly or cumulative goal* is realized, the assistant receives a $25 bonus. If neither the monthly nor the cumulative goal is reached the bonus is missed, but if it is made up in a later month it will be paid at that time.

This provides your assistant with an easily understood system of financial reward and gives the assistant a continuing interest in productivity as you both perform the necessary activities to guarantee ultimate success.

It is interesting to note that the assistant's bonus structure also drives *your* behavior in the key skill of prospecting. Part of their bonus depends on your ability to consistently obtain referrals. Two-way accountability is built into this system. Yours – in the area of getting quality referrals – and the assistant's – in terms of scheduling quality appointments that will lead to New Facts and Cases Opened on New Clients.

An important part of this bonus system is your *daily* supervision meeting with your assistant. Keeping your *Success Manual* data is the primary method of tracking the assistant's monthly bonus. You will be more inclined to get referred leads if you know your assistant will be tracking and following up on them daily as part of his or her own compensation.

Part 2

Using OCS with Today's Tools and Technology

Chapter 6

OCS and Today's Financial Services Professional

Changes in the Financial Industry – Is Everything Different Now?

Repeal of the Glass-Steagall Act and New Technologies

It is true that the financial services industry is highly dynamic. From 1933 through 1999, the Glass-Steagall Act (officially the Banking Act of 1933) legally separated the various segments of our industry. Banks, stock brokerage, and insurance companies all were required to operate independently of one another. Congress repealed the Act in 1999 and began the great movement toward convergence and consolidation. Convergence is the term used to describe the new reality of large financial companies offering a complete range of financial services. Put bluntly, everyone will sell everything.

Will Financial Services Professionals be Replaced by Online Services?

Added to the legal and organizational changes is the impact of mass computerization and the Internet. The power of the Internet brought about virtually instant access to worldwide communication and phenomenal amounts of information. This access allows a direct connection between companies and the consumer. The elimination of the middleman is being called Disintermediation. Traditionally, middlemen provided information, consultation, service, and sales coordination. Now, much of this can be done on-line.

As disintermediation continues, costs are reduced, market inefficiencies are eliminated, and products begin to compete with increasingly smaller margins. The marginalization or commoditization of many products will certainly reduce commission structures. As business costs rise with inflation and commission rates fall with purer market competition, the question arises, will Financial Services Professionals be able to sustain a profitable business? Will a whole new way of doing business be required in order to survive?

Let's look at these questions carefully because they are at the heart of the entire premise of this book and the One Card System. Indications are that direct marketing by companies via mass mailing, telemarketing, or online quotes and sales will not replace the financial services professional – primarily because a relationship that is built upon trust is not a commodity! The Client is not just buying a product – he or she is buying the knowledge and solutions of a professional, and the peace of mind that he or she is in good hands. Even though people can now purchase prescriptions and medications online, it will not replace their desire to consult with a doctor who understands them and their history. Moreover, they will be willing to pay more for personalized medical guidance. The Internet, on the other hand, can't listen, understand, appreciate or care. You can see, therefore, that a career built upon a model of transactional selling will always be in jeopardy.

The purpose of this book is to teach Financial Services Professionals how to achieve personal freedom throughout their professional careers. In our view, a business philosophy built upon client building and creating and sustaining trusting relationships is fundamental to long-term success in the financial services career. It is true that the business environment has changed and will continue to change. The irony, however, is that the traditional building blocks of the One Card System – referred lead prospecting, complete values-oriented fact finding, needs-based solutions, and regular client contact and review – are even more important now than ever before! It is our belief that if these skills are lost then the individual producer will fall to the decreasing margins and increased competition of transaction based selling. The reality is – for today's Financial Services Professional – that the One Card System will help you stand out from your peers.

The New Model for a Successful Financial Services Professional

The Crucial Issue of Client Control

The successful Financial Services Professional of the future will be the person who earns the trust of the client and, therefore, also enjoys greater control of the client relationship. Successful people today have incredibly busy lives. They are looking for ways to simplify the tremendous amount of information they must process. In some ways, the information explosion of the Internet and smart phones has created even more demands upon their time and attention.

In order to simplify their financial lives, some of these busy people will want what has become known as one-stop shop approach to their financial affairs. That is, they will want the convenience of having their banking, investing, insurance, and financial planning all handled in one place with one trusted financial advisor and one comprehensive summary report. As industry convergence combines with increasing technological power, that wish will become more and more possible. However, not everyone will want this. Some will want a variety of professionals handling the different areas of their financial life. And still others will prefer the transactional model to handle their own needs using a self-service approach.

The financial services mega-companies that once were banks, insurance companies, and brokerage houses will all compete to bring Clients under their umbrella of services. The belief is that as a Client adds to the number of services he or she has with one company, the more convenient and efficient it becomes for that Client to stay with that company. In short, everyone will be competing for client control.

Who will win? At times, it appears that the winner will be the most technologically sophisticated company that generates the largest number of automated client contacts or touches such as discount offerings for multiple services. Our belief is that the professional who is referred, who understands the Client, who follows-up and creates a trusting relationship will ultimately guide that Client's actions. As such, that professional will be highly compensated.

The Client Control Model

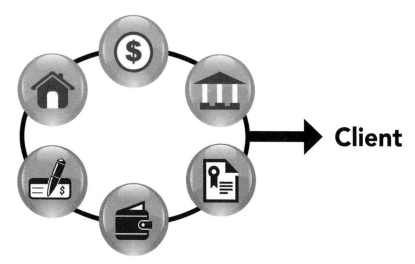

Client

The successful Financial Services Professional of the future won't have to be an expert at everything, but he or she will need to know how to find Clients and create trust. The specific expertise needed for a particular Client problem will be available through his or her company or companies. Real time video and Web conferencing will allow a local professional to bring in a national or international expert. Expertise will become a commodity while client control will become the paramount position. The ultimate winner will be the professional who is perceived by the Client to be his or her trusted Financial Services Professional. *Trust* will become synonymous with client control and client control will become synonymous with success.

How Will the One Card System Help?

When you look at the philosophy, the administrative tools, and the Sales Cycle skills embodied within the One Card System, you will see that it actually is a technology for creating and sustaining long-term, trusting business relationships. It is a system for becoming a Trusted Financial Services Professional. In this regard, it is the ideal system for competing and succeeding in today's business environment.

The One Card System as a *Franchise Model*

It is estimated that approximately 80 percent of all small business startups in the United States fail within the first five years. On the other hand, it is estimated that approximately 90 percent of all existing franchise startups (an established franchise opening another outlet) are still in business five years later. Why the enormous difference? What is it that makes franchises successful?

The answer clearly lies in the fact that franchises have standardized methods and procedures. They don't change the way they do business with each new customer. They identify what works and then they repeat it. Franchises turn problems into processes. And, franchises measure, measure, measure. That is, they quantify what they are doing so they can scientifically evaluate the effect of anything they change.

The One Card System (OCS) is indeed *a proven system*. It is the result of twenty-five years of research, testing, and improvement and more than forty years of effective implementation. It is *the* franchise model that integrates all of the elements needed to make your financial services business succeed. More than that, however, it also provides the administrative systems for tracking your business activity and production. Consequently – and this is a big advantage – it allows you to quantify your business activites so you can understand and predict your business outcomes. In its entirety, the OCS includes all the tools, instructions, and methods for building your business. It provides the technology for creating trusting relationships and a substantial client base.

The OCS and Technological Advancement

One of the questions that is often asked about the OCS is, "How does the OCS utilize and stay current with the continuing technological advancements?" After all, wasn't the OCS developed during the 1960s in a pre-computer work environment? Although today there are several powerful technological options for using the OCS, it is useful to review the historical and technological development of the OCS.

To begin with, keep in mind that the OCS is an integrated system consisting of two major components, each of which can be utilized with varying levels of electronic automation. The first of these is a system for prompting regular contact with your Suspects, Prospects, and Clients. The technology utilized for this task during the inception of the OCS was a card file which used index cards. While this manual approach may seem primitive to today's computer-savy generation, it is still in use today by thousands of highly successful Financial Services Professionals around the world. This system remains simple, inexpensive, fast, efficient, and not subject to breakdown. It is still used extensively because it works!

The second major component of the OCS is a system for recording sales-related activity on a daily basis. The collection of this data formed the basis for O. Alfred Granum's extensive research. Initially, activity data for Granum's Financial Services Professionals (then called Agents) was collected in spiral notebooks. This data was transferred to a series of tables and analyzed. These notebooks were later formalized and published as what we know today as the OCS *Success Manual*. The *Success Manual* continues to be used today by thousands of successful Financial Services Professionals to record and track their sales activity and production.

The Original OCS Research
Spiral Notebooks

So, how has the OCS kept pace with technology? Although the *Success Manual* has proven to be a simple, inexpensive, and effective way to record activity and production, it lacks the power to automatically analyze the data. In the early 1990's Dr. Barry Alberstein created a Microsoft® Excel worksheet that completely and automatically analyzed the data recorded in the *Success Manual*. This became the *Career Activity Management Report* or the *CAM® Report*. Through recent development, the program is now known as the *Career Activity Management(CAM) System™ (discussed in detail in Chapter 8 of this book)* it is now a comprehensive online system that tracks client inventory and preforms many of the functions of the previously manual system. It is designed to work hand in hand with the *OCS Productivity Planner* (discussed in detail in a later chapter) to greatly streamline all OCS activities.

In addition, there is an extensive array of commercial customer relationship management (CRM) software programs available such as Microsoft® Outlook or ACT, which are discussed in the next chapter. Any of these programs can be used to automate the functions of the OCS Card File.

The Career Activity Management (CAM) Report ©

Report Prepared For **Sam Baker**

Report Date 11/20/2005

Enter your data upon the completion of each month- All Calculations Are Automatic.

Business Activity / Submitted / Placed

Mnth	Days worked	Apointmts Made	Apointmts Kept	Dials	Telephone Reach	Apmts	Meals	Qual Suspts	Referl Atmpts	Refrls Obtain	New Seens	New Facts	Cases Opened	Closes	Points	Core Sales	Other Sales	New Accnts	Core FYC	Other FYC	Core Sales	Other Sales	New Accnts	Core FYC	Other FYC	Company Credits
Goals	17	80	60	400	140	70	17	50	20	40	14	13	20	25	100	9	5	6	$6,000	$2,000	9	4	5	$6,500	$1,000	$7,500
							1 Pt.	5Pts				1 Pt.	1 Pt.	1 Pt.	1Pt.											
Jan	14	56	42	390	72	40	13	34	18	33	14	15	25	20	90	5	4	5	$3,300	$1,700	8	2	5	$6,121	$130	$6,251
Feb	19	78	63	421	89	44	15	48	26	44	14	13	22	28	102	6	5	6	$4,738	$5,007	5	5	3	$2,557	$1,142	$3,699
Mar	18	72	59	380	69	42	19	56	21	50	13	13	25	23	108	5	6	5	$5,360	$4,462	7	6	6	$7,627	$5,174	$12,801
Apr	19	78	61	412	75	41	15	44	18	43	12	12	22	26	97	8	4	6	$7,625	$2,710	7	3	6	$5,492	$853	$6,345
May	17	82	66	441	93	46	17	62	24	59	15	14	26	25	113	8	5	6	$13,695	$1,000	6	5	6	$6,629	$3,242	$9,871
Jun															0											
Jul															0											
Aug															0											
Sep															0											
Oct															0											
Nov															0											
Dec															0											
Year to Date Total	87	366	291	2,044	398	213	79	244	107	229	68	67	120	122	510	32	24	28	$34,708	$14,879	33.0	21.0	26.0	$28,426	$10,541	$38,967
Average per month	17	73	58	409	80	43	16	49	21	46	14	13	24	24	102	6	5	6	6942	2976	7	4	5	5685	2108	7793

(your monthly average times 12 months - Green equals at or above goal - Red equals behind goal)

Annualized Activity and Production: 209 | 878 | 698 | 4906 | 955 | 511 | 190 | 586 | 257 | 550 | 163 | 161 | 288 | 293 | 1224 | 77 | 58 | 67 | $83,299 | $35,710 | 79 | 50 | 62 | $68,222 | $25,298 | $93,521

Active Client Count **408**

Inventory Report
Short Term $21,250
Long Term $42,500
Underwriting In $16,530

Cummulative Report

Activity	Dollar value of each Activity in Paid for Commission
Day Worked	$448
Appointment Made	$106
Appointment Kept	$134
Dial	$19
Reach	$98
Apmt Made by Phone	$183
Lunch (Business Meal)	$493
Qualified Suspect	$160
Referral Attempt	$364
Referral Obtained	$170
New Seen	$573
Factfinder Interview	$582
Case Opened	$325
Closing Interview	$319
Efficiency Point	$76

Average number of activities per:

Activity	Sale	Day	New Client
Day Worked	1.6		3.3
Appointment Made	6.8	4.2	14.1
Appointment Kept	5.4	3.3	11.2
Dial	37.9	23.5	78.6
Reach	7.4	4.6	15.3
Apmt Made by Phone	3.9	2.4	8.2
Lunch (Business Meal)	1.5	0.9	3.0
Qualified Suspect	4.5	2.8	9.4
Referral Attempt	2.0	1.2	4.1
Referral Obtained	4.2	2.6	8.8
New Seen	1.3	0.8	2.6
Factfinder Interview	1.2	0.8	2.6
Case Opened	2.2	1.4	4.6
Closing Interview	2.3	1.4	4.7
Efficiency Point	9.4	5.9	19.6

Key Efficiency Ratios and Benchmarks for the Year to Date

	Actual	Goals	OCS
Phoning Efficiency			
Dials to Reaches	19%	35%	33%
Reaches to Appointments Made	54%	50%	50%
Appointment Efficiency			
Appointments Made to Kept %	80%	75%	67%
Referrals Obtained per Attempt	2.14	2.00	3
Qualified Suspects to Facts %	27%	26%	30%
New Seens to Facts %	99%	93%	80%
Facts to Cases Opened %	179%	65%	80-150%
Cases Opened to Closes %	102%	125%	150%
Selling Efficiency			
Cases Opened to Total Sales Submitted %	47%	70%	
Closes to Total Sales Submitted %	46%	56%	
Ave. Paid FYC per Core Sale	$861	$889	
Ave. Paid FYC per Other Sale	$502	$400	
Core Sales Underwriting Success	82%	89%	95%
Points Per Day	5.86	6.00	5
Points per Kept Appointment	1.75	1.67	1.5 - 2

* Suspects & New Facts are the "10" and the "3" of the famous "10-3-1" New Client Acquisition Ratio.

© 2000-2005 Alberstein Consulting

The OCS Offers Flexibility

Consider your options. You can use a completely manual version of the OCS. This is time tested, reliable, and the best way to learn the system. You can go to the other end of the continuum and use a completely automated approach. Or, you can use a blended system of manual elements combined with computerized components. A blend that leans more toward the manual system might use the OCS Card File system, the *Success Manual*, the *OCS Productivity Planner*, and a commercial CRM data base program. A more computer based blended system might combine the *OCS Productivity Planner* with the *CAM System*™ to take full advantage of the online tools now available. The OCS is very flexible and the choice is yours.

Note: update this graphic

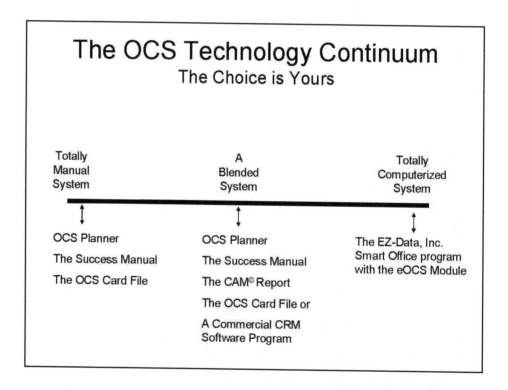

The OCS Technology Continuum
The Choice is Yours

Totally Manual System	A Blended System	Totally Computerized System
OCS Planner	OCS Planner	The EZ-Data, Inc. Smart Office program with the eOCS Module
The Success Manual	The Success Manual	
The OCS Card File	The CAM© Report	
	The OCS Card File or	
	A Commercial CRM Software Program	

What Is Really Important?

The critical issue isn't whether you use a software or paper version of the system. What is paramount is that you fully understand how the system works and what it is doing for you. You need to understand the role of each OCS component and why these actions are important for your success. It truly doesn't matter whether or not the process is automated; rather, it is essential that you understand and follow the process!

In this book we recommend you get started with a manual approach. If you learn the basic system and why it has been constructed in this way, you will then be in a position to succeed with more automated tools. It is this understanding that will fully empower you. If you jump directly to automated tools, put in a few names, and then believe you are using the One Card System, you will have missed it all!

Take the time to learn the manual system as outlined previously and in the final section on Converting to the One Card System. Then and only then, if you wish, transfer your knowledge and understanding to a blended or completely computerized version. We promise you it will be a valuable investment of your professional time and will bring you the sense of control offered by the OCS.

Newer Technologies for
The Financial Services Professional

Whether you choose to use the One Card System or not, there are many newer technology tools that will simplify and improve the lives of today's Financial Services Professionals.

Technology, software, computing, and communication devices are changing at an amazing rate. Consequently it is nearly impossible to cover all the tools currently available and even more difficult to try to anticipate what will be available tomorrow! Our purpose here is to review some of the basic tools currently available and discuss why understanding and using new technologies is important to today's Financial Services Professional. While we have attempted to include many of the more common tools, we did not deliberately include or exclude and particular vendor. The fact that a product is included here is not meant to suggest that these products are superior to others or that their inclusion represents an endorsement by the authors. We have attempted to mention products and services simply as a way of introducing the concepts these provide, not as a comprehensive or approved list.

We want to give the reader an overview of how the new technologies can improve their knowledge, research, practice processes, and management systems. Clearly the times dictate that these need a fresh look.

Human Capacity and Why We Need Technology

The 7 ± 2 Limitation

The human brain is powerful and amazing, but even the brain has its limitations. The study of these limitations is often referred to as the psychology of human capacity. George Miller, a cognitive psychologist at Princeton University, published research in 1956 that suggested the maximum number of objects the average human can hold in working memory is seven, plus or minus two. Recent research supports this earlier finding, while other current studies suggest that the number may actually be as low as four items. In either case our capacity is clearly limited. One way of thinking about this is to imagine we have 7 ± 2 (from five to nine) slots in our brain to hold short term information. This means if we write out a to-do list of twenty-five items and we lose the list, we will only be able to remember 7 ± 2 items. We simply aren't biologically equipped to keep track of large databases.

Successful career requirements

Think about this for a moment. Clearly we can't build a substantial client base and a successful practice with this biological limitation. As suggested by the original Granum research – and validated over several decades – Financial Services Professionals need to identify and acquire approximately 1,000 clients throughout their career to maximize success. According to his research this translates to identifying, contacting, and tracking approximately 10,000 qualified candidates (qualified suspects) over the length of one's career. Considering human capacity, it's easy to see why this would be virtually impossible without the use of a process and system.

Overload and anxiety

What happens if we try to jam more information into the slots and exceed their capacity? The result is a sense of cognitive overload and a feeling of anxiety. Imagine someone giving you a lengthy series of instructions on how to get to their home and you try to remember it all without writing it down or using a GPS. After a few landmarks and turns you will begin to get anxious as you realize you can't remember all of the details. Overload creates anxiety, and anxiety is a feeling we really don't like. We will do almost anything to avoid it. It can be compared to the feeling one gets when being held under water for too long, and again, we don't like it! Many Financial Services Professionals spend their professional lives feeling as though they are standing in a pool of water up to – but not covering – their noses. They aren't drowning, but they aren't interested in anyone making any waves either! They are constantly experiencing mild anxiety, on the verge of severe anxiety. But, if we can only handle 7 ± 2 items, isn't this under water feeling inevitable? The answer is yes, unless we have a system or process that will capture and hold the items for us. Many of today's tools – including OCS – will help you keep your head above water!

How does anxiety affect us?

Anxiety almost inevitably leads to behaviors designed to keep the water level low. These behaviors are called *avoidance behaviors* because we avoid the immediate anxiety caused by doing what is necessary, but not easy or pleasant. These avoidance behaviors are only effective in the short run because they *temporarily* lower the water level to relieve anxiety. It is only temporary because the tasks remain to be done, and the anxiety water level rises again. So, reading *The Wall Street Journal* or reorganizing our office may relieve the anxiety of doing the immediate required task for awhile, but the feeling will not last for long. The problem, of course, is that these avoidance behaviors interfere with our capacity to actually accomplish what we need to do to build a clientele. This failure to undertake the appropriate activities to accomplish our business requirements only creates more anxiety – which, in turn, motivates more avoidance. It's a vicious cycle. What then is the answer to our limited human capacity?

The necessity of a system

The only consistently successful answer to this question is to have a system for guiding your professional practice. If you have a mastered process for your business tasks you won't require all of the seven slots in order complete the necessary activities. A key element here is that your system must be able to **capture** (identify and record) the desired tasks, and then **assign** a specific time to complete them. This process of capturing and assigning is critical to anxiety management and also beneficial to ultimate success.

The role of technology

Technology provides us with the tools to conduct our desired business process. It's interesting that today we associate the word technology with automation and computerization. However, this isn't the case. *Merriam-Webster*® dictionary defines technology as, "a manner of accomplishing a task especially using processes, methods, or knowledge". No mention of automation or computers. So, it's accurate to say that a pencil, calendar, index cards, and a notebook provide the technology to implement the One Card System. Combine this with your phone and you have a simple but powerful system to capture, assign, and carry out your business process with minimal anxiety.

Now consider using the art, psychology, concepts, and processes contained within the time tested One Card System and supplementing it with the latest technological innovations to manage the system. You will combine the best system with the latest tools to minimize the stress and anxiety from your daily work life.

With this in mind, let's review some of the tools readily available to today's Financial Services Professional and consider how you can incorporate them into your business process.

The benefits of new technology

A clear benefit of today's technology is the ability to access huge amounts of information. The time savings are enormous. Consider the number of steps involved in the research when Dr. Alberstein was writing the dissertation for his doctorate:

1. Go to the campus library.

2. Review a reference book for a study or article of interest.

3. Read the article and check for useful references listed at the conclusion of the article.

4. Wait in line at the copier and copy the article bibliography.

5. Go to the library index card catalog and look for the location of the text that contained the first useful article on the copied list.

6. Locate the book, copy the article of interest, and repeat the process for each of the required articles.

The complete research process took months! Now, consider the same research today using high speed Internet at home. The same amount of research can be done in a fraction of the time without ever needing to leave your chair!

It is obvious that effectively utilizing new technology can greatly improve our available information, save time, and make us more efficient and effective. Notice it says *"effectively utilizing new technology."* The fact that a technology is new doesn't necessarily make it valuable or beneficial. While it may be new and potentially beneficial, if not utilized properly, the technology will not automatically create efficiency or effectiveness. You can buy the latest smart phone but it won't be of additional value unless you learn how to use the new features. You must also be careful that a new technology doesn't become an avoidance behavior in itself. Surfing the Web in the office doesn't add to our efficiency or effectiveness!

Using Today's Tools to Increase Industry Knowledge and Skills

Surfing the Web for fun may not be of much help, but the Internet used effectively is a virtually unlimited storehouse of helpful information. Let's look at a few Web sites that you could use to increase your knowledge base and provide valuable tools for your practice. Remember this is only a partial list of hundreds of valuable tools.

Google - www.Google.com

Google, of course, needs no introduction. It is an enormous program designed to search the Web for virtually any topic imaginable as well as provide a wide range of computing tools and services. In addition to providing easy access to billions of Web pages, Google has many special features to help you find exactly what you're looking for. Google runs over one million servers in data centers around the world, and processes over one billion search requests and about twenty-four petabytes of user-generated data every day (there are a million gigabytes in a petabyte). Almost any computer search begins with checking Google. We will return to Google in our discussion of using technology to help prospecting.

Bing - www.Bing.com

Bing (formerly Live Search, Windows Live Search, and MSN Search) is another huge Internet search service, but from Microsoft®. As with Google, it offers an extensive range of search features as well as computing tools and services.

LIMRA, The Life Insurance and Market Research Association - www.Limra.com

LIMRA is a worldwide organization dedicated to the financial services industry. Its Web site contains up to date information regarding current issues and state of the industry. A wide range of research and educational programs of value to Financial Services Professionals is also available.

Hoopis Performance Network - www.Hoopis.com

The Hoopis Performance Network is a Web based subscription service offering an extensive range of interviews and information for financial services professionals.

National Underwriter Advanced Markets Service – www. advisorFX.com

National Underwrtier Advanced Markets Service (AMAFX) provides the most comprehensive advanced planning research database available today. The content is dedicated to assisting financial advisors who serve business owners, wealthy families and corporations with their complex planning issues. AMAFX provides excellent coverage of estate planning, wealth transfer planning, business succession planning, trusts, IRAs, 401(k)'s, wealth management, and benefits planning. The service provides more depth of content than any other platform available. Users are provided with over 50 Practice Aid illustrations describing complex concepts in an easy to understand narrative style so that they can then share them with their clients. AMAFX takes the complex concepts and makes them simple.

TAX FACTS Online – www.taxfactsonline.com

Tax Facts Online offers the extensive data contained within the renowned *Tax Facts on Insurance & Employee Benefits* and *Tax Facts on Investments* Source Books in a single convenient and easy-to-use online resource. One of the most trusted authoritative resources available today delivers a fully searchable online solution that is updated whenever changes occur.

Back Room Technician® by Advisys – www.advisys.com

Back Room Technician and echoWealth are used at each stage of the sales cycle: from prospecting and approach to needs analysis, recommendation and closing. They help increase sales, attract high level recruits, train representatives, introduce new product and marketing initiatives and improve customer service. Our products are powered by Advisys, the first turnkey Web services platform for automating advice-driven solutions.

Profiles and NaviPlan by EISI – www.eisi.com

Clear, easy-to-use needs analysis software for financial assessments. EISI products allow a financial advisor to complete a simple analysis in just minutes or a sophisticated financial plan. Profiles Forecaster is an easy-to-learn, goals-based application that keeps data entry to a minimum. You can tailor action-oriented results in a clear, ready-to-present format. It's ideal for qualifying prospects and providing a basic financial assessment to investors. NaviPlan Select is a powerful yet flexible program that lets you pick your plan. For simple or sophisticated financial plans – you always have exactly what you need. It's the very latest in financial planning technology, backed by more than twenty years of experience. So you can manage your clients' dreams and have total confidence in the plan you present.

The Virtual Sales Assistant (VSA) – www.fsonline.com

The Virtual Sales Assistant has been described as an interactive library, but it is much more than that. It is truly a very knowledgeable assistant that can put virtually everything you need to operate a financial practice at your fingertips. The Virtual Assistant is the only product that offers Financial Snapshots, Priority Approaches, and Priority Planning Reviews. It also includes our popular Virtual Advisor, a twice monthly publication providing ideas on how to make sales using The Virtual Assistant, as well as executive summaries of events that affect financial advisors. Hundreds of Personalized Reports for your clients and prospects are included along with prospect approach letters, PowerPoint presentations, dozens of financial and needs calculators, detailed Tax Information, and Advanced Planning Books and Tools.

Audible - www.Audible.com

Audible is a powerful tool for busy people who wish they had more time to read and prefer to listen to written content. Audible.com is a leading provider of digital spoken audio information and entertainment on the Internet. Audible content contains over 85,000 audio programs including audiobooks, magazines, newspapers, entertainment, and business information. These programs are downloaded and played back on PCs, CDs, or AudibleReady® computer-based and wireless mobile devices. This is the new high tech alternative to books on tape. You can listen to books or articles while driving or exercising using your iPod, iPad, or cell phone. It's reasonably priced and the narration is of the highest quality.

Copytalk Mobile Scribe Services - www.Copytalk.com

Copytalk is a dictation transcription service. Immediately after a meeting with a client you can dictate the case history update using your cell phone. The transcription is processed by people rather than computers, and the results are emailed to you or your assistant the following day. The emailed transcription can be edited and pasted into your electronic case history file in either your CRM or CAM System™. You can also use the service to update clients or dictate daily activity totals or follow-up tasks to your assistant who can enter them into your automated system.

Using Social Networking Services to Improve Prospecting

The knowledge that can gained from the vast information on the Web is exciting, but how can you use it to create practical improvements to your business process? Most experienced Financial Services Professionals will agree that the process of obtaining quality introductions to potential clients is the single most important skill in achieving success in this career. You need the names of people before you can possibly meet or help them. Research on the Internet can be of significant help for this purpose.

To maximize the number of introductions you wish to obtain during your prospecting opportunities, there are two types of names you want to get from your nominator:

- Names of people both you and the nominator know, but to whom you have not been introduced.

- Names of people that the nominator knows but you do not.

We want a process that maximizes both.

Six-Step Prospecting Language

Later in this book, you will learn about O. Alfred Granum's famous Six-Step Prospecting Language, which has been time tested in every conceivable market. It is powerful and it works. Part of the power comes from the fact that it feeds names we already know as well as categories that prompt additional names from the nominator. The point is that combining the six-step language with other techniques will maximize the total number of referrals obtained in an interview.

Use Prompting Lists to Increase Referrals

During conversations with others, personal observations, or actual discussions with your Prospect or Client, you likely have the names of people who are friends or associates of your Prospect or Client. One approach is to bring up names of these people during the Fact Finding Interview and ask your Prospect or Client for a referral. While these names are valuable, you usually won't come up with enough names to meet your goals. How can you come in fully prepared to walk away with the highest number of referrals possible? The answer may be in the use of Prompting Lists.

A prompting list is simply a list of people whom the nominator might recognize. You can take advantage of social networking sites to build your list. For example, if your client is an Optometrist, then the prompting list might contain a list of members of the local Optometric Association or Optometrists found through a Google search. If the prospect is a member of an engineering or law firm, the list could be a roster of firm members or members of an appropriate professional association. If they are simply members of the Order of the Mystic Knights of the Sea, then we want a list of Order members! With the explosion of social networking sites, you have a wide range of tools available to locate these names.

Recognition versus Recall Memory

Why is a prompting list so valuable? The answer is that prompting lists rely on recognition memory. Psychologists have long understood the difference between recognition and recall memory. When you ask a client to think of people who might benefit from your services, you are asking the client to utilize recall memory. That is, you are asking them to try to recall people they know. This requires more work on the part of the client, and remembering the limits on human capacity you will be lucky to obtain even a few names. Recognition memory, on the other hand, is much easier for the client and much more powerful. All you are asking is if they recognize or remember any of the people on your list. It is not unusual to obtain ten or twenty names (introductions) using this technique. Often viewing the list stimulates remembering other names not on the list. Clearly a prompting list is a powerful necessity in prospecting.

Tools for Building Prompting Lists

Where can you get such lists? First you need to check online. Use a search engine like the aforementioned Google or Bing and start entering search words. You will be amazed. Most professional organizations or companies have a Web page and often have listed member directories. If not, most sites offer directions as to how to obtain them. After obtaining the list you can edit it and then either print it out for the client to view, or show the list on your tablet computer such as an iPad or PlayBook. The use of a tablet device makes for a smooth transition to the prospecting topic and identifies you as someone who keeps up with the latest innovation.

To excel in any area generally comes as a result of careful preparation. Prospecting is no different. If you are going to be able to calmly feed names and categories you must have prepared these lists in advance of your meetings. We have already discussed the importance of preparing a relevant prompting list prior to our meeting. An even more efficient approach is having your assistant routinely prepare such lists for you. There are two key points here. One, you can't view prospecting as an Add-on to the really important task of selling. It is a critical process in your success and must be treated as such. Second, as the great life insurance sales professional Ben Feldman once said, "If it's a problem, make it a process and it won't be a problem anymore." The more you can systematize your prospecting process and the preparation for that process, the greater your success! Consider the following social networking sites when preparing prompting lists.

LinkedIn – www.linkedin.com

LinkedIn is rapidly becoming an essential tool for Financial Services Professionals. It is well worth joining and taking the time to master. It is a very powerful prospecting tool.

LinkedIn is a business-related social networking site which, as of March 2011 reports having more than 100 million registered users spanning more than 200 countries and territories worldwide. The site is available in English, French, German, Italian, Portuguese, and Spanish and reports approximately 21.4 million unique U.S. visitors each month.

One purpose of the site is to allow registered users to maintain a list of contact details of people with whom they have some level of relationship, called *Connections*. Users can invite anyone (whether a site user or not) to become a connection. However, if the recipient of an invitation selects "I don't know", this counts against the person inviting them, and after five such IDKs a member cannot invite another to connect without first supplying their recipient mail address.

This list of connections can then be used in a number of ways:

- A contact network is built up consisting of your direct connections, the connections of each of their connections (termed *second-degree connections*) and also the connections of second-degree connections (termed *third-degree connections*). This can be used to gain an introduction to someone through a mutual contact.

- It can then be used to find jobs, people, and business opportunities recommended by someone in one's contact network.

- LinkedIn also allows users to research companies. When typing the name of a given company in the search box, statistics about the company are provided. These may include the ratio of female to male employees, the percentage of the most common titles/positions held within the company, the location of the company's headquarters and offices, or a list of present and former employees – which makes for a valuable prompting list.

Facebook – www.facebook.com

Facebook is a social networking service and Web site which, as of January 2011, reports having more than 600 million active users. Users can create profiles with photos, lists of personal interests, contact information, and other personal information. Users can communicate with friends and other users through private or public messages and a chat feature. Additionally, users may join common-interest user groups, organized by workplace, school, or other characteristics. In order to access a user's full site information, you must be friends with that person.

Although Facebook is the largest and most commonly used social networking program, one must be very careful in using it as a prospecting tool. Its primary purpose is for communication between friends and acquaintances, not for business networking. However, it's possible to view a list of your Prospect's friends even if you don't happen to be Facebook Friends with the prospect. From this, you can create a prompting list or cross-reference these names through another site (such as LinkedIn) to identify characteristics that would make them a potentially good prospect for your business.

Client Communication

Almost everyone today understands the importance of regular contact with clients. The One Card System includes regular contact with Qualified Suspects, Prospects and Clients. Clearly this regular contact is a perfect task for new technology.

How often should you contact clientele?

There is a great deal of debate about how often a Financial Services Professional should contact his or her Suspects, Prospects, and Clients. Given today's technological options, daily contact would not be out of the question. This, of course, would be foolish. The One Card System suggests a *voice to voice* contact with potential and existing clients twice a year. In today's financial services environment many advisors are managing client investment portfolios in addition to handling their risk management issues. Some industry coaches suggest quarterly or even monthly contact for these clients. The appropriate frequency of contact depends upon the nature and expectations of the client, as well as the quality of the professional relationship. It is the authors' view that twice a year is sufficient for risk based clients and quarterly is appropriate for investment clients.

What are the most effective means of communication?

The answer most often given to this question is to ask your clients how they would prefer to be communicated with. The typical choices have been by phone, letter, email, or in person. Today we have added the incredibly powerful medium of Web conferencing (sometimes referred to as Webinars) and Skype. Again, OCS developers and successful users still believe that a voice-to-voice contact twice a year is sufficient to sustain the quality of the relationship and uncover the potential for additional business. Web conferencing now offers another voice to voice opportunity in addition to the phone call or in-person meeting. For your active clients, it is recommended you see them face to face once a year as one of your two required contacts.

While the wisdom of this advice is sound, reaching Suspects, Prospects, or Clients by phone is becoming increasing difficult. In this case, the technology of voice mail, caller ID, receptionists, and No Call lists works against us, not for us. One answer is email. Today, many busy people don't answer or regularly check their phone messages but always check their email. Given this you might consider contacting your clientele via both phone and email. Many advisors today are using email to request appointments, confirm appointments, introduce new information or ideas, and generally communicate with their clientele. Email is also commonly used to schedule Webinar meetings and to invite additional attendees.

Many advisors utilize services that deliver either professional newsletter-type material or personal messages such as "Happy Thanksgiving" by email on a scheduled basis. It's important to recognize the fine line between the value of regular contact and the possibility of being viewed as an aggressive marketing pest or spammer.

Web Conferencing

The word **Webinar** is short for Web-based Seminar. The original idea was to be able to present seminar type material via the Web. Today, Web Conferencing has added the ability to interact with attendees and even conduct polls and record your events. This communication method has become widely accepted, affordable, commonly used, and almost essential to many businesses. It is now possible to hold nearly real time meetings with individuals or large groups where computer monitors, voice, and visual transmission can be shared virtually anywhere in the world. The impact it can have on your practice is phenomenal. Today's advisor can utilize Web conferences to take or update facts, show proposals, meet with a joint work partner, present to a board of directors, and even have a spouse conference in on your live meeting. Here are three popular services:

GoToMeeting™ – www.gotomeeting.com

GoToMeeting™ is a Web-hosted service created and marketed by Citrix, a division of Citrix Systems. It is a remote meeting and desktop sharing software that enables the user to meet with other computer users, customers, clients or colleagues via the Internet in real-time. GoToMeeting™ was designed to allow the desktop view of a host computer to be broadcast to a group of computers connected to the host through the Internet. Transmissions are protected with high-security encryption and optional passwords. By combining a Web-hosted subscription service with software installed on the host computer, transmissions can be passed through highly restrictive firewalls.

Microsoft® Live Meeting – http://www.microsoft.com/online/office-live-meeting.asp

Microsoft® Office Live Meeting is a powerful Web conferencing program that is installed on a user's PC. The software is available for the attendee as a free download from the Microsoft® Web site.

WebEx – www.Webex.com

WebEx Communications Inc. is a Cisco company that provides online meeting, Web conferencing and videoconferencing applications. The Webex program provides an interactive whiteboard which makes it excellent for training purposes.

Customer Relationship Management (CRM) programs

Since human capacity severely limits our ability to mentally keep track of information, a Customer Relationship Management program is essential today. These programs are generally built around client records and range from simple contact lists containing names, addresses, email addresses, and phone numbers to sophisticated programs that contain real time totals of investments, insurance, cash, and net worth.

These programs can keep track of who is in your client base and provide tools for contacting them. Consequently, the ability to synchronize with your cell phone is important so today's CRMs provide the ability to filter and sort contacts, send email, and create mail merged documents. Since these programs can be expensive and time-consuming to set up and learn, be sure to check the complexity of use as well as the ability to import and export data. This becomes increasingly important should you decide to change programs at a later date. Here is a partial list of some options.

Microsoft® Outlook

Microsoft® Outlook is a widely used, powerful personal information manager program that offers a wide variety of features, including email, calendar, task manager, contact manager, note taking, journal, and Web browsing. Many other CRM programs include the ability to exchange information with Outlook.

Act!

ACT! (Sage ACT!) is a CRM that reports having over 2.7 million registered users and includes features such as contact management, calendar, communication tools, the ability to track prospective customers, reports, and the ability to synchronize data from other applications or over the Web.

Advisor's Assistant

Advisors Assistant from Client Marketing Systems is a Web-based full featured CRM program widely used in the financial services industry.

Proprietary CRM Programs

Many companies in the financial services industry have created their own CRM programs for use by their representatives. Often these programs include the ability to track the products the customers own and/or the contents of their investment portfolios.

Using New Technology in Practice Management

We have looked at ways in which recent technological tools provide new power and efficiency in research, prospecting, client communication, and client data storage. We also have reviewed how technology greatly assists us in overcoming our mental limitations in building our practice.

Taken individually, these programs provide an excellent array of tools, with each providing a specific function or purpose and can be integrated with the processes of the One Card System. Many carriers have developed proprietary CRM-related systems, so it is recommended that you check with your primary carrier and agency manager to determine if an automated system is available to use in conjunction with OCS. For those who do not have access to a carrier-specific system, a new tool is available that integrates OCS into a comprehensive system designed exclusively for the financial services profession. The features of the *CAM System*™ are described in detail in Chapter 8 of this book.

Chapter 7

The Productivity Planner – Simplifying the Manual or Automated Approach

The *Productivity Planner* is a key tool for Financial Services Professionals using OCS today. It functions as an annual appointment calendar, while capturing the full power of the One Card System. It combines the business functions of the original monthly *Control Booklets* and *Success Manual* in one comprehensive planning, appointment and activity-tracking calendar. It also works seamlessly with both the manual OCS Card File approach and the new *Alberstein CAM® System* (discussed in next chapter) to help guide and analyze your relationship-building activities and work plan.

The Design of the Productivity Planner

The *Productivity Planner* is divided into three sections: **Planning, Appointments** and **Success Manual.** Three divider tabs are included to use as place markers for each of these sections. These dividers also serve as a reference for the quick codes you will use to record the results of activities in each section.

Planning Tab: This tab is placed in the planning pages for the current month on which you are working. This

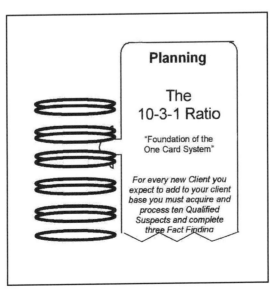

Planning

The
10-3-1 Ratio

"Foundation of the
One Card System"

*For every new Client you
expect to add to your client
base you must acquire and
process ten Qualified
Suspects and complete
three Fact Finding*

allows you to quickly record the results of your Birthday and Review contacts.

Appointments Tab: This tab is inserted between the appointment pages of the current week for ease of reference to your weekly work plan.

Success Manual Tab: This tab is placed between the current month's *Success Manual* pages and provides quick codes to be used to record and evaluate the results of each day's activity.

The Planning Section

The first section of your *Productivity Planner* sets the stage for effective organization, beginning with a big picture view of your practice. First, you will develop your annual plan by establishing:

- How much do you want to earn over the next year?

- How many Clients do you need to add to your client base to achieve your income needs?

- How much and what kind of activity will be necessary?

Once you have formulated your goals for the year you can begin turning those goals into reality.

Annual Day View Calendar

The Granum research found that his agency's highly successful professionals generally worked 200 *focused* "field days" each year. These were considered *Rule #1 Days* in which the representative focused exclusively on "seeing people or working to see people". That is, the representative was either conducting business appointments or calling to schedule appointments during these days.

The Annual Day View Calendar allows you to look at your year as a whole. Record nonselling commitments such as conferences, educational seminars, holidays or vacations. You should establish a goal that your annual work plan includes a minimum of 200 focused field days. The *Productivity Planner* includes a second calendar for the following year to allow you to note the dates of future events as you learn of them.

Sample Section of the Annual Day View Calendar page

	Monday	Tuesday	Wednesday	Thursday	Friday	Sat/Sun
JUNE				1	2	3 / 4
	5	6	7	8	9	10 / 11 **MDRT**
	12 ←	13 **MDRT**	14 →	15	16 Monthly Planning	17 / 18 Father's Day
	19	20	21	22	23	24 / 25
	26	27	28	29	30 **ChFC Exam**	

Personal Financial Planning Sheet

The Personal Financial Planning worksheet follows the annual calendar pages and is used to identify your income needs for the year. This exercise helps you to stay focused on the bottom line by zeroing in on the amount of business you must produce each and every week in order to meet your pre-defined financial objectives.

Your Activity Work Plan

The next step is to complete the Career Activity Management Worksheet, which helps you establish the activity levels that will be required in order to achive your income goals. If you are new to the business, we recommend targeting the activity levels outlined in the Progressive Expectations section of Chapter 5 in this book. As you continue to track your activity and production data, you can begin to formulate work plans that are tailored to your skills and average case size. The following illustration represents the activity plan of an experienced Financial Services Professional. Newer representatives will require much higher levels of activity in the areas of Prospecting and Fact Finding in order to meet the Fast Start criteria discussed in earlier chapters.

The Career Activity Management (CAM) Report© Worksheet

Goals	Business Activity					Meals (1 Point)	Qual Suspts (.5 Points)	Refrl Atmpts	Refrls Obtain	New Seens (1 Point)	New Facts (1 Point)	Cases Opened (1 Point)	Closes	Points	Submitted					Placed					Company Cedits
	Appointments Made	Kept	Dials	Telephoning Reach	Appts	Meals	Qual Suspts	Refrl Atmpts	Refrls Obtain	New Seens	New Facts	Cases Opened	Closes	Points	Core Sales	Other Sales	New Accnts	Core FYC	Other FYC	Core Sales	Other Sales	New Accnts	Core FYC	Other FYC	Company Cedits
Daily	4.8	3.6	30.0	12.0	4.2	0.7	4.8	1.2	3.6	1.2	1.1	1.3	1.4	7.0	0.6	0.1	0.4	$510	$180	0.5	0.1	0.3	$480	$180	$600
Weekly	24	18	150	60	21	4	24	6	18	6	5	7	7	35	3	1	2	$2,550	$900	3	1	2	$2,400	$900	$3,000
Monthly	80	60	500	200	70	12	80	20	60	20	18	22	24	116	10	2	6	$8,500	$3,000	9	2	5	$8,000	$3,000	$10,000
Yearly	960	720	6000	2400	840	144	960	240	720	240	216	264	288	1392	120	24	72	$102,000	$36,000	108	24	60	$96,000	$36,000	$120,000

The CAM Report Monthly Summary Form

It is well known that measuring results improves ongoing performance. The *CAM© Report Monthly* Summary Form, illustrated on the following page, is used to measure your month-to-month progress toward your goals. It builds to an annual summary of the activity and production information collected in the *Success Manual* section of your *Productivity Planner*.

If your company is not using a proprietary activity analysis program, the *Alberstein CAM© System* can be used along with the *Productivity Planner*. The data from the Monthly Summary form can then be entered into the *CAM® System* (described in the next chapter) for a detailed analysis of your activity levels and trends, Sales Cycle skills, commission value of activities, average case size, new client acquisition ratio (10-3-1 ratio) and more. These diagnostics are exceedingly valuable in helping you to achieve your work plan, and as a basis for next year's planning.

Career Activity Management (CAM) Report© Monthly Summary Form

Month	Days Worked	Business Activity					1 Point / .5 Point		1 Point		1 Point		1 Point		Points	Submitted					Placed					
		Appointments Made	Kept	Dials	Telephoning Reach	Appts	Meals	Qual Suspts	Refrl Attmpts	Refrls Obtain	New Seens	New Facts	Cases Opened	Closes		Core Sales	Other Sales	New Accnts	Core FYC	Other FYC	Core Sales	Other Sales	New Accnts	Core FYC	Other FYC	Company Credits
Monthly Plan	17	80	60	400	140	70	17	50	20	40	14	13	20	25	100	9	5	6	800	2000	8	4	5	6500	1000	7500
January	14	56	42	390	72	40	13	34	18	33	14	15	25	20	90	5	4	5	3300	1700	8	2	5	6121	130	6251
February	19	78	63	421	89	44	15	48	26	44	14	13	22	28	102	6	5	6	4738	5007	5	5	3	2557	1142	3699
March	18	72	59	380	69	42	19	56	21	50	13	13	25	23	108	5	6	5	5350	4462	7	6	6	7627	5174	12,801
April	19	78	61	412	75	41	15	44	18	43	12	12	22	26	97	8	4	6	7625	2710	7	3	6	5492	853	6345
May	17	82	66	441	93	46	17	62	24	59	15	14	26	25	113	8	5	6	13,695	1,000	6	5	6	6629	3242	9871
June																										
July																										
August																										
September																										
October																										
November																										
December																										

Building a Financial Services Clientele

The Career Activity Management (CAM) Report ©

Report Prepared For Sam Baker   **Report Date** 11/20/2005

Enter your data upon the completion of each month- All Calculations Are Automatic.

Month	Days worked	Made	Kept	Dials	Reach	Aprmts	Meals	Qual Suspts	Referl Atmpts	Refrls Obtain	New Seens	New Facts	Cases Opened	Closes	Points	Core Sales	Other Sales	New Acnts	Core FYC	Other FYC	Core Sales	Other Sales	New Acnts	Core FYC	Other FYC	Company Credits
		Appointmts		Telephone												Submitted					Placed					
Goals		80	60	400	140	70	17	50	20	40	14	13	20	25	100	9	5	6	$8,000	$2,000	9	4	5	$6,500	$1,000	$7,500
								5Pts				1 Pt	1 Pt	1 Pt	1 Pt	1Pt										
Jan	14	56	42	390	72	40	13	34	18	33	14	15	25	20	90	5	4	6	$3,300	$1,700	5	2	5	$6,121	$130	$6,251
Feb	19	78	63	421	89	44	15	48	26	44	14	13	22	28	102	6	5	6	$4,738	$5,007	5	5	3	$2,557	$1,142	$3,699
Mar	18	72	59	380	69	42	19	56	21	50	13	13	25	23	108	5	6	5	$6,350	$4,462	7	6	6	$7,627	$5,174	$12,801
Apr	19	78	61	412	75	41	15	44	18	43	12	12	22	26	97	8	4	6	$7,625	$2,710	7	3	6	$5,492	$853	$6,345
May	17	82	66	441	93	46	17	62	24	59	15	14	26	25	113	8	5	6	$13,695	$1,000	6	5	6	$6,629	$3,242	$9,871
Jun															0											
Jul															0											
Aug															0											
Sep															0											
Oct															0											
Nov															0											
Dec															0											
Year to Date Total	87	366	291	2,044	398	213	79	244	107	229	68	67	120	122	510	32	24	28	$34,708	$14,879	33.0	21.0	26.0	$28,426	$10,541	$38,967
Average per month	17	73	58	409	80	43	16	49	21	46	14	13	24	24	102	6	5	6	6942	2976	7	4	5	5685	2108	7793
Annualized Activity and Production	209	878	698	4906	965	511	190	586	257	550	163	161	288	293	1224	77	56	67	$83,299	$35,710	79	50	62	$68,222	$25,298	$93,521

(your monthly average times 12 months - Green equals at or above goal - Red equals behind goal)

Active Client Count 408

Inventory Report
Short Term $21,250   Long Term $42,500   In Underwriting $16,530

Cumulative Report

Activity	Dollar value of each Activity in Paid for Commission	Sale	Day	New Client
		Average number of activities per:		
Day Worked	$448	1.6		3.3
Appointment Made	$106	6.8	4.2	14.1
Appointment Kept	$134	5.4	3.3	11.2
Dial	$19	37.9	23.5	78.6
Reach	$98	7.4	4.6	15.3
Aprmt Made by Phone	$183	3.9	2.4	8.2
Lunch (Business Meal)	$493	1.5	0.9	3.0
Qualified Suspect	$160	4.5	2.8	9.4
Referral Attempt	$364	2.0	1.2	4.1
Referral Obtained	$170	4.2	2.6	8.8
New Seen	$573	1.3	0.8	2.6
Factfinder Interview	$582	1.2	0.8	2.6
Case Opened	$325	2.2	1.4	4.6
Closing Interview	$319	2.3	1.4	4.7
Efficiency Point	$76	9.4	5.9	19.6

Key Efficiency Ratios and Benchmarks for the Year to Date

	Actual	Goals	OCS
Phoning Efficiency			
Dials to Reaches	19%	35%	33%
Reaches to Appointments Made	54%	50%	50%
Appointment Efficiency			
Appointments Made to Kept %	80%	75%	67%
Referrals Obtained per Attempt	2.14	2.00	3
Qualified Suspects to Facts %	27%	26%	30%
New Seens to Facts %	99%	93%	80%
Facts to Cases Opened %	179%	65%	80-150%
Cases Opened to Closes %	102%	125%	150%
Selling Efficiency			
Cases Opened to Total Sales Submitted %	47%	70%	70%
Closes to Total Sales Submitted %	46%	56%	56%
Ave. Paid FYC per Core Sale	$861	$889	
Ave. Paid FYC per Other Sale	$502	$400	
Core Sales Underwriting Success	82%	89%	95%
Points Per Day	5.86	6.00	5
Points per Kept Appointment	1.75	1.67	1.5 - 2

* Suspects & New Facts are the "10" and the "3" of the famous "10-3-1" New Client Acquisition Ratio.

© 2000-2005 Alberstein Consulting

Production Graph

The next pages of the *Productivity Planner* features the *Production Graph* – an easy to maintain and motivating visual record of your progress during the year. Blank spaces on the vertical axis allow you to scale the graph to your own first year commission goal. At the beginning of the year, draw an ascending line in black ink representing your cumulative first year commission goal. Plot your cumulative year to date achievement with a colored bar at the end of each month. Your objective is to "stay above" your FYC goal line! The table at the bottom of the graph is designed to help you numerically determine how your actual performance compares to your goals.

Sample Production Graph
(Cumulative FYC Results through May)

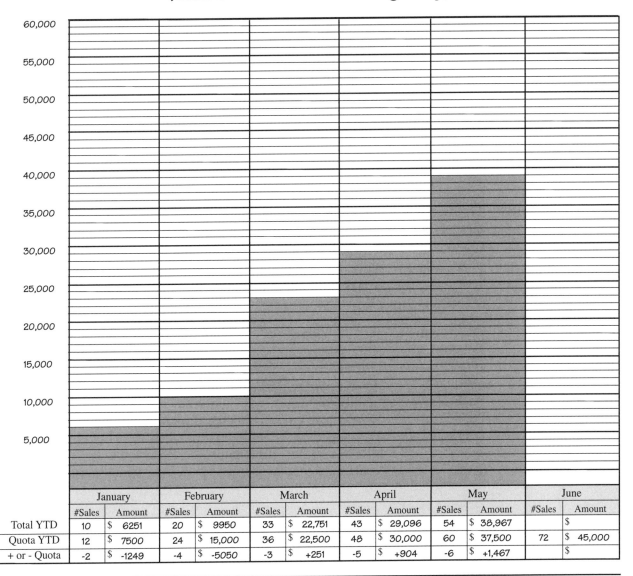

	January		February		March		April		May		June	
	#Sales	Amount	#Sales	Amount	#Sales	Amount	#Sales	Amount	#Sales	Amount	#Sales	Amount
Total YTD	10	$ 6251	20	$ 9950	33	$ 22,751	43	$ 29,096	54	$ 38,967		$
Quota YTD	12	$ 7500	24	$ 15,000	36	$ 22,500	48	$ 30,000	60	$ 37,500	72	$ 45,000
+ or - Quota	-2	$ -1249	-4	$ -5050	-3	$ +251	-5	$ +904	-6	$ +1,467		$

Production Record

The *Production Record* table is designed to keep you clearly focused on the goal of achieving Million Dollar Round Table (MDRT) qualifying status. On this table, you will list all applications that have been approved and placed in force at the end of each month. You will then the amount of production still required to qualify for MDRT, Court of the Table, or Top of the Table. Each month you'll have a clear vision of your progress and an understanding of how far you have left to go. Along with the *Production Record* are pages for use in the Annual Review described in Chapter 5. On these pages, you will create an ongoing history of results from New Facts Surveys, sales from Qualified Suspects, and cases opened by month.

	INSURED OR ACCOUNT OWNER	POLICY OR ACCOUNT NUMBER	LIFE OR CASE CR.	EFFECTIVE DATE	COMPANY PRODUCTION CREDIT	PLAN	MDRT CREDIT	LEFT TO GO
PRODUCTION RECORD								
1								
2								
3								
4								
5								
6								
7								
8								
9								
10								
11								
12								
13								
14								
15								
16								
17								
18								
19								
20								
21								
22								

Monthly Planning

This section of the *Productivity Planner* will guide you through the vital monthly planning process, which is conducted the third Friday of each month. Simply follow the instructions outlined at the bottom of the page. During this session, you will simply follow the instructions are included at the bottom of each calendar page.

Monday	Tuesday	Wednesday	Thursday	Friday	Saturday	Sunday
			1	**2** 10:30 Client | Builder 12:30 Mtg.	**3** Study ChFC	**4**
5	**6**	**7**	**8**	**9**	**10** Fly to San Diego for MDRT	**11** MDRT
12	**13**	**14**	**15**	**16** Monthly Planning	**17** Study ChFC	**18** Father's Day
	← MDRT ANNUAL MTG. →					
19	**20**	**21**	**22**	**23**	**24** Study ChFC	**25**
26	**27**	**28**	**29**	**30** 1:00 ChFC ↓ Exam		

OCS Monthly Planning Process

The third Friday of the month is the recommended day for OCS monthly planning. An investment of only 60 minutes in this task will dramatically improve your Client Building effectiveness. Check off each activity as you complete it.

☑ Mark out non-selling times and days (agency or firm meetings, conferences, training classes, vacations).

☑ Calculate the total number of days available for selling activities.

☑ Determine your daily OCS point goal for this month:

$$\frac{100}{\text{Monthly Point Goal}} \div \frac{17}{\text{Selling Days}} = \frac{6}{\text{Daily Point Goal}}$$

☑ Using the OCS Card File, complete the Automatic Contacts page: Birthday / Review / Other.

☑ Assign Automatic Contacts to the top of the appropriate day.

☑ Move the yellow Qualified Suspect cards filed for the upcoming month to the appropriate tabs of the 1-31 section of the OCS Card File.

❑ Update annual progress for your:
   Production Record (calculate MDRT status).
   Production Graph (calculate YTD progress).

❑ Prepare for Client Builder Meeting.

❑ Update CAM™ Report.

Automatic Contacts Page

An *Automatics Contacts* page is adjacent to each *Month at a Glance* page in the monthly planning section. The One Card System prompts you to contact all active Prospects and Clients twice a year: once at or near their birthdays and again approximately six months later. These Automatic Contacts are critically important in sustaining the relationships that lead to a loyal clientele, resulting in higher retention, repeat sales, and ongoing referrals. These pages are used to record the names of all of the Prospects and Clients you plan to contact during the month.

Birthday Automatics

The purpose of the *Birthday Automatic* list is to prompt a phone call of congratulatory greetings and, perhaps, an invitation to a birthday lunch. These luncheon meetings provide excellent opportunities for referred lead prospecting or other marketing efforts. To identify the individuals with birthdays in the month you are planning, simply go to the alphabetical section of your OCS Card File and run your finger along the exposed tabs for that month. Pull these cards up – not out – and record the name and birthday in the Birthdays column. Then transfer the names to the top of the day you plan to make the contact. When a birthday lunch (BL) is desired, schedule the call at least one week prior to the actual date.

Review Automatics

Review Automatics represent your second planned contact for the year. The purpose of these listed Automatics is to trigger a telephone call six months after the birthday to offer to conduct a review of their insurance and financial program. Identify names of Review Automatics in much the same manner as for *Birthday Automatics*; simply go the alphabetical section of your OCS Card File and locate the exposed tabs representing the month that is six months *prior to* the one you are planning. Pull the cards up – not out – and record the names in the Reviews and Other column. Then transfer the names to the day you wish to make the call, *within the first ten calendar days of the month*. You will want to schedule Reviews as early in the month as possible in order for business to result during the same month.

It is both efficient and effective to limit automatic contacts to twice per year. However, if a Prospect makes a justifiable request for a future call back at a non-automatic time, or you desire additional Client contact, record his or her name in the Review and Other column of the appropriate month's Automatics page. Once you do so, the *Productivity Planner* will automatically prompt you to make the call at the agreed upon time.

View of the Automatics List After the Monthly Planning Session

June	(June Birthdays)			(December Birthdays)	2006
Day	**Birthdays**	**Results**		**Reviews and Other**	**Results**
9	Allen, C.			Abbott, S.	
26	Bergstrom, J.			Chen, P.	
2	Carter, K.			Donovan, K.	
6	Gonzalez, T.			Ellis, G.	
28	Kohler, A.			Ivorsen, K.	
23	Lowenthal, L.			Martinez, A.	
6	Mills, H.			Matthews, J.	
14	Nolan, C.			O'Niel, B.	
7	Parker, E.			Rollins, S.	
19	Rawlston, P.			Tanaka, N.	
21	Sorenson, T.			Taylor, C.	

Unfinished Priority Work

Space has been provided in the lower section of the *Automatic Contacts* page to record progress on any longer term tasks or projects, such as work pertaining to education goals or more complex or advanced cases. This section will remind you of these important activities.

Record Results

The Results columns on the *Automatic Contacts* page will be blank at the beginning of the month but will be updated as contacts or appointments are completed. This allows you to evaluate your effectiveness with these calls. After all, these calls provide excellent opportunities for relationship building, prospecting and repeat sales. A quick list of the appointment codes are included on the Appointments Divider Tab.

Month-End View of the Automatics Page

June   2006

Day	Birthdays	Results	Reviews and Other	Results
9	Allen, C.	✓	Abbott, S.	CO - LTC
26	Bergstrom, J.	✓	Chen, P.	✓
2	Carter, K.	BL, 3 QS	Donovan, K.	CO-TC
6	Gonzalez, T.	✓	Ellis, G.	✓
28	Kohler, A.	✓	Ivorsen, K.	CO-TC, 2QS
23	Lowenthal, L.	BL, 2 QS, CO	Martinez, A.	CO - EQ
6	Mills, H.	BL, 4 QS	Matthews, J.	DF
14	Nolan, C.	✓	O'Niel, B.	CO-VA, 1QS
7	Parker, E.	✓	Rollins, S.	✓
19	Rawlston, P.	BL, 4QS	Tanaka, N.	✓
21	Sorenson, T.	✓	Taylor, C.	QF
15	Tabor, W.	BL 6 QS	Ungstaad, L.	CO-DI
5	Wallace, D.	✓	Vaneli, E.	CO-EQ
30	Williams, B.	BL, CO	Warren, P.	✓
11	Young, D.	BL, 4 QS		
16	Zeder, F.	BL, 3 QS		
Unfinished Priority Work				
Complete ChFC course by June 30th — Passed Exam!				

The Weekly Appointments Section

Following the *Monthly Planning* section and *Automatic Contacts* pages are the Weekly Appointment pages. This section helps to ensure that you properly execute your monthly work plan. All planned Automatic contacts, scheduled appointments, and office work activities are listed here, making sure that nothing is overlooked. The *Weekly Appointment* pages are divided into three sections that break the daily work plan into smaller segments of activity so your day doesn't seem overwhelming.

Top Section

The top section is for tracking scheduled Automatic contacts and Phone activity. Each morning, pull the file folders for the names listed at the top of that day. When you make the call, the complete file and Case History should be in front of you so appropriate notes can be made, and to review previous conversations for valuable background information. When you reach the individuals on the list, cross off the name by drawing a line through it. If you fail to reach someone, draw a wavy line through the name and move it forward to the next appropriate day. Record phone activity, as you dial, using the dot and check codes that are printed on the Appointments divider tab.

Birthdays			Birthdays			Birthdays		
6 Gonzalez			7 Parker	6 Gonzalez		15 Tabor		
11 Young			15 Tabor					
Automatic Contacts			Automatic Contacts			Automatic Contacts		
Matthews	Rolling	Lake	Tanaka	Ungstaad		Vanelli	Taylor	
O'Niel	Ellis		Taylor	Rollins		Warren		

Dialing Codes

- Use a dot every time a dial is made.

- ✓ Change the dot to a check mark if the individual is reached and spoken with.

- ✗ Cross the check mark with a slash mark when no appointment is obtained but the Suspect grants permission to "stay in touch."

✕ Cross the check mark with a double slash if an appointment scheduled.

Middle Section

The middle section of the Weekly Appointment pages is used to schedule appointments and other business activities. Use the quick codes located on the Appointments divider tab to record the results of your daily activities as they are completed.

Activity	Results
7:00 Preparation Time	
7:30	
8:00 (Case Prep: Ivorsen)	
8:30	
9:00 Telephoning	
9:30	
10:00	
10:30 Collins, A. – CL (here)	✗
11:00 (VA Pres; decision ✗6/9)	
11:30 Mills, H. – BL@ Palimino's	
12:00 (✗)4 QS)	
12:30	
1:00	
1:30	
2:00 Tollefson, B. – AP	✗
2:30 (FF, CO)	
3:00	
3:30	
4:00 Mackey, P. – AP	
4:30 (Resch'd to 6/8)	
5:00 Admin.	
5:30	
6:00	
6:30 Abbott – CL (here)	✗
7:00 (Bot. LTC, 2QS)	
7:30	
8:00	
To Do / Notes	
Case Prep: Ivorsen	

Appointment Results Codes

			Birthdays					Birthdays					Birthdays		
						6	Gonzalez	7	Parker	6	Gonzalez	15	Tabor		
						11	Young	15	Tabor						

		Automatic Contacts				Automatic Contacts				Automatic Contacts		
Matthews	Rolling	Lake	Tanaka	Ungstaad		Vanelli	Taylor	
O'Niel	Ellis		Taylor	Rollins		Warren		

$\checkmark$ = Appointment Scheduled

✗ = Appointment Kept

BL = Birthday Lunch

QS = Qualified Suspects obtained

AP = Approach Appointment (New Seen)

FF = Fact Finding Interview

CO = Case Opened

CL = Closing Interview

Del = Delivery Interview

R = Review

RL = Review Lunch

Lower Section

The lower portion of the *Weekly Appointment* pages provides you the opportunity to create a visual picture of each day's activities. These activities will be recorded later in the *Success Manual* section of the *Productivity Planner*. It allows you to numerically total your *daily* and *weekly* activities and expenses. **It is *not* a substitute for the Success Manual,** which provides a monthly summary – using actual names – so you can track progress on specific cases. This section helps you stay on top of the daily activities and points required to meet your financial goals.

				CAM™ Report Weekly Total			
				Appts. Made	23	New Facts	4
Appts. Made 5	Daily OCS Points		Appts. Made 4	Daily OCS Points		Appts. Kept	20	Cases Open	7
Appts. Kept 5	Meals	1	Appts. Kept 4	Meals	1	Dials	149	Closes	7
Dials 30	QS#	5	Dials 28	QS#	8	Reaches	48	Total Points	36.5
Reaches 8	Facts	1	Reaches 9	Facts	1	Appts.	23	Core Sales	6
Appts. 4	CO	2	Appts. 5	CO	1	Meals	5	Other Sales	1
RA: 2 RO: 5	Closes	1	RA: 3 RO: 8	Closes	2	Qual. Susp.	27	New Accts.	2
New Seens 1	Total	7.5 pts	New Seens -0-	Total	9 pts	RA: 10 RO: 27	Core FYC	4250
Expenses:	Mileage:		Expenses:	Mileage:		New Seens 5	Other FYC	2500

Success Manual Section

The back section of the *Productivity Planner* incorporates the *Success Manual*. The Success Manual provides a visual indication of the overall health of your practice by recording monthly activity with detailed information on Suspects and case names. The use of the *Success Manual* is covered in detail in Chapter 4 of this book.

To help you understand how the *Weekly Appointments* section works with the *Success Manual*, the following pages contain three sets of illustrations that graphically demonstrate the correlation of the information for these two sections.

- The first example illustrates sample Weekly Appointment pages *as they would appear on Monday morning,* at the beginning of a weekly work plan.

- The second example illustrates how these same pages would *appear on Friday afternoon,* after the accomplishments of the week have been recorded.

- The final illustration will demonstrate the month-to-date *Success Manual*, and its use of names to summarize and expand upon the weekly view. The quick codes for the *Success Manual* can be found on the divider tab for that section. Refer back to Chapter 4 in this book for a more thorough explanation of how to record and analyze activity data in the *Success Manual*.

Sample Weekly Appointment Pages

5 Monday	*156/210*		**6 Tuesday**	*157/209*		**7 Wednesday**	*158/208*	

Birthdays

	Monday				Tuesday			Wednesday	
6	Gonzalez			7	Parker				
11	Young			15	Tabor				

Automatic Contacts

Monday: Matthews, Rollins, Lake, O'Niel, Ellis

Tuesday: Tanaka, Ungstaad, Taylor

Wednesday: Vanelli, Warren

Activity / Results

Time	Monday	Tuesday	Wednesday
7:00	Preparation Time	Preparation Time	Preparation Time
7:30	↓		
8:00	↓	↓	↓
8:30			
9:00	Telephoning	Telephoning	Telephoning
9:30	↓	↓	↓
10:00			
10:30	Fredricks, N. – AP	Collins, A. – CL (here)	Jacobs, T. – CL
11:00	(Fredricks Industries)		
11:30		Mills, H. – BL@ Palimino's	Martinez, A & N –Review
12:00			(lunch here)
12:30			
1:00	Wallace, D. – BL@ Palimino's		Harris, D. – AP
1:30			
2:00		Tollefson, B. – AP	
2:30			
3:00	Ivorsen, K & J – Review		York, M. – CL
3:30			
4:00		Mackey, P. – AP	
4:30			
5:00	Kraus, M & T – CL	Admin.	Admin.
5:30		↓	↓
6:00			
6:30	Admin.	Abbott – CL (here)	
7:00			
7:30			
8:00			

To Do / Notes

Monday: Case Prep: Torrelli

Tuesday:

Wednesday:

	Monday	Daily OCS Points		Tuesday	Daily OCS Points		Wednesday	Daily OCS Points
Appts. Made								
Appts. Kept		Meals			Meals			Meals
Dials		QS#			QS#			QS#
Reaches		Facts			Facts			Facts
Appts.		CO			CO			CO
RA: RO:		Closes			Closes			Closes
New Seens		Total			Total			Total
Expenses:	Mileage:		Expenses:	Mileage:		Expenses:	Mileage:	

At the Beginning of the Week

8 Thursday — 159/207

Birthdays

| 19 | Rawlston | | |
| 16 | Zeder | | |

Automatic Contacts

Activity		Results
7:00	Preparation Time	
7:30		
8:00		
8:30		
9:00	Telephoning	
9:30		
10:00		
10:30		
11:00		
11:30	Donovan, K. - Review	
12:00	(lunch here)	
12:30		
1:00	Stuart, C. - AP	
1:30		
2:00	Torrelli, M - CL	
2:30		
3:00		
3:30		
4:00		
4:30		
5:00		
5:30		
6:00		
6:30		
7:00		
7:30		
8:00		

To Do / Notes

Appts. Made		Daily OCS Points	
Appts. Kept		Meals	
Dials		QS#	
Reaches		Facts	
Appts.		CO	
RA: RO:		Closes	
New Seens		Total	
Expenses:		Mileage:	

9 Friday — 160/206

Birthdays

| 9 | Allen | | |
| 14 | Nolan | | |

Automatic Contacts

Activity		Results
7:00	Preparation Time	
7:30		
8:00		
8:30		
9:00	Telephoning	
9:30		
10:00		
10:30		
11:00		
11:30		
12:00		
12:30		
1:00		
1:30		
2:00		
2:30		
3:00		
3:30		
4:00		
4:30		
5:00		
5:30		
6:00		
6:30		
7:00		
7:30		
8:00		

To Do / Notes

Appts. Made		Daily OCS Points	
Appts. Kept		Meals	
Dials		QS#	
Reaches		Facts	
Appts.		CO	
RA: RO:		Closes	
New Seens		Total	
Expenses:		Mileage:	

10 Saturday — 161/205

Activity	Results
10:00 - Flight to	
San Diego	

To Do / Notes

11 Sunday — 155/211

MDRT
ANNUAL
MTG.

To Do / Notes

CAM™ Report Weekly Total

Appts. Made		New Facts	
Appts. Kept		Cases Open	
Dials		Closes	
Reaches		Total Points	
Appts.		Core Sales	
Meals		Other Sales	
Qual. Susp.		New Accts.	
RA: RO:		Core FYC	
New Seens		Other FYC	

Sample Weekly Appointment Pages

5 Monday		156/210
Birthdays		

6	Gonzalez		
11	Young		

Automatic Contacts		
Matthews	Rollins	Lake
O'Niel	Ellis	

Activity	**Results**
7:00 Preparation Time	
7:30	
8:00 (Case Prep: Torrelli)	
8:30	
9:00 Telephoning	
9:30	
10:00	
10:30 Fredricks, N. – AP ✗	
11:00 (Fredricks Industries)	
11:30 (FF, CO -401k)	
12:00	
12:30	
1:00 Wallace, D. – BL@ Palimino's	
1:30 (✗- 3QS)	
2:00	
2:30	
3:00 Ivorsen, K & J – Review	
3:30 (✗ U, CO-TC)	
4:00	
4:30	
5:00 Kraus, M & T – CL ✗	
5:30 (Bot. 2 Life, 2QS)	
6:00	
6:30 Admin.	
7:00	
7:30	
8:00	

To Do / Notes
Case Prep: Torrelli

Appts. Made	4	**Daily OCS Points**	
Appts. Kept	4	Meals	1
Dials	25	QS#	5
Reaches	9	Facts	1
Appts.	4	CO	2
RA: 2 RO: 5		Closes	1
New Seens	1	Total	8.5 pts.
Expenses:		Mileage:	

6 Tuesday		157/209
Birthdays		

7	Parker	6	Gonzalez
15	Tabor		

Automatic Contacts		
Tanaka	Ungstaad	
Taylor	Rollins	

Activity	**Results**
7:00 Preparation Time	
7:30	
8:00 (Case Prep: Ivorsen)	
8:30	
9:00 Telephoning	
9:30	
10:00	
10:30 Collins, A. – CL (here) ✗	
11:00 (VA Pres; decision ✗6/9)	
11:30 Mills, H. – BL@ Palimino's	
12:00 (✗ 4QS)	
12:30	
1:00	
1:30	
2:00 Tollefson, B. – AP ✗	
2:30 (FF. CO)	
3:00	
3:30	
4:00 Mackey, P. – AP	
4:30 (Resch'd to 6/8)	
5:00 Admin.	
5:30	
6:00	
6:30 Abbott – CL (here) ✗	
7:00 (Bot. LTC, 2QS)	
7:30	
8:00	

To Do / Notes
Case Prep: Ivorsen

Appts. Made	5	**Daily OCS Points**	
Appts. Kept	4	Meals	1
Dials	36	QS#	6
Reaches	11	Facts	1
Appts.	5	CO	1
RA: 2 RO: 6		Closes	2
New Seens	1	Total	8 pts.
Expenses:		Mileage:	

7 Wednesday		158/208
Birthdays		

15	Tabor		

Automatic Contacts		
Vanelti	Taylor	
Warren		

Activity	**Results**
7:00 Preparation Time	
7:30	
8:00 (Case Prep: Tollefson)	
8:30	
9:00 Telephoning	
9:30	
10:00	
10:30 Jacobs, T. – CL	
11:00 (Resch'd to 6/15)	
11:30 Martinez, A & N –Review	
12:00 (lunch here) ✗ (U, CO -EQ)	
12:30	
1:00 Harris, D. – AP ✗	
1:30 (next ✗ 6/9 for FF)	
2:00	
2:30	
3:00 York, M. – CL ✗	
3:30 (Bot. DI - 3QS)	
4:00	
4:30	
5:00 Admin.	
5:30	
6:00	
6:30 Clark, G&S -FF	
7:00 (Resch'd to 6/20)	
7:30	
8:00	

To Do / Notes
Case Prep: Tollefson
Order Abbott Paramed

Appts. Made	5	**Daily OCS Points**	
Appts. Kept	3	Meals	1
Dials	30	QS#	3
Reaches	11	Facts	-0-
Appts.	5	CO	1
RA: 1 RO: 3		Closes	1
New Seens	1	Total	4.5 pts.
Expenses:		Mileage:	

As They Appear at the End of the Week

8 Thursday				159/207

Birthdays

19	~~Rawlston~~			
16	~~Zeder~~			

Automatic Contacts

	~~Warren~~			

Activity		Results
7:00	Preparation Time	
7:30	↓	
8:00		
8:30		
9:00	Telephoning	
9:30	↓	
10:00	Lake, P. - Delivery ✓	
10:30	(4QS)	
11:00		
11:30	Donovan, K. - Review ✓	
12:00	(lunch here) (U, CO-TC)	
12:30		
1:00	Stuart, C. - AP ✓	
1:30	(next ✓ 6/15 for FF)	
2:00	Torrelli, M - CL	
2:30	(EP Pres; Decision ✓ 6/15)	
3:00		
3:30		
4:00	Mackey, P.- AP ✓	
4:30	(FF, CO - Life, 1QS)	
5:00		
5:30	Admin.	
6:00	↓ (Case Prep: Martinez)	
6:30		
7:00		
7:30		
8:00		

To Do / Notes
Case Prep: Martinez
Order York Paramed

Appts. Made	5	**Daily OCS Points**	
Appts. Kept	5	Meals	1
Dials	30	QS#	5
Reaches	8	Facts	1
Appts.	4	CO	2
RA: 2 RO: 5		Closes	1
New Seens	1	Total	7.5 pts.
Expenses:		Mileage:	

---

9 Friday				160/206

Birthdays

9	~~Allen~~	16	~~Zeder~~
14	~~Nolan~~		

Automatic Contacts

	~~Fredricks~~			

Activity		Results
7:00	Preparation Time	
7:30		
8:00	(Case Prep: Mackey)	
8:30	↓	
9:00	Telephoning	
9:30	↓	
10:00		
10:30	Ivorsen, K&J - CL (here)	
11:00	✓ (Bot. VL, 2QS)	
11:30	Young, D. - BL (2 early)	
12:00	@Palm Ct. ✓ (4QS)	
12:30		
1:00	Harris, D - FF ✓	
1:30	(FF, CO - DI & Ovhd. Exp.)	
2:00		
2:30		
3:00	Collins, A - CL2 ✓	
3:30	(Bot. VA, 2 QS)	
4:00		
4:30	Admin	
5:00		
5:30	↓	
6:00		
6:30		
7:00		
7:30		
8:00		

To Do / Notes
Case Prep: ~~Mackey~~

Appts. Made	4	**Daily OCS Points**	
Appts. Kept	4	Meals	1
Dials	28	QS#	8
Reaches	9	Facts	1
Appts.	5	CO	1
RA: 3 RO: 8		Closes	2
New Seens	~~0~~	Total	9 pts.
Expenses:		Mileage:	

---

10 Saturday		161/205

Activity	Results
10:00 - Flight to	
San Diego	
↓	

To Do / Notes

11 Sunday	155/211

↑

MDRT
ANNUAL
MTG.

↓

To Do / Notes

CAM™ Report Weekly Total			
Appts. Made	23	New Facts	4
Appts. Kept	20	Cases Open	7
Dials	149	Closes	7
Reaches	48	Total Points	36.5
Appts.	23	Core Sales	6
Meals	5	Other Sales	1
Qual. Susp.	27	New Accts.	2
RA:10 RO:	27	Core FYC	4250
New Seens	5	Other FYC	2500

QUALIFIED SUSPECTS								
Date	Name	Nominator & Initials	Where Secured	How To Be Promoted	Age	Income	Occupation	CO, A, DF, 31
2	Harris, D.	KC	BL	NL	38	100	Bus.Own.	(CO)
↓	Vaughn, T.	↓	↓	↓	36	75	ElecEng.	DF
5	Fulton, J.	DW	BL	NL	30	45	Asst. Prof.	DF
	Ericks, W.				39	100	Prof.	31
↓	Harvey, B.	↓	↓	↓	40	100	Prof.	DF
5	Hoffman, J.	MK	CL	NL	42	150	Lawyer	31
↓	Colter, M.	↓	↓	↓	35	60	Paralegal	DF
6	Aperlee, D.	HM	BL	NL	58	200	Vet	31
	Aperlee, D.Jr				32	100	Vet	31
	Zimmer, H				62	–	Ret. Vet	DF
↓	Franklin, T	↓	↓	↓	55	200	Bus. Own	31
6	Cullen, K.	SH	CL	NL	66	–	Ret.	DF
↓	Tobian, G.	↓	↓	↓	68	–	Ret.	31
7	Sang, C.	MY	CL	DL	26	30	Intern	
	Cantwell, P				25	30	Intern	
↓	Gianni, F.	↓	↓	↓	26	30	Intern	
8	Lake, L	PL	Del.	DL	38	120	Builder	
	Lake, T.				40	60	Teacher	
	Sawyer, A				36	60	Land. Arch	
↓	Flores, V	↓	↓	↓	40	80	Corp.Mgr	
8	Brahn, N	PM	FF	DL	36	75	Pharm.Rep	
9	Iverson, C	KI	CL	DL	38	60	Surg. RN	
↓	Iverson, D.	↓	↓	↓	35	50	Phys.Thrp.	
9	Howell, G.	DY	BL	NL	55	200	Devlpr.	
	Kanter, M.				50	150	Bldr.	
	Suzuki, T.				42	100	Eng.	
↓	Yost, I.	↓	↓	↓	36	80	Eng.	
9	Castez, A.	AC	CL	NL	68	–	Ret.	
↓	Louritzen,E	↓	↓	↓	70	–	Ret.	

NEW FACTS

Torrelli, M.

Jacobs, T.

Collins, A.

Fredricks, N.

Tollefson, B.

Mackey, P.

Harris, D.

CASES OPENED							
Date	Name	Action Date	Category	New Facts?	Illustration	Amount	Sold, A, DF
1	Torrelli, M	6/15	3	Y	EP	450 L / 2700 DI	
1	Jacobs, T	6/15	3	N	EQ	IRA ROLLOVER	
1	Kraus, M	–	4	U	L	2 Juv 100K ea.	I $
2	Collins, A	–	3	Y	VA	125 K SPDA	I
2	Abbott, S	–	1	U	LTC	4 K/mo	I $
5	Fredricks Industries	6/19	3	Y	BUS	401(k)	
5	Ivorsen, K	–	TC	U	L	250VL	I $
6	Tollefson, B	6/16	3	Y	L	500 L	
7	Martinez, A	6/19	1	U	EQ	Mut. Fd.	
8	Donovan, K	6/16	TC	U	L	100 WL	
8	Mackey, P	6/15	3	Y	L	685L	
9	Harris, D	6/16	3	Y	DI	DI & OH. Exp.	

Success Manual Pages

CLOSING INTERVIEWS

Date	Name	Attempt # / Time Lag	Type Case
5	Kraus, M	5 / 1	L
6	Collins, A	4 / 1	VA
6	Abbott, S	6 / 1	LTC
7	York, M	1 / 2	DI
8	Torrelli, M	0 / 1	EP
9	Ivorsen, K	7 / 1	L
9	Collins, A	4 / 2	VA

BUSINESS — SENT TO THE HOME OFFICE

Date	Name	Category	Amount (000)	Type	Annualized FYC
6	Kraus, P.	4	100	WL	300
6	Kraus, A	4	100	WL	320
7	Abbott, S	!	3	LTC	1500
8	York, M	3	2.5	DI	730
9	Ivorsen, K	TC	250	VL	1400
9	Collins, A	3	100	VA	2500

Placed In Force

Date	Name	Category	Amount (000)	Type	Annualized FYC
8	Lake, L.	3	500	WL	1810
8	Lake, T.	3	500	T	400

ACTIVITY AND EFFICIENCY POINTS

Date of the Month	Appts. Scheduled	Appts. Kept	Dialed	Reached	Appts.	1 pt MEALS — Name / Results	Qualified Suspects (.5 pts)	Referrals Attempts	Referrals Obtained	Approaches	New Facts (1 pt)	Cases Opened (1 pt)	Closing Interviews (1 pt)	Points
1	4	3	28	6	3		0	0	0	2	2	3	0	5
2	3	3	26	7	4	Carter (BL) 2QS	2	1	2	1	1	2	0	5
3/4	STUDY ChFC →													
WK	7	6	54	13	7	1	2	1	2	3	3	5	0	10
5	4	4	25	9	4	Wallace (BL) 3QS	5	2	5	1	1	2	1	8.5
6	5	4	36	11	5	Mills (BL) 4QS	6	2	6	1	1	1	2	8
7	5	3	30	11	5	Martinez (R) U, CO	3	1	3	1	0	1	1	4.5
8	5	5	30	8	4	Donovan (R) U, CO	5	2	5	2	1	2	1	7.5
9	4	4	28	9	5	Young (BL) 4QS	8	3	8	0	1	1	2	9
10/11	MDRT →													
WK	23/30	20/26	149/203	48/61	23/30	5/6	27/29	10/11	27/29	5/8	4/7	7/12	7/7	36.5/46.5
12														
13														
14														
15														
16														
17														
18														
19														
20														
21														
22														
23														
24														
25														
26														
27														
28														
29														
30														
31														

Conclusion

The *Productivity Planner* is a unique tool for today's Financial Services Professional. Your business goals, work plan, appointments, accomplishments and your *Success Manual* are all in one place. The *Productivity Planner* is the Command Center for your practice.

Running a successful financial services practice is challenging. It can be compared to cooking on a four burner stove: one burner for prospecting, another for phone activities, a third for opening cases, and the fourth for closing. The goal is to monitor the activities on all four burners to create the perfect meal. Without a system, we jump from one task to another hobbled by confusion and anxiety.

The *Productivity Planner* allows you to free your mind by systematically capturing tasks and assigning them to a date and time. It provides you with a clear plan to follow and it monitors your progress. When the *Productivity Planner* is used in conjunction with *OCS Card File*, the *One Thousand Clients* book, and the analytical power of the Alberstein *CAM® System* (discussed next), you have the perfect combination to fully utilize the power of the One Card System.

Chapter 8

The CAM System™ – An Automated Solution

While the first section of this book focused on the original concept and research behind the system and its validity today, we recognize that technology and automation are an integral part of everyday work and personal lives. Today's Financial Services Professionals prefer a system that integrates with automated systems and tools that they already use in their work. While we recommend you begin using the system in its original manual format, it's only logical that once you understand the system and how to implement it in your practice that you will transition to an approach that capitalizes on the latest innovations. For those representatives whose carriers do not have a proprietary system in place, we recommend the new *Career Activity Management (CAM) System™*. When combined with the *Productivity Planner*, the *CAM System* provides all of the functions of the original OCS and much more.

The CAM System™

The *Career Activity Management (CAM) System™* is a web based practice management system specifically designed for the financial services industry. It provides representatives with the ability to analyze and manage their practices by tracking goals, activity, production, inventory, and relationships. It provides a complete range of reports, analytical tools, and charts including strong forecasting and coaching modules. In short, the *CAM System*, combined with the *Productivity Planner*, includes everything needed to organize and manage a financial services practice.

The new *CAM System*™ was created by Dr. Barry Alberstein and Delia Alberstein, co-authors of this text. As a consulting psychologist to the financial services industry for over thirty years, Dr. Alberstein has conducted more than 3,500 Client Builder (productivity enhancement) meetings. This provided the opportunity to personally listen to and analyze more than 20,000 monthly activity and production reports from advisors. As a result of this analysis, The *CAM System* includes what are considered to be the key elements in an effective financial services practice management system:

- Setting goals and refining work plans,

- Analyzing and managing activity and production

- Organizing and evaluating Suspect, Prospect, and Client inventories

- Managing and coordinating tasks with an assistant

- Scheduling the ongoing the contacts that build relationships, capture cross sales, and lead to a growing base of clients and referrals.

Like the original manual approach to the One Card System, the *CAM System* helps you to understand the science of your business by providing the ability to control and predict outcomes. Imagine the impact on your practice when you can control and predict the outcomes of your business efforts and activities! Through observation, measurement, and analysis, the system helps you to truly understand the science of your sales process and the building of a successful financial services practice.

In the area of activity management, the *CAM System* provides a comprehensive analysis of your activity and production patterns, and your skill in moving suspects and prospects through the client acquisition process. When opportunities for improvement are identified, the *CAM System* also provides proven coaching suggestions that will help get you back on track and maximize your productivity.

From the original Granum research, it was established that throughout your career you must identify, qualify, contact, and see tens of thousands of individuals (entities) in order to build a profitable clientele. The *CAM System* helps you to organize, evaluate, and process these large inventories of Qualified Suspects and Prospects. Just as importantly, it will help you to evaluate both the quantity and quality of your existing Clientele.

And finally, it cannot be emphasized enough that this is a relationship building business. Early trusted relationships are built through personal introductions, in-depth fact-finding, and following through on your commitments in a timely manner. The *CAM System* will help you meet your commitments during the sales cycle, while keeping track of the numerous tasks, activities, and appointments required each week. It also helps you sustain Prospect and Client relationships through the systematic contacts recommended by the One Card System.

If used properly and consistently, the *CAM System* will help you to understand the relationship between your activities and your business results. It provides the management tools and proven coaching techniques to help you identify your strengths and correct obstacles to growth. It allows you to run your financial services practice in an objective, businesslike manner that keeps you on target for meeting your short-term and long-term career goals.

An Overview of The CAM System™

The *CAM System*™ handles the three major areas required to build and manage a successful practice: Activity, Inventory, and Relationships.

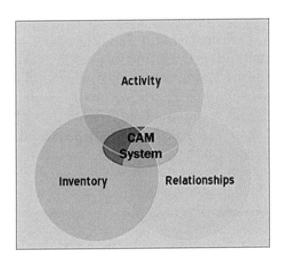

With three simple steps you can organize, analyze, and control your practice with clarity and efficiency. After entering your goals, sales activity, and inventory from your *Productivity Planner* and other sources used in your practice, you'll be ready to tap the power of the *CAM System*. And, because the system is Web based, you can easily exchange information with an assistant, coach, or marketing team.

The *CAM System* was designed to be easy to use, with only two entry screens – one for goals and activities and another for entering inventory (inventory can also be imported from other systems, using CSV files). After logging into the system, a menu of short cut buttons link to the main functions of the program, making the *CAM System* easy to use on Web-enabled tablets, such as the iPad or PlayBook.

Goals and Work Plans

The first step in working with the *CAM System* is to enter your goals and work plans – which you will have already established in your *Productivity Planner*. If you will be utilizing the *CAM System* to track your progress toward your annual activity and production goals, you would begin by entering your desired **monthly goals**. If you are new to the business we highly recommend setting your monthly activity goals at the Fast Start levels discussed elsewhere in this text or at the levels recommended by your manager based on the historical performance of successful people in your firm. The *CAM System* will then generate a Work Plan showing you the amount of activity required each field day and week of the year.

Work Plan Summary

Name: Chris Sample

Report Date: 5/30/2011

	Days Wrkd	Appts Schd	Appts Kept	Tel Dials	Tel Rchs	Tel Apmt	Meal	Leads (QS)	Refr Atmp	Refr Obtn	New Seens	New Facts	Case Opnd	Clos	Pts	Core Sls	Othr Sls	New Clnts	Core FYC	Other FYC	Core Sales	Other Sales	New Clnts	Core FYC	Other FYC	Total FYC
								Business Activity											**Submitted**				**Placed**			
Daily Plan	1	4.4	3.3	25.0	5.6	2.8	0.8	3.3	0.8	2.8	1.0	0.8	1.1	1.4	5.8	0.5	0.2	0.2	$428	$183	0.4	0.2	0.2	$389	$167	$556
Weekly Plan	5	22.2	16.7	125.0	27.8	13.9	4.2	16.7	4.2	13.9	5.0	4.2	5.6	6.9	29.2	2.5	1.1	1.1	$2,139	$917	2.2	1.1	1.1	$1,944	$833	$2,778
Monthly Plan	18	80	60	450	100	50	15	60	15	50	18	15	20	25	105	9	4	4	$7,700	$3,300	8	4	4	$7,000	$3,000	$10,000
Yearly Plan	216	960	720	5400	1200	600	180	720	180	600	216	180	240	300	1260	108	48	48	$92,400	$39,600	96	48	48	$84,000	$36,000	$120,000

As you build your records over time, the *CAM System* will help you track your activity and production patterns, your sales cycle skills, and your average case size. This will allow you to fine tune future work plans according to your income goals, markets, and actual historical performance.

Activity Management

The OCS client building philosophy recognizes that it is not possible to predict which prospects will become clients. We can't control precisely who will buy, nor how much or how often our clients will purchase our products and services. We can control, however, our sales activity, and we know from the extensive Granum OCS research that there is a direct correlation between activity and results. Only through consistent and accurate recordkeeping, measurement, and analysis can we come to understand the correlation between our activities and sales results. The combination of the *Productivity Planner* and the *CAM System* provide the perfect tools for creating this understanding.

Daily Record Keeping – The Role of the OCS Productivity Planner

Before we can analyze our activity and production data we must first collect and record it on a daily basis. The *Productivity Planner* is your tool for recording daily activities and accomplishments. Jot down your results from your phone and appointment setting activities as they occur throughout the day. At the end of each day, record your activity totals on the appointment pages, and at the end of the week, enter your weekly totals into the *CAM System*.

You will record the following in your *Productivity Planner* on a daily basis:

- Dialing Activity and Results

- Appointments Scheduled and their Results

- Jotting down the Sales Cycle Activity names and accomplishments

- Calculating daily and weekly activity totals

You will discover that the *Productivity Planner* is actually one of the fastest recording devices and is much more efficient than entering data into an automated system as it occurs! For example, the dot and check notation system explained in Chapter 7 is a quick and easy way to record phone activity as you dial. Available appointment times can be easily identified. Scheduling an appointment is a snap; just write the name of the individual in the appointment time slot. After completing an appointment note the results of the meeting on the appointment page. At the end of the day, tally your activity results and jot down the totals in the activity summary section of the appointment pages. These results will be entered into the *CAM System* on a weekly basis to minimize the amount of time you spend on data entry.

Entering your *Productivity Planner* Activity into the *CAM System*

The *Productivity Planner* is portable, easy to use, and will help you capture daily accomplishments that will be totaled at the end of each week or month and entered into the *CAM System*. Working together, these two tools will help you track and evaluate the correlation between your business activities, skills, and results.

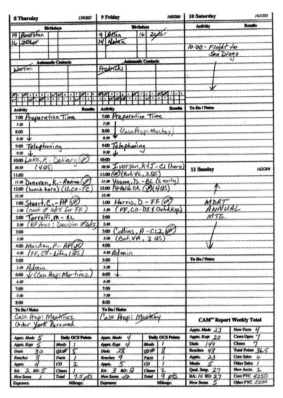

The CAM System™ Activity Entry Screen

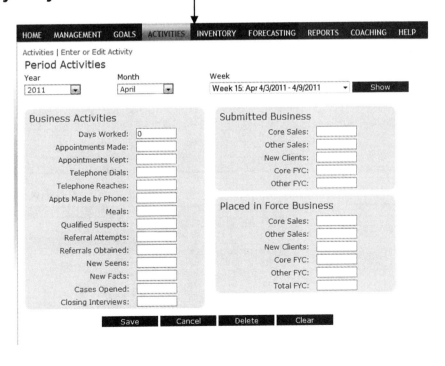

CAM Activity Analysis Report

The benefit of entering weekly activity into the *CAM System* is enormous! With the click of a button you'll be able to generate the *CAM Activity Analysis Report*, which provides a comprehensive analysis of your activity patterns, sales cycle skills, and the resulting production for any period of time you select. This Report provides a detailed picture of your activity, skills, production, and inventory – *all on a single page*. The analysis includes:

- Year-to-date totals, monthly averages, and annualized projections;

- Simple color-coded display of your progress toward your personal goals;

- A full range of graphs, allowing you to track your performance visually;

- Revenue calculations of each business activity, as well as the number you're averaging per sale, per day, and per *new* client account;

Activity Analysis Report

Name: Chris Sample

Report Period: 1/1/2011 - 3/31/2011

	Days Wrkd	Apmts Schd	Apmts Kept	Tel Dials	Tel Rchs	Tel Apmts	Meal	Leads (QS)	Refr Atmp	Refr Obtn	New Seens	New Facts	Case Opnd	Clos Intvs	Pts	Core Sls	Othr Sls	New Clnts	Core FYC	Other FYC	Core Sales	Other Sales	New Clnts	Core FYC	Other FYC	Total FYC
Goals	18	80	60	450	100	50	15	60	15	50	18	15	20	25	105	9.0	4.0	4.0	$7,700	$3,300	8.0	4.0	4.0	$7,000	$3,000	$10,000
Jan 11	20	71	57	397	105	50	17	64	19	62	14	13	18	25	105	6.5	3.0	4.5	$8,537	$3,600	8.0	3.5	3.5	$6,636	$3,598	$10,234
Feb 11	21	76	60	366	88	48	16	63	15	54	17	14	17	29	108	12.0	4.0	6.0	$8,235	$2,172	7.0	3.0	5.0	$6,200	$2,772	$8,972
Mar 11	23	90	68	451	109	58	15	72	18	61	15	14	21	28	114	12.5	8.0	7.0	$8,656	$4,800	9.0	7.0	6.0	$7,646	$3,550	$11,196
Monthly Averages																										
	21	79	62	405	101	52	16	66	17	59	15	14	19	27	109	10.0	5.0	6.0	$8,476	$3,524	8.0	4.0	5.0	$6,827	$3,307	$10,134
YTD Totals																										
	64	237	185	1214	302	156	48	199	52	177	46	41	56	82	326	31.0	15.0	17.5	$25,428	$10,572	24.0	13.5	14.5	$20,482	$9,920	$30,402
Annualized Projections																										
	256	948	740	4856	1208	624	192	796	208	708	184	164	224	328	1306	124.0	60.0	70.0	$101,712	$42,288	96.0	54.0	58.0	$81,928	$39,680	$121,608

Activity Values and Averages

Activity	Dollar value of each in Paid for FYC	Sale	Day	New Client
Days Worked	$475	1.7	1.0	4.4
Apptmts Scheduled	$128	6.3	3.7	16.3
Appointments Kept	$164	4.9	2.9	12.8
Dials	$25	32.4	19.0	83.7
Reached	$101	8.1	4.7	20.8
Apmts Made by Phone	$195	4.2	2.4	10.8
Business Meals	N/A	1.3	0.8	3.3
Qualified Suspects	$153	5.3	3.1	13.7
Referral Attempts	$585	1.4	0.8	3.6
Referrals Obtained	$172	4.7	2.8	12.2
New Seens	$661	1.2	0.7	3.2
New Facts	$742	1.1	0.6	2.8
Cases Opened	$543	1.5	0.9	3.9
Closing Interviews	$371	2.2	1.3	5.7
Efficiency Points	$93	8.7	5.1	22.5

* New Leads & New Facts are the "10" and the "3" of the famous "10-3-1" New Client Acquisition Ratio.

Key Skill Ratios

Phoning Efficiency	Actual	Goals
Dials to Reached	25 %	22 %
Reaches to Appointments Made	52 %	50 %
Appointment Efficiency		
Appointments Scheduled to Kept %	78 %	75 %
Referrals Obtained per Attempt	3.40	3.33
QS to New Facts	21 %	25 %
New Seens to New Facts %	89 %	83 %
New Facts to Cases Opened %	137 %	133 %
Cases Opened to Closing Interviews %	146 %	125 %
Selling Efficiency		
Cases Opened to Total Sales Submitted %	82 %	65 %
Closes to Total Sales Submitted %	56 %	52 %
Average Placed FYC per Core Sale	$853	$875
Average Placed FYC per Other Sale	$735	$750
Core Sales Underwriting Success	77 %	89 %
Points Per Day Worked	5.10	5.83
Points per Kept Appointment	1.76	1.75

Inventory Report

Short Term Inventory	
# of Cases:	7
Weighted FYC:	$9,830

Long Term Inventory	
# of Cases:	2
Weighted FYC:	$2,625

Submitted Inventory	
# of Cases:	7
Weighted FYC:	$5,482

Active Clients	
# of Clients:	268.00
Future $ Value:	$265,234

- Identification of your conversion ratios and key skill indicators as you move cases through the decision process;

- A summary of the values of your Open Case and Submitted Case Inventories; and

- A display of your future revenue estimates from your active clientele.

Coaching Tips

When opportunities for improvement are identified in the Activity Analysis Report, the Coaching section of the *CAM System* contains a virtual treasure trove of coaching tips! This section contains practical and proven suggestions from Dr. Barry Alberstein, which are a result of over 30 years of industry consulting. Dr. Alberstein has personally analyzed over 20,000 monthly activity and production reports from both new and experienced producers. His coaching practice includes numerous MDRT, Court of the Table, and Top of the Table members as well as advisors just beginning their careers. The *CAM System* incorporates much of his proven coaching guidance and identifies possible problems and recommends practical solutions. It's like having a built-in personal coach!

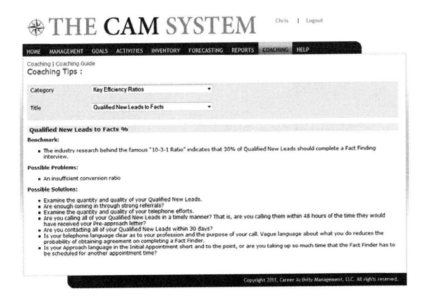

Activity & Production Graphs

All of the data included in the Activity and Analysis Report can also be displayed in a graphic format. Your balance of activities and production, cumulative progress toward your goals, and trends analysis graphs are all included.

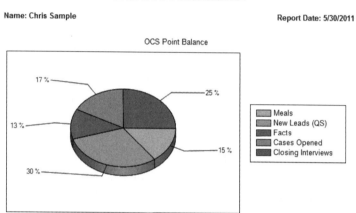

CAM OCS Point Balance

Name: Chris Sample   Report Date: 5/30/2011

OCS Point Balance

17 %
13 %
30 %
25 %
15 %

- Meals
- New Leads (QS)
- Facts
- Cases Opened
- Closing Interviews

Forecasting

The *CAM System* is also ideal for year-end planning and quarterly adjustments using the Forecasting module to generate a customized work plan driven by your personal revenue goals. The resulting plan will show the activity required to reach your earnings goal, based on your own historical performance!

Name: Chris Sample   **Projected Work Plan**   Report Date: 5/31/2011

Required Business Activities

	Appt Schd	Appt Kept	Tel Dials	Tel Reaches	Tel Appts. Schd.	Business Meals	New Leads (QS)	Referral Attempts	Referrals Obtained	New Seen	New Facts	Cases Opened	Closing Interviews	Points
Daily	3.6	2.8	18.5	4.6	2.4	0.7	3.0	0.8	2.7	0.7	0.6	0.9	1.3	5.0
Weekly	18.1	14.1	92.4	23.0	11.9	3.7	15.2	4.0	13.5	3.5	3.1	4.3	6.3	24.9
Monthly	65	51	333	83	43	13	55	14	49	13	11	15	23	90
Yearly	780	609	3993	993	513	158	655	171	582	151	135	184	270	1074

Estimated New Clients Required: 55

Estimated Annual Sales Required: 123.35

The Forecasting module also includes a powerful "What If?" production calculator that allows you to evaluate the effect of varying your average case size, number of closes, or closing ratio. By modifying any of the three variables you can immediately see the impact on your annual projected First Year Commission revenue.

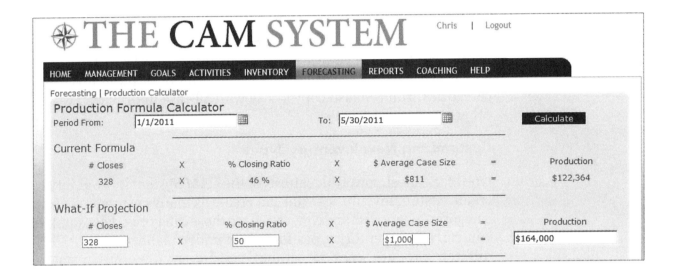

Inventory Management

One of the unique features of the *CAM System* is its inventory control module. Effective inventory control is essential to managing a financial services practice. The term inventory generally refers to the number of cases that the Financial Services Professional is currently working on. Through the *CAM System's* inventory management tool, you can track cases through the sales cycle, schedule tasks, and follow up with prospects and clients on a timely basis. These practices are essential in case management, building trust and sustaining your valuable relationships. The *CAM System* stores the case details and case history notes for all of your Suspects, Prospects, and Clients. Follow-up dates and tasks can be assigned, and cases can be moved through the sales cycle with the click of a button. The *CAM System* can even track recurring follow ups, such as birthdays and age changes.

Types of Predefined Inventories

As mentioned, the term inventory generally refers to Open Cases and cases that have been submitted to underwriting or the home office for approval. The *CAM System's* predefined inventory types include inventory categories for Short Term cases opened (expecting a decision within six weeks), Long Term cases opened (longer than six weeks), and Submitted Cases. Predefined inventory types also include Completed Cases, Incomplete Cases, Qualified Suspects, Prospects, Active Clients, and Inactive Clients. As you enter the data on a new lead or case you can assign that person or entity to one or more of these inventory categories. You can also copy a case with all case information to any other inventory category.

Customizing New Inventory Types

One of the most powerful features of the *CAM System* is the ability to create custom inventories. You can create as many custom inventory categories as you wish and copy cases into those categories. For example, you can add inventory types for assets under management (AUM), different product types, target markets, and even recruiting stages. You can then generate inventory reports for any of the customized categories. This ability to add inventory categories makes the program very flexible.

Generating Inventory Reports

Reports can be generated for each individual inventory category, or combinations of inventories, and can be sorted by any variable such as case size or follow-up date. The reports will tally the number of cases in the inventory as well as the total expected First Year Commission and a weighted probability total of expected First Year Commission. This is very helpful in predicting future revenue. Reports also include phone numbers, scheduled follow-up dates, tasks and reasons, as well as other case data for a complete view of any given inventory category.

Name: Chris Sample

CAM Inventory Report

Case Inventory

Report Date: 5/31/2011

Number of Cases:		14
Total Expected FYC:		$20,436
Total Weighted FYC:		$15,613

#	Date	Inv. Type	Name	Source	Age	Occupation	Income	Category	Case Type	Wtd FYC	Phone	Next Follow Up	Reason
1	3/10/11	Short Term Cases	Baxter, Bill	Center of Influence	48	Dentist	$300,000	Jack Morris, CPA referral	DI	$1600	M:678-403-5928 B:234-876-4000 H:234-567-2938	3/29/2011	Closing Interview
2	3/10/11	Short Term Cases	Wang, Steven	Center of Influence	44	VP Marketing - Dynasoft	$175,000	Jack Morris, CPA referral	401(k) rollover	$1760	M:203-676-9823 B:420-362-2105	3/31/2011	Decision Interview
3	3/25/11	Short Term Cases	Davis, Jack	Marketing Campaign	33	M.D. - Residency	$80,000	Univ. Med. School Intiative	Life / DI	$480	H:203-660-8813	3/30/2011	Closing Interview
4	3/25/11	Short Term Cases	Torelli, Mark & Marie	Center of Influence	45	Owner - Restaurant	$200,000	Jack Morris, CPA referral	EE Benefits / Retirement Plan	$2500	M:203-725-3467 B:203-440-4000 H:203-662-9384	4/1/2011	Pick up policies & ee census
5	3/26/11	Short Term Cases	Olson, Dorothy	Referral	62	Retired	$80,000	Karen Masters referral	LTC	$640	M:203-849-2094 H:203-393-4755	4/1/2011	Decision & Application
6	3/24/11	Short Term Cases	Tabor, James & Donna	Referral	50	MD	$250,000	Mike Daniels, MD referral	Retirement Planning	$2250	M:203-615-1756 H:203-344-1457	4/6/2011	Present Analysis / Recommendations
7	3/23/11	Short Term Cases	Fulton, Teresa	Referral	37	Professor - Math	$100,000	Joan Seymour referral	Life	$600	M:(203) 788-2390 H:(345) 456-3456	3/29/2011	Closing Interview
8	3/15/10	Submitted Cases	Hartwell, Kathy	Referral	35	Dental Hygienist	$60,000	Existing Client	Life	$760	M:203-412-3580	4/1/2011	Call with u/w Status Update
9	2/25/11	Submitted Cases	Reynolds, Dan	Referral	44	Business Owner	$150,000	Existing Client	DI Increase	$676	M:203-234-5678 B:203-345-5000 H:203-345-7075	4/1/2011	Delivery / Discuss 2009 Plan contribution
10	3/27/11	Submitted Cases	Martinez, Robert	Referral	36	Nurse Practicioner	$110,000	New	Life / DI	$1017	M:203-910-5349 B:203-278-9441 H:203-982-3982	4/15/2011	Underwriting status update
11	3/25/11	Submitted Cases	Nelson, Mark	Referral	37	Engineer	$115,000	Existing Client	Term Conversion	$630	M:202-810-9247 H:202-967-8935	4/15/2011	Delivery
12	3/26/11	Submitted Cases	Masters, Karen	Referral	43	Attorney	$185,000	John Olson referral	Life	$900	M:333-456-2345 B:222-333-4444	4/15/2011	Check u/w status
13	3/28/11	Submitted Cases	Hernandez, Alex	Center of Influence	42	Business Owner - Elec. Supply	$250,000	Jay Jones, CPA referral	Life / Key Person	$1140	B:203-445-6600	4/19/2011	Underwriting status
14	3/22/11	Submitted Cases	Dupree, Jackie	Referral	34	Dentist	$150,000	Existing Client	DI Increase	$660	M:425-784-2846 B:202-772-1422 H:202-435-9057	4/25/2011	Delivery

Instant Viewing of Case Details from Report Lists

Perhaps one of the most exciting and convenient features of the *CAM System* inventory module is the ability of the program to instantly display the complete case details of any case on an inventory list. Simply click on a name on the list to open a view of the case details for that individual, including the case timeline and case history notes.

Masters, Karen

Client Info

Inventory Type	Submitted Cases
Name	Masters, Karen
Date Obtained	3/10/2011
Source	Referral
Age	43
Occupation	Attorney
Income	$185,000
Optional	John Olson referral
Net Worth	$250,000
AUM	
Category	3

Contact Info

Email	k.masters@bplaw.com
Business Phone	222-333-4444
Mobile Phone	333-456-2345
Home Phone	345-495-2869
Home Address	

345 Shady Lane

Anytown		US	34567

Business Address

Boylston & Patterson, LLP

123 Main St.

Anytown		US	34567

Case Info

Case Type	Life
Amount	$1,000,000
Company	Diamond Live
FYC Estimate	$1,000
Closing Probability	90%

Follow-Up Info

Next Follow Up:	4/5/2011	Qual. Plan Contribution
Optl. Follow up 1:		
Optl. Follow up 2:		
Optl. Follow up 3:		
Optl. Follow up 4:		

Case Timeline

Date Obtained	Initial Facts	Case Opened	Decision Intvw.	Date Submitted	Date Completed	Active Client
3/10/2011	3/20/2011	3/20/2011	3/26/2011	3/28/2011		

FYC Submitted	FYC Earned
$1,000	

Case Notes

Case Notes - Karen Masters

Date: 3-10-11
Event: Initial call
Purpose: Sch. appt.
Results: Referred by John Olson (cousin of Karen). Karen was very receptive. Recently moved to area w/ one son (Anthony) to be closer to her family.
Wants to re-evaluate her financial situation. Intial appt. 3/22/11 here at 4PM for facts. Instructed what to bring.

Inventory Information Graphs

These reports provide graphs that show important demographic information such as the number of cases in your chosen inventory distributed by buyer age, income, and source of the case. It also shows the First Year Commission of the cases distributed by age, income, and source. This information can be used to evaluate both the quantity *and* quality of your inventory.

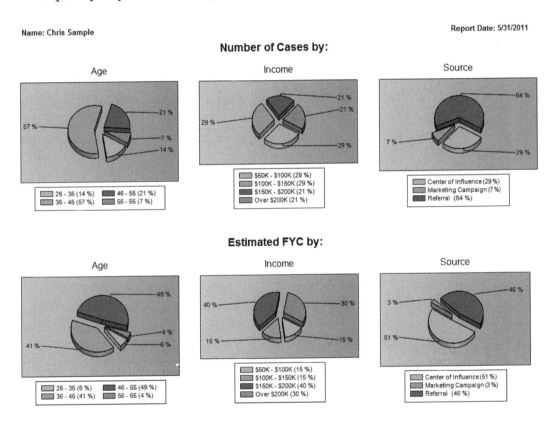

Name: Chris Sample   Report Date: 5/31/2011

Number of Cases by:

Age — 57 %, 21 %, 7 %, 14 %
26 - 35 (14 %)   46 - 55 (21 %)
36 - 45 (57 %)   56 - 65 (7 %)

Income — 29 %, 21 %, 21 %, 29 %
$50K - $100K (29 %)
$100K - $150K (29 %)
$150K - $200K (21 %)
Over $200K (21 %)

Source — 64 %, 7 %, 29 %
Center of Influence (29 %)
Marketing Campaign (7 %)
Referral (64 %)

Estimated FYC by:

Age — 49 %, 4 %, 6 %, 41 %
26 - 35 (6 %)   46 - 55 (49 %)
36 - 45 (41 %)   56 - 65 (4 %)

Income — 40 %, 30 %, 15 %, 15 %
$50K - $100K (15 %)
$100K - $150K (15 %)
$150K - $200K (40 %)
Over $200K (30 %)

Source — 46 %, 3 %, 51 %
Center of Influence (51 %)
Marketing Campaign (3 %)
Referral (46 %)

Because the *CAM System* is Web based, you (or your assistant), can view, edit, and share individual case notes and details. The inventory section also allows email, printing, and file exporting to Microsoft Word™, Excel™, and PDF file formats. The simplicity and flexibility of The CAM System™ inventory module offers unprecedented power for inventory management.

Relationship Management

Perhaps nothing is more important in building *and* sustaining a significant clientele than staying in touch and following up with your prospects and clients. This is the heart of the One Card System and managing client relationships. The *CAM System* provides the ability to generate Follow Up Reports that show all of your appointments and tasks for any selected time period. For example, if you are conducting your monthly planning session, you can set the date range to cover only the upcoming month. All birthdays and reviews would be identified, as well as any scheduled appointments or tasks. This allows you to assign important contacts and case management tasks to your calendar or to an assistant.

Using the Follow Up Report to Organize Dialing

The Follow Up Report can also be used to organize your day and your daily phone session. Simply set the date range for the current day to view all the telephone contacts, appointments, and tasks that are scheduled. During the phone session, the case details can be pulled up on the screen to record any notes or future actions. You can even open a list of browser tabs for all of the people you wish to call during that phoning session. As you complete each phone contact you simply close the browser tab for that case and the next case automatically opens for your viewing and editing. At the end of the phone session, the refreshed Follow Up Report can be printed and taken into the field, allowing you to make calls between appointments to any individuals you were unable to reach.

Follow Up Report

Name: Chris Sample

Report Period: 3/29/2011 - 3/29/2011

#	Inv. Type	Name	Category	Case Type	Phone	Email	Follow-Up Date	Reason
3	New Leads(QS)	Harvey, Beth	Jackie DuPree DDS referral		B:203-778-9045	elizabeth.harvey@nicesmile.com	3/29/2011	Call for init. appt.
4	New Leads(QS)	Vauhn, Timothy	Pat Stevens referral		M:425-710-7834	tim.vaughn@optics.com	3/29/2011	Call for init. appt.
6	New Leads(QS)	Ericks, Wayne	Jay Seymour referral		B:203-778-3469	wayne.ericks@any.univ.com	3/29/2011	Call for init. appt.
9	New Leads(QS)	Carson, Andy	Beth Hartwell referral		M:(345) 236-5689 H:(456) 345-5678	acarson@aol.com	3/29/2011	Call for init. appt.
10	New Leads(QS)	Aperlee, David	Rob Jackson, DVM referral		B:203-567-3545	daperlee@countryvet.com	3/29/2011	Call for init. appt.
11	New Leads(QS)	Davis, Bob	Grant Harris refrl		B:345-923-0934		3/29/2011	Call for init. appt.
13	New Leads(QS)	Downs, John	ref. by Dorothy Hamilton		M:425-345-6907	jdowns@yahoo.com	3/29/2011	Call for init. appt.
2	Long Term Cases	Peterson, Ralph	Existing Client	Buy / Sell - Life & DI	M:203-778-8822 B:203-446-2300	ralph@petersonsupply.com	3/29/2011	Call re: meeting with attorney
5	Incomplete Cases	Collins, Alice	New	Buy / Sell funding	B:203-377-1700	a.collins@dkmg.com	3/29/2011	call to sch. lunch w/ Alice & Carl Morris to update facts
1	Short Term Cases	Baxter, Bill	Jack Morris, CPA referral	DI	M:678-403-5928 B:234-876-4000 H:234-567-2938	bbaxter@gmail.com	3/29/2011	Closing Interview
7	Short Term Cases	Fulton, Teresa	Joan Seymour referral	Life	M:(203) 788-2390 H:(345) 456-3456	teresa.fulton@any.univ.com	3/29/2011	Closing Interview
8	New Leads(QS)	Colter, Margaret	John Dole, JD referral				3/29/2011	Initial Interview
12	New Leads(QS)	Nelson, Jane	Gary Johnson referral		B:503-234-4565		3/29/2011	Initial Interview

Clicking on any name will open the case details for that name

The Importance of Following Up

Of course it is important to follow up on current open cases and regularly contact our clientele. Granum determined that approximately 20 percent of an active clientele, when properly served, will purchase again in any given year, if you keep in touch. But what about the people you have taken facts on and even presented a proposal, only to be delayed or rebuffed? These cases may seemingly be lost, but they are very important. In the *CAM System™* inventory module we would move them to the Incomplete inventory category for future contact. Why is this so important?

The Granum research revealed some very important statistics that should guide your inventory management. The findings showed that 40 percent of New Clients defer their initial purchase to the second or third year of contact. Therefore, it is critically important to keep in touch with the people that show interest but do not buy in the first year. These are the people who are captured in the Incomplete inventory category. If you do not follow up with your incomplete cases, they will be lost and you will have let this 40 percent block of potential new clients slip away. Remember, these are people you have already invested considerable time in finding and developing. Their future referrals may be lost as well, which adds to the importance of proper follow up.

Are the OCS Cards Still Useful?

The OCS Card File can, of course, help you to guide your follow up contacts and help organize your phone activity. The cards have been used successfully for years and still work beautifully. We still recommend their use for the first three to six months of using the system. They are portable, simple, and quick. So, the question often arises, "Long term, does the *CAM System* replace the OCS Card File?" The answer is ... it's up to you!

Some advisors prefer a combination of the two; tracking suspects with yellow cards and only entering names into the *CAM System* after an initial meeting or taking facts. This reduces the amount of time entering data and deleting records of those Suspects who don't move on to become Prospects. Others prefer to be completely electronic and enter all qualified suspects into the *CAM System*. Either way, you will be able to manage large volumes of suspects, prospects, and clients and keep in touch on a regular basis.

Because of the power of technology, however, the *CAM System* offers the additional benefits of being able to easily organize, sort, and evaluate inventory. You can better manage and assign tasks and share information with an assistant. Revenue estimates help you manage cash flow and demographic information can be easily evaluated to determine your most profitable sources and markets.

The *CAM System* will guide the sound inventory management that is essential for properly servicing clients and growing a successful practice. It will store the case details and notes and remind you to contact prospects and clients at the appropriate time. It will help you follow through on commitments, build relationships and maximize your client building opportunities.

Conclusion

Without a doubt we live in changing times. Things we now take for granted like Google, Smart phones, and Web-based conferencing simply didn't exist only a few years ago. The word Google is now a verb in the dictionary! In an attempt to keep pace, the *CAM System* was developed to harness the power of this dynamic new technology. Our desire is to provide financial services professionals with the finest practice management system available and, as such, we are dedicated to constantly improving the program as technology allows. By helping financial services professionals to build successful practices, they can, in turn, help an ever growing number of clients with the challenges of obtaining financial security and freedom.

Part 3

Critical Soft Skills for Client Building

Chapter 9

Mastering the Sales Cycle

Introduction

Your business can be viewed as an interaction between three elements: Knowledge, or the Science, of the business; Mastery of the Soft Skills and Art of the sales cycle; and the Administration and Organization of the business.

1. The Science is built upon the activity and production data you collect in your *Productivity Planner* and analyze with your *CAM System*. This provides you with the knowledge needed to predict future outcomes based upon current activities. Additionally, it allows you to evaluate your sales cycle soft skills to identify both your strengths and skill deficits.

2. The Soft Skills, or Art, of the business are comprised of the language and sales skills that compose the steps of Client Acquisition that are graphically represented as the Sales Cycle.

3. The Administration of your practice is guided by the components of your One Card System, such as your *Productivity Planner, Card File,* or *CAM System.*

To fully succeed in your career, you need to master all three: how to predict and control future outcomes; the language and skills of the Sales Cycle; and how to administer your practice. The remainder of this book covers the soft skills required to master the Sales Cycle. They will, in effect, teach you the selling skills, or the Art, of the business. Prior to moving into the first segment of the Sales Cycle, it is important to set the stage with a discussion of the philosophy behind the process.

The Philosophy of a Consultative Sales Process

Consultative Selling vs. Transaction-Based Selling

When you enter the sales field in America today, you will encounter one of two basic sales philosophies: 1.) product-driven, transaction-based selling, or 2.) need-based, relationship-driven selling. These are often referred to as Transaction Selling and Consultative Selling.

Transaction Selling

Product-driven, transaction-based selling emphasizes the importance of the immediate sale and focuses on three factors:

1. Product Price

2. Product Features and Benefits

3. Warranties and Guarantees

The product is the central focus of the sale and is generally viewed as a commodity. The profit is viewed as a result of a successful transaction with the buyer, who is often referred to as the Customer. The margins in these products are under constant pressure from competition, and the greater the dissemination of market information through factors such as the Internet, the slimmer the margins become.

Consultative Selling

"The profit is in the relationship, not in the sale."

A consultative selling philosophy focuses on understanding the needs and wants of the Client. It is often referred to as a Needs-based relationship-driven sales process. It views products in the same way a physician views medications. They are tools to help solve a Client's problems or achieve her goals. Notice that the buyer is now referred to as a Client. This implies a longer term professional relationship. The Financial Services Professional acts more as a financial consultant than a salesperson. In this philosophy it is often said that, "The profit is in the relationship, not in the sale." The client is actually buying professional guidance and expertise. When we see a physician we aren't buying the medication but the physician's knowledge, experience, and guidance. The consultative sales philosophy emphasizes the same elements, along with highly developed relationship and communication skills.

Which Is Better: Transaction or Consultative Selling?

The answer is neither. One philosophy is not smarter, more ethical, or inherently more effective. It all depends upon what you are selling. If you are selling products that are consumer commodities such as personal computers or athletic footwear, a transactional sales process appears most efficient. If, on the other hand, you are selling products that require a more complete understanding of your Client and his or her unique situation, then a consultative approach is far superior. A consultative sales model becomes essential as the complexity of the Client's situation increases.

The Client Building philosophy stresses making the individual a Client by listening to and focusing on his or her financial needs, goals, and objectives. The specific product is secondary to the act of first understanding and then recommending.

Although the One Card System can function as an efficient administration system for either approach, it is designed as a comprehensive system for forming and sustaining long-term profitable Client relationships using a consultative sales process.

The *Right* Triangle of Selling

The Client Building philosophy is built upon a Consultative Sales Process. Consultative selling begins by gaining a clear understanding of your Prospect's situation and concerns. As we are gaining this understanding we are following a model for the sale. This model is often referred to as the *Right* Triangle of the Sale.

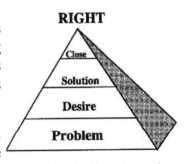

The *Right* triangle looks like the first of the two illustrations shown. The "right" triangle stands upon a firm foundation of facts. Within the triangle itself, the base is the Problem, next comes the assessment and stimulation of Desire, then the Solution, and finally the Close.

Too Often We Turn the Triangle Over

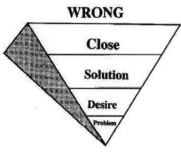

WRONG

Close

Solution

Desire

Problem

**Balanced Precariously
Upon A Point**

Unfortunately, all too often the Financial Services Professional flips the focus and the *Right* triangle ends up standing on its point. Set up in this manner, it is precariously balanced and apt to tip over. We give inadequate attention to the identification of the Problem and creation of the Desire. Therefore, we end up with a presentation top-heavy with forced closing attempts.

Geometry Equals Reality!

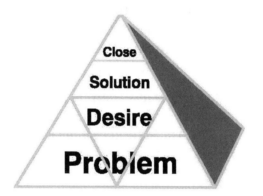

Close

Solution

Desire

Problem

When the bottom two sections – the Problem and Desire – are combined, they take up three times more area in the *Right* triangle as the top two. This geometric ratio is an accurate representation of the relative importance of the four steps. Identifying the Problem and creating Desire are about three times more important (and three times more difficult) as presenting the Solution and conducting the Close. If the first two steps are done properly, the last two are relatively easy.

The Benefits of the Sales Cycle

The Wheel of Client Acquisition

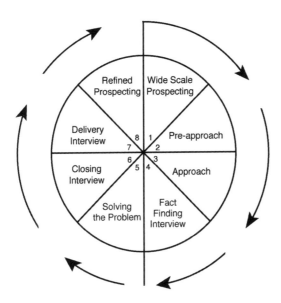

A Clear Track up the *Right* Triangle

Correctly followed, the Sales Cycle provides a clear set of steps that will guide you up the *Right* triangle to sales success. In essence, it gives you a track to run on.

Leads the Prospect to a Buying Decision

Since the client acquisition process is built upon the philosophy of the *Right* triangle, it psychologically leads the Prospect to a buying decision based upon his or her needs and objectives.

Reduces Confusion and Anxiety

This business can be overwhelming, and it is important to have a system such as the OCS to help you keep all the balls in the air. Following the Sales Cycle allows you to cover one step at a time and understand where you are in the sales process. It gives you a clear objective for each step. Without this understanding, the process becomes too confusing and you can become paralyzed by the resulting anxiety.

Offers a Sense of Accomplishment

It has been said that this is a business of delayed rewards and delayed punishments. The timing of those rewards, or psychological reinforcement, is often more important than the eventual amount of the reward. By viewing the client acquisition process as a cycle made up of separate steps, you can feel a sense of accomplishment (positive reinforcement) as you move successfully through each one.

Mastery Is the Key

Mastery Equals Confidence

Anxiety can prevent you from accomplishing your goals. Sometimes this anxiety flows from a lack of self-confidence. In this case, how can you build confidence? The best answer lies in *mastering* the material required for success. After all, confidence doesn't come from a general familiarity, but from mastery.

Steps for Mastering the Sales Cycle Language

It should be stressed that simply listening to someone else perform – in person or on an audio or video tape – does not accomplish mastery of the material. You must work at it yourself in order to acquire persuasive sales skills. Consider the following steps:

How to master persuasive sales skills.

1. *Start* with a word-for-word written version of the language you wish to master.

2. *Read* it into a recorder.

3. *Listen* to your recording and correct the script as necessary so that it reads the way you wish to speak it.

4. *Read* the corrected version into the recorder.

5. *Listen* without the script, outlining as you listen.

6. *Speak* into the recorder from your outline only.

7. *Listen* to your recording with script and outline before you, correcting the outline as necessary.

8. *Repeat* steps 4 through 7 until you are completely satisfied.

Mastery Allows You to Focus on Communication

It is absolutely necessary to practice on your own using the recorder until you feel adequately prepared. The purpose of practice is to allow you to make mistakes and correct them without any financial consequences. As they say, "Practice makes perfect."

Your presentation should be so ingrained that you can direct your attention toward the finer points of communication rather than to the words you are saying. Only then are you free to use your intellect and talents to fully observe what is going on with your Prospect. When you are focused on what you are going to say, you often miss what is most important.

The purpose of practice is to allow you to make mistakes and correct them without any financial consequences.

The Critical Importance of a Sense of Urgency

We Create Emotion through Our Own Beliefs

In addition to the proposal and the words used during the sales presentation, of equal – if not greater – importance is the emotional climate you create. Psychologists tell us that our "thoughts are catching." If you deeply believe in the need for the product you are recommending – if you believe the individuals ought to take action immediately – you will convey this sense of mission to your Prospects.

We Must Convey a Sense of Urgency

Although we begin by focusing on the problem, it does not mean that we are encouraging a slow, deliberate approach to the solution. If we convey a sense of urgency by the manner in which we conduct ourselves from beginning to end, the probability of inducing action is tremendously improved!

Convey a sense of urgency by the manner in which we conduct ourselves.

This sense of urgency cannot be overly stressed! It must begin when the lead is obtained. Process every new lead immediately. Send the pre-approach communication within twenty-four hours of hearing about the person. Call this individual within forty-eight hours of the day he or she will have received the communication. At the end of the Fact Finding Interview, schedule the appointment for the Closing Interview.

Teach Your Prospects How to Do Business with You

If you have been prompt and diligent through all of the steps you will be in character and consistent when you urge your Prospect to action at the end of your Closing Interview. Conversely, if you are slow and sloppy, you prove by your deeds that you do not think immediate action is too important – so you probably won't get it!

Top Financial Services Professionals bring a sense of urgency to every interview, while the unsuccessful person acts passively. While words and phrases are important, the great professional can succeed with the least motivating words delivered with winning intensity, while the weak representative frequently resorts to power phrases with docility. To a top professional, the next session – whether pre-approach, approach, fact finding, or closing – is not merely *a challenge*, but *the challenge*, while to a mediocre representative the next appointment serves only to help reach a daily quota of calls.

We Always Communicate Something

Projecting a sense of urgency leads to action.

This sense of urgency that comes so naturally to the superior professional leads directly to action. A passive presentation, on the other hand, leads directly to "Let me think it over." An intense desire to lead creates boldness and conviction on the part of the great professionals, and their obvious sincerity of purpose is almost instantly communicated. Weaker representatives communicate too. However, they reveal that they do not care very much and that there is very little at stake either for them or their Prospects.

What is the *Art*?

What is the *art* of the business anyway? It is the art of moving people to action. The art of merchandising insurance and other financial products is the moving of people to action, as contrasted with obtaining their passive agreement in the acceptance of a logical idea.

The Art of business is moving people to action.

The Important Thing Is Action

When Aeschines the Greek spoke, the people nudged each other and said, "How well he speaks." But when Demosthenes spoke, they brandished their swords and their spears and said, "Let's march against Philip of Macedonia!" This is an excellent example of enthusiasm motivating people to action.

Our Profession Is Motivation

To succeed, you should spend a portion of your time searching for ideas that will move people's minds – when ideas move people's minds, people move to action! Where can you find these motivating ideas? Everywhere! They are all around you.

As you read through the following ideas, look for the common denominator – for the thread that runs through these ideas and binds them together.

Aristides the Just

A very old idea first: Two thousand years before the birth of Christ, an Athenian Statesman, Aristides the Just, said,

"Not houses finely roofed, nor the stones of walls well builded; nay, nor canals and dockyards make the city, but *men*—men able to use their opportunities!"

Dr. S. S. Huebner

Almost 2,000 years after the birth of Christ and 4,000 years from the time of Aristides, a school teacher, Dr. Huebner, picked up the thought, embellished it, merchandised it, dramatized it, sold it, preached it, and taught it. Now we use it practically every day under the label HLV for Human Life Value.

Persuasion and Leadership – Abraham Lincoln

In discussing persuasion and leadership, President Lincoln said,

"When the conduct of men is designed to be influenced, persuasion—kind unassuming persuasion—should be adopted. It is an old and true maxim that a drop of honey catches more flies than a gallon of gall.

"So with men. If you would win a man to your cause, first convince him that you are his sincere friend. Therein is a drop of honey that catches his heart, which say what he will, when once gained, you will find but little trouble in convincing his judgment of the justice of your cause, if indeed that cause is a just one.

"On the contrary, assume to dictate his judgment or command his action, he will retreat within himself, close all avenues of his head and heart, and though your cause be naked truth itself and though you throw it with more than Herculean force and precision, you will no more be able to pierce him than to penetrate the hard shell of a tortoise with a rye straw.

"Such is a man and so he must be understood by those who would lead him, even to his own best interest."

On the Lighter Side – Abraham Lincoln

"That argument of yours seems to me to be about as thick as soup made by boiling the shadow of a sparrow which had starved to death."

Pauline Jeffries, an Architect of the One Card System

"With earnest patient diligence, helping associates to see that their most important function is to help the Prospect find out what it is that he, the Prospect, really wants to do! Because once any man knows what it is he wants to do, he will work and fight to find ways to make his want come true!"

Unknown

"When Mr. Anxiety comes to call, don't invite him in for a drink. Take him outside where sunshine and fresh air and oxygen and exercise will exorcise him!"

Stephen Leacock

"How strange it is, our little procession of life! The child says, 'When I am a big boy.' But what is that? The big boy says, 'When I grow up.' And then, grown up...married...'What is that after all?' The thought changes to 'When I am able to retire.' And then, when retirement comes, he looks back over the landscape traversed; a cold wind seems to sweep over it; somehow he has missed it all, and it is gone. Life, we learn too late, is in the living, in the tissue of every day and hour."

The Common Denominator

Search for ideas that move people's minds.

Did you spot the common denominator, the thread that binds these thoughts together? The common denominator is simply that these ideas happened to appeal to the authors. And that is the important concept suggested to you! It is not important what appeals to others. What is important is what appeals to *you*. This search for ideas that will move people's minds may seem like a nebulous, abstract thing, but if you bring it close to home and understand what it really is, a search for ideas that move you, it's not difficult at all.

Search for Ideas that Move You

Dedicate yourself to a search for ideas that move your mind. When you find one, seize it and assimilate it – make it a part of yourself. If it is good enough, it will spur you to action. As you go into action and pilot a course in which you passionately believe, your excitement communicates itself and you become unstoppable!

Chapter 10

Identifying Suspects Through Six Step Prospecting and Three Step Promotion

The Importance of Referrals?

To build a clientele of sufficient quantity and quality you need a constant flow of high quality Suspects. But, where do you find them? There are many sources of potential Suspects. Newspapers and phonebooks are filled with names, but calling the majority of them would be a waste of time. You should focus on meeting only those individuals who are likely to meet your criteria of intelligence, responsibility, and financial potential. The best way to identify these individuals is through the eyes of a nominator. It is generally easier to obtain a quality Client from a third-party nominated referred lead than through any other method of prospecting.

Whether you call them referred leads, referrals, prestige introductions, personal introductions, or just introductions, they are the fuel that drives the engine of a financial services business. Referred lead prospecting and in-depth values-oriented fact finding are the two master skills of the business. Obtaining referrals not only enhances the relationship between you and the nominator, it also dramatically cuts the trust development time with a new Qualified Suspect. Furthermore, it is undoubtedly the fastest way to build case size. Referrals are the great practice accelerator.

In today's world of voice mail, caller ID, call screening, No Call Lists, e-mail SPAM, and piles of junk mail, it is almost impossible to build a successful business using direct mail and cold calls. These approaches just won't work anymore. Mastering referred lead prospecting is no longer a great option: it is a non-negotiable necessity.

Referrals Dramatically Reduce the Time Required to Establish Trust

Referrals are the great accelerator of your business.

Consider this scenario. You call a Suspect you have not been referred to: someone who knows nothing about you and with whom you have no third party influence. You do a good enough job on your introduction, Fact-finding, and recommendations that he buys something from you and becomes a Client. Now ask yourself, "Does this Client now consider me his trusted Financial Services Professional?" The answer is a decisive, "No!" How long will it take to earn that level of trust? In most cases it probably will take several years of regular contact and excellent service to earn this designation.

But, suppose you were warmly referred to the same person by someone he or she knows and respects? What if, after meeting you did the exact same fine professional job? How long would it then take for you to be recognized as his or her trusted Financial Services Professional? It could be as little as a few months or weeks! Being referred by a respected nominator dramatically reduces the time required to establish trust in the professional relationship. This, in turn, accelerates both the rate at which you obtain referrals from the new client and the speed at which you build your clientele.

What Is Prospecting?

Prospecting means discovering *who* – specifically, who measures up on three counts:

1. Who has intelligence?

2. Who has a deep sense of responsibility?

3. Who has outstanding economic potential?

Have Enough Quantity to Ensure Sufficient Quality

The more people you have a chance to evaluate, the higher the quality of those you finally select. The heights you reach will be dependent upon the quality of your Clientele, which is in turn a function of your preliminary screening. Your job is to look at many people through the eyes of your nominators and to eliminate all except those who measure up to your standards. Only by looking at quantity is it possible to select quality!

A Sense of Purpose

If you believe that you are prospecting just to gather names, sell something, make money, and move on, then you will always feel that pursuing referrals is somewhat unprofessional, demeaning, or uncomfortable. When you understand that it is the only way you will be able to consistently find people who need your help, then you are ready to begin the journey toward becoming a master prospector.

Simply put, you must understand and believe that you are presenting financial services to do something FOR someone rather than TO someone. Stop and seriously think about the good that you can do. How much money is brought into a community by the lifetime work of a successful Financial Services Professional? How many families, businesses, children, and grandchildren are dramatically benefited? Your work is powerful and it is critical. Clearly it is a profession to be honored.

Your work is powerful and critical.

A Process: Prospecting and Promotion

It is important to first recognize that the overall prospecting process is actually divided into two distinct phases: prospecting and promotion. Prospecting is the process of identifying and qualifying names. Promotion is the process of obtaining and utilizing the influence of the nominator. Prospecting without promotion is like breathing with one lung. You can live, but it is difficult to flourish.

The Six Step Prospecting and Three Step Promotion Process

This famous referred lead prospecting process comes from the creator of the *One Card System*, O. Alfred Granum, CLU. It has been time tested in every conceivable market. It is powerful and it works. Part of the power comes from the fact that it feeds names we already know as well as categories that prompt additional names from the nominator. Furthermore, the process is designed to obtain the active endorsement of the nominator or turn names into introductions.

The actual Six Step Prospecting and Three Step Promotion language appears later in this chapter. When the 6-3 process is used in combination with other techniques, such as prompting lists (name rosters of professional associations, clubs, or companies), you will be prepared to maximize the total number of referrals obtained in an interview.

There are two additional key points here. First, we can't view the referred lead prospecting process as merely an add-on to the really important task of selling. It is a critical process in our success and must be treated as such. Second, as the great producer Ben Feldman once said, "If it's a problem, make it a process and it won't be a problem anymore." The more systematic our prospecting process and the preparation for that process, the greater our success.

The Importance of Preparation

Obviously, all outstanding performances in any area of endeavor are the result of careful preparation. The skill of referred lead prospecting is no exception. Without preparation you will greatly restrict the number of referrals obtained. Remember, to sustain a growing practice you need to obtain between forty and eighty Qualified Suspects every month. At least 75 percent of these should be referrals. Without sufficient preparation, the probability of this happening is very small. If you aren't obtaining an average of at least three referrals per request, you probably aren't taking enough time to prepare.

Outstanding performances are the result of careful preparation.

The Critical Prospecting Outline

An exceedingly important part of your preparation for stronger opportunities (those that occur after the completion of a closing interview, delivery, or birthday lunch) is the advance preparation of a Prospecting Outline. Prepare this by reviewing the Case History, Facts form, or Confidential Questionnaire, and extract names that can be introduced for qualification purposes. Also search for any categories or situational clues that might trigger the prospective nominator to think of additional names.

A List of Names and Categories to Be Fed

Prepare a list for every nominator. List every name and category that is to be fed for qualification purposes. This is a separate document from the prompting list and is very important. You will use this as a reminder of the names and categories you want to explore with the nominator. Additionally, if you take the time to prepare an outline, the probability that you will actually pursue referrals increases dramatically.

Maximizing the Names We Already Know

Your Prospecting Outline will include the names of friends or associates of your nominator – many picked up from personal observations or previous conversations with the nominator. These are valuable and you will want to discuss these names with the nominator for qualification and endorsement. But there can be a limit to how many names you can bring up in a meeting because of your limited supply and time. How can you speed up the process and make it easier for your nominator? One way is the use of prompting lists.

The Psychology of Prompting Lists

As discussed previously in this book, retrieving names strictly from our memory is called Recall Memory. Recognizing a name that is presented to us is called Recognition Memory – which is far more powerful and much faster than recall memory. When someone looks at a list to see if there are any people they might know and can help you out with, they will recognize far more names than if asked to suggest names without the use of a list. It is common for a nominator to quickly check off five or ten names in just a few seconds. You will want to use prompting lists to take advantage of the power of recognition memory.

Prompting lists tap the power of recognition memory.

The Use of Prompting Lists

A prompting list is simply a list of people whom the nominator might recognize. It can be a list of names you assembled and printed out or it can be a published list of some kind. If, for example, the nominator is a Real Estate Agent, the prompting list may be composed of members of the local Realtors Association or the Real Estate Offices listed in a local directory.

Where Can You Get Prompting Lists?

The information for prompting lists can be found in many places. Association rosters, company Web sites, and financial reports are good sources. Of course, the Internet is a very powerful source. Entering a key word into Google will provide an amazing amount of information. Most professional organizations or companies have member directories on their Web sites. If not, they often provide directions as to how to obtain them. Even though preparing prompting lists takes some time, it is well worth the effort.

Maximizing the Names We Don't Know Going into the Interview

In addition to prompting lists, we can utilize categories to stimulate the nominator's thinking. There are numerous sources of such categories, but here are some that are frequently used:

- Who do you know that owns a successful business?

- Who would you say is your most trusted advisor or professional?

- With whom do you socialize, play golf, or play other sports? (Any appropriate sport or activity will do.)

- Who are church members, business associates, professionals you work with or admire?

- If you won a free cruise for yourself and three other couples, whom would you invite to go on the cruise with you?

- If you were hosting a dinner party, who would be your two favorite couples to invite?

- If you had to pick one person that you felt really had a chance to make a mark or rise to the top of his or her business or profession, whom would that be? (This is the 5th Step, or Pinpoint Question, in Six Step Prospecting from the *One Card System* by O. Alfred Granum.)

- "I'm looking for people like you; people who are intelligent, responsible, and want the best strategies to grow and protect their assets." Who comes to mind?

- If you were starting a business of your own, who would be the first three people you would call?

Additional Categories for Direct Suggestion or Prompting Lists

- Associates mentioned when the nominator's position in the organizational structure of the company is discussed

- Guardians

- Relatives

- Professional Advisors

- Professional Associations

- Business Organizations

- Social, Volunteer, or Religious Organizations

- Residential Neighborhoods

- Geographic Business Districts or Office Buildings

- Present or Past Place of Employment

Consider a Visual Aid for Prompting Categories

Some Financial Services Professionals prefer to use a visual prompting sheet for categories, such as the one illustrated next, with the nominator's name in the center to emphasize his or her importance. The use of this type of graphic is most effective in face-to-face meetings, where categories can be explored thoroughly. However, the graphic can also be mailed or emailed to receptive Clients with an appropriate explanation.

You Are A Center of Influence

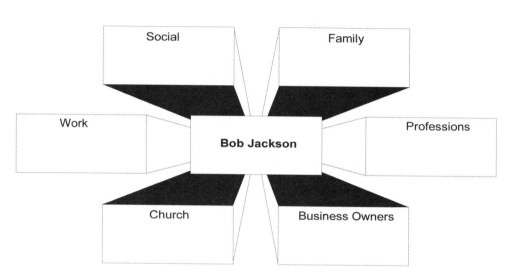

Scripting for 6-3 Prospecting and Promotion

Six Step Prospecting

The classic 6-3 Prospecting & Promotion language, developed by O. Alfred Granum, is based upon sound psychological principles and has been proven in thousands of professional practices around the world. It is the base from which almost all other prospecting language has been developed.

The purpose of the prospecting step is to identify the names and qualifying information of individuals who are likely candidates for your services. As the name implies, there are six steps to the basic prospecting method.

1. Get an affirmative

2. Feed a name

3. Qualify

4. Who else?

5. Pinpoint

6. Double-step ahead

These six steps, combined with the three Promotion steps, are the heart and soul of the prospecting process. They may be used in a number of different settings and contexts, but the basic principles always remain the same.

1. Get an Affirmative

The purpose of the first step is to begin the prospecting process on a positive note.

Begin the process on a positive note.

"Now that you've had a chance to see something of the work I do, tell me frankly, how do you feel about what you've seen so far?"

Wait for a response. If the nominator clearly expresses strong appreciation for the work you have done, you may proceed to the next step of the process. If, on the other hand, the nominator's initial response is brief, it may simply be a "socially appropriate" response. If that happens proceed by getting a second affirmative.

"Thank you. However, I'm not just looking for compliments. It's important for me to get honest feedback on my work. Given what we have done so far, how have you felt about the process?"

If the first affirmative is simply a socially acceptable response, it is the second affirmative that creates a commitment in the individual's mind. Next, use the following phrase to transition to the second step.

"Thank you. I appreciate your thoughts. With that in mind I'd like to ask your thoughts on another matter."

2. Feed a Name or Category

"Earlier you spoke highly of Barbara Powell and I'd like to share what I do with her. (No pause.) Approximately how old is Barbara?"

3. Qualify the Suspect in Depth

Notice that there is *no pause* between the feeding of a specific name and the first qualification question for Step Three. Your objective is to immediately start a conversation about the person you are considering, thereby reducing the possibility of an objection.

Ask your qualification questions in the same order every time. By doing so, you avoid overlooking anything and it will be easier to reconstruct your notes. You will record the qualifying information on your Prospecting Outline.

- Exact spelling of the full name

- Age

- Residence and business address

- Phone numbers

- Company and title

- Spouse, spouse's employment, and children

- Ultimate potential and present income

Many of your potential Suspects will be in dual income families, so choose one and then proceed.

Explore the individual's potential first, then their current situation.

"You've indicated that the Powells are a respected couple and I'd like to share what I do with them. (No pause.) About how old are they? And what does Barbara do in her career? What is her position at the XYZ Company?"

Now ask any further appropriate in depth qualifying questions before moving on to economics.

"Would you be willing to guess as to what Barbara's ultimate potential might be?"

"And what would that mean to her economically?"

"What is your estimate of how well she is doing now?"

By asking about ultimate *potential* first (deliberately leaving out the word *income)*, it is usually easy to get the nominator to respond. Then, having discussed the future, it is natural to go on to ask about the individual's present situation.

4. Who Else Comes to Mind?

"If your mind works like mine, as you were telling me about Barbara and Don, perhaps the names of other people flashed through your mind. If that happened, who else came to mind?"

Pursue the "who else" track as long as it is productive, and then feed another name or category for qualification. However, even though things may be going smoothly, make sure to save enough time at the end of the prospecting session to obtain promotional help.

5. Pinpoint

Begin the next step by turning your outline face down and saying:

"Thank you. This has been very helpful. Now, I'd like to ask you to open your mind wide for a moment and think of five people you know here in the Chicago area. (Pause for a moment.)

If you had to identify just one, who in your opinion has the very best opportunity to really make a mark in his or her business or profession, to really rise to the top, who would that person be?"

The pinpoint question helps you prospect toward individuals with higher economic potential.

Allow your nominator time to respond on his or her own first, but if someone doesn't come to mind, then orient the nominator's thinking toward business associates or acquaintances, social interests, college friends, clubs, or personal hobbies. If this doesn't work, go back to the previously discussed group of persons and have them pinpoint the best one of them.

Whether the nominator comes up with a new name or goes back to one previously suggested, it is vitally important in setting the stage for the Double-Step-Ahead question by having him or her concentrate on the individual being discussed. If a new person is being discussed, the necessity for discussion of that person is obvious. If you are referred back to someone previously mentioned, review his or her information. In either case, conclude by saying:

"I can see, based on what you've told me, that you think highly of Dennis. But tell me, what is it about Dennis that makes him stand out in your mind as having such unusual potential?"

6. Double-Step Ahead

When the nominator answers the previous question, go on to the final step by saying:

"Bill, from all you have told me it appears that you know Dennis reasonably well. Is that so?"

Allow him to acknowledge that he does know the individual well.

"Fine, knowing him as well as you do, would you put yourself in his position for just a moment, and think from his point of view. Tell me, who would Dennis be apt to know well here in the Chicago area?"

This question gives you a double jump ahead. You not only know where to go next, but you also know, before you even meet the *next* Suspect, where you might be able to go from that individual, when the time comes. This adds tremendous strength to what might otherwise be relatively weak suspecting opportunities, such as those that occur on the phone or at the end of the approach. If you get an affirmative from the individual, having a specific name to suggest for qualification greatly improves the chances of obtaining that individual's cooperation.

Remember, too, that if specific names cannot be obtained through the use of the Double-Step Ahead question, knowledge of general areas of interest can be almost equally useful. If you know before you call on a Suspect that he or she is a member of the South Shore Country Club, was in the Navy, is active in the community church, and graduated from Princeton, you obviously have a number of areas to explore as you attempt to obtain future Suspecting cooperation.

Continuing with a Prompting List

If the situation is appropriate you may smoothly transition to your prompting list following your Six-Step Prospecting language.

"Thank you, this has been very helpful. If you don't mind, I'd like your thoughts on something else for a moment.

Bill, you're an Optometrist and that's a professional group with which I'm doing more and more work. I brought along a list of some of the optometrists that I'm planning to introduce myself to and I wonder if there are any that you know and could help me out with? Maybe you could take a moment to check off any that you know or are friendly with." (Hand him the list and your pen).

Three Step Promotion

Prospecting is finding out <u>who</u>. Promotion is utilizing the influence of the nominator.

We said earlier that Prospecting is finding out *who*. Promotion, on the other hand, means *obtaining and utilizing the influence of the nominator* to meet the Suspect under favorable circumstances. The classic promotion process consists of three steps:

1. Describe

2. Challenge

3. Summarize and Stress

1. Describe

"Now I'd like to describe the procedure I normally use in introducing myself to a potential Client. I write a brief letter (or email message) outlining the type of work I do. Then, I call to ask the individual for an appointment. That's entirely up to them. When it's appropriate to do so, I ask the person who has told me about the individual to add a brief note of introduction."

2. Challenge

Do not pause at this point but move on as you point to the first name that was qualified and challenge the nominator's influence by saying:

"Looking at these people who we previously discussed and starting with the first one, Barbara Powell, tell me, do you feel that you know Barbara well enough and have a comfortable enough relationship with her that it would be appropriate for you to add a note of introduction?"

If the nominator shows some doubt or hesitation, ask if it would be all right to tell Barbara that you know (and, if appropriate, have worked with) the nominator. If this is satisfactory, you will later add a phrase, mentioning the nominator's name, to your own introduction.

On the other hand, if the nominator does not want to be involved with the first Suspect, make it clear that you will not mention his or her name. This raises confidence in you and increases the probability of better cooperation as you move to the next Suspect.

3. Summarize and Stress

Having checked every name to determine what level of promotional help your nominator can give, *summarize and stress* this way:

"Fine, now to summarize. When I get back to my office, I will write letters (email messages) to these people and will call them. In the cases of those with whom you feel comfortable, I'll send the letters that include your note of introduction (or, I'll mention your name in my email message)."

Let him or her see you make a notation at the bottom of your prospecting outline as to the date you will make your phone calls, and then go on as follows:

"The important thing I would like to stress is that it is <u>you</u> and your influence and prestige that are important. Without them, I'm only a stranger. But with your introduction, the probability of my being able to meet these people under favorable circumstances is greatly increased. Then, it's entirely up to them, of course, as to whether they wish to continue a relationship with me.

"There are two reasons why I hope to meet them. The first is obvious, they sound like respected and interesting people. The second reason is perhaps more important. All of these people will discuss their financial goals with someone, sometime, and I hope to have the opportunity to participate in that discussion. As you know, I feel strongly about providing quality and service, so I truly appreciate your support."

Get the Nominator's Note on Letters or Brochures

If the person agrees, glance at your watch and say:

"May I take another five minutes? These are the letters (or brochures) I'll be sending. If you could take another couple of minutes, you might add your notes of introduction right now. Anything with your signature would be fine."

At this point, give the nominator the appropriate number of pre-approach letters, complete except for the inside name and address, and let them add their notes. If you are using brochures rather than letters simply give them several and show them some endorsed examples. You might carry a sheet of sample notes to give them an idea of what others have said. What they say isn't nearly as important as the presence of their signature.

Overcoming Resistance

When Will Resistance Occur?

If nominators are ever going to give you resistance, the odds are very high that they will do it at Step 2, when you suggest a specific name and ask a qualification question.

The Benefit of the Double Affirmative

Remember that you don't suggest the name and ask a qualifying question unless you have first obtained a *strong* affirmative. If your nominator's first response had appeared to be simply a socially appropriate response, then you would have used the language suggested earlier for obtaining a double affirmative.

"...I'm not just looking for compliments, Bill. It's important for me to get honest feedback on my work. Given what we've done so far, how have you felt about the process?"

Receiving a strong affirmative greatly reduces the probability of resistance. If you do run into trouble, however, the material that follows should give you a good chance to overcome it and move on.

Three Steps in Overcoming Resistance

1. Draw the venom and pull the sting

2. Backtrack the affirmative

3. Describe your desired Suspect and your introduction

1. Draw the Venom and Pull the Sting

When resistance is encountered, such as, "I don't like to meddle in other people's affairs," draw the venom and pull the sting by being most concerned and understanding. Begin by asking your nominator if he or she has had a bad experience in the past with referring professionals. Allow them to briefly state their concerns and then promptly move on to the process of overcoming resistance.

2. Backtrack the Affirmative

Then, backtrack the affirmative by saying:

"I certainly understand how you feel, Bill. That's why I was so careful a moment ago to ask you how you felt about me and my work. If you've been uncomfortable with what we've done, then I guess I have to improve. I'm hoping, however, that you meant it when you said that you appreciated the job I've done."

At this point the nominator will almost certainly assure you that *you* are fine. They will probably go on to share that it is the involvement in the personal affairs of others that is really what they want to avoid.

3. Describe Your Desired Suspect and Your Introduction

With a sigh of relief, you can continue by describing the characteristics of the individuals you are seeking, and the introduction procedure that you use.

"I can understand your reluctance to involve yourself. Perhaps it would help if I described the types of individuals who tend to be interested in my services and how I introduce myself to them.

"You know, the phone book is full of the names of thousands of people. I could write them letters, call them on the phone and make lots of appointments. But, for most of them, it would be a waste of their time. This is because we know that, well, many people are reluctant to take on the responsibility of significant long-range planning. Consequently, I'm looking to work with quality people; people who are like you, intelligent, responsible individuals with good economic potential. People who want to grow and protect their assets.

"I normally introduce myself by writing a brief letter outlining the type of work I do. I call on the phone to ask if the individual would like to see me. That's entirely up to them. (No pause.) In that light, could you help me with Barbara Powell? How do you think she measures up on the scales of intelligence, responsibility, and economic potential?"

If the nominator answers the qualification question, you are then back on the track of cooperation. You can then proceed with the next steps in the Six Step Prospecting, that of qualifying the Suspect you have suggested, and then probing for more names.

However, if the nominator is still hesitant, you might present the following irrefutable argument. It is a fact that all of these people will speak to someone, someday about their financial goals.

I understand. However, you might consider this: all of these people are going to discuss their financial goals with someone, sometime. All I'm really looking for is the opportunity to be able to participate in that discussion. As you know, I feel very strongly about providing quality and service. So, on that basis, do you feel Barbara Powell is the type of individual to whom I should introduce myself?"

The Gracious Exit language is your "escape hatch." It allows you to end the conversation on a positive note.

The Gracious Exit

However, if this doesn't work and your nominator still resists, don't push any harder. We are not trying to win battles and lose wars. Here we can utilize the Graceful Exit language.

"Fair enough, Bill, I understand and appreciate how you feel. Would you be comfortable with this? If you should hear of someone who is actively looking for a Financial Services Professional, would you be comfortable mentioning my name?"

Nominators will almost certainly agree to this and will assure you that their hesitation has nothing to do with you personally. This allows you to end the conversation on a positive note with the nominator agreeing to refer you under the right circumstances. *So, you have nothing to lose and everything to gain by engaging in the referred lead prospecting process.*

What if the Nominator Offers to Call, Write, or Email the Nominees?

This is an interesting question because the offer could either be a very generous offer of assistance or a subtle form of resistance. If the nominator suggests that you not call the Suspects until <u>after</u> he or she has called or emailed them, then you are probably dealing with a form of resistance. You might consider the following response in this situation:

"I truly appreciate your offer, but I'd prefer to send the letters (or call) myself for two reasons. First of all, there's no reason you should have to do my job. You've already been helpful in offering your support. And secondly, you're busy enough. Does that seem reasonable?"

If the nominator again states that he or she would prefer that you not call the Suspect until they have communicated, then back off graciously and honor that request.

"If that is most comfortable for you then that would be fine. I really do appreciate you taking the time to contact these people. What is a reasonable time to check back with you on this? Would a week seem about right?"

A Different Perspective on Rejection

Sometimes nominators simply refuse to offer introductions and Suspects refuse to meet with us. Often we take this as personal rejection. We shouldn't. The nominator is rejecting the referral process, not us. Additionally, resistant Suspects are selecting *themselves* out. Long-range planning for financial security requires people who are willing to face their responsibilities, and many won't. We aren't on trial – they are.

A Series of Selection Gates

Picture the client acquisition process as one of leading or helping people through a series of gates in concentric fences. The Suspects who become Prospects and successfully negotiate the fences to become Clients are permanently corralled in the innermost section. They are the lucky ones. Those who cannot make it are left outside. It's not that they reject you; it's just a fact of life that many cannot measure up to your requirements.

Think of it this way. Milling about outside the outer fence are the thousands of people you can contact, if you wish. Your first job is to open the outer gates just a crack and select only those who meet the objective tests of age, income, and future expectations. These people are admitted through the first gate.

Establish Your Minimal Acceptable Profile (MAP)

It is valuable to stop and think about what minimum qualifications are necessary for your Suspects to be invited into your practice. Obviously, not everyone measures up. Take the time to identify and write down your MAP for new Suspects in your *One Thousand Clients* book.

Progressive Sifting and Winnowing

From then on, you must sift out those who have the subjective qualities you are seeking. You do so by opening successive gates, describing the green pastures within, and inviting those who wish to do so to pass through with you. Once safely inside the inner circle, the gates are closed and the Clients are kept there by providing them with ongoing service. The successive gates include your preapproach grid, the approach mesh, the fact finding and analysis screen, and, finally, the fine inner sieve.

The Final Sieve of Becoming a Client

The inner sieve is the ultimate test in determining whether original Suspects, newly qualified as Prospects by having passed successfully through all gates but the last, are to become Clients. To get those Prospects through that inner sieve, they must purchase something from you.

The Prospects must buy at least a part of the solution to their problems to gain admittance to the final section where they are entitled to the highest grade of service. It isn't easy, for a large number of Suspects will have to be screened to end up with a few high quality Clients.

When is the Best Time to Pursue Referrals?

There are stronger prospecting situations and weaker ones. The weaker ones occur at the end of the Pre-Approach and the Approach Interview. They are weaker because the nominator has not yet had the opportunity to experience the benefits of your work.

Nevertheless, even these weaker opportunities should be utilized by individuals who are new to the industry, and by any others who are not generating a satisfactory flow of good Suspects every year.

The stronger prospecting opportunities occur as an integral part of your Fact Finding Interviews, Closing Interviews, Delivery Interviews, Client Reviews, and birthday lunches.

Quantity Determines Quality

Obtaining large numbers of referrals is the best way to increase your case size. The higher the quantity of referrals, the greater the probability of some high quality Suspects appearing in the mix. Referred lead prospecting is very much like panning for gold. In one scoop of gravel (one request) there may be nothing, or there may be a few small grains of gold. The probability of finding a good sized gold nugget, however, goes up with the number of scoops. To a large extent, quantity determines quality. Keep score!

Referrals are the best way to increase case size.

Prospecting through Personal Observation

Personal Observation – An Overlooked Set of Skills

We have emphasized the importance of maximizing referrals, but it is important not to overlook another very powerful way to bring Qualified Suspects into your practice – prospecting through personal observation. Every day Financial Services Professionals see and often speak with lots of people they would love to introduce to their practice. Businesses you frequent, people in your office building, people you observe at clubs and meetings – they are all possible Suspects.

The problem is that many Financial Services Professionals simply don't know how to approach someone in a way that would allow them to contact them later on a favorable basis. The best way to guide people to a discussion about your practice is to get them to ask you what you do for a living.

How to Get People to Ask You What You Do:

Imagine you are talking to someone in a social setting such as a party or networking event and you want him or her to ask you what you do for a living. Begin the process by simply asking <u>them</u> what they do for a living.

"I'm curious. What career are you in?"

If they answer with an occupation that is not represented in your client base, then say:

"That's interesting, I don't think I have any gemologists (whatever they are) in my practice."

If they answer with an occupation that is represented, then say:

"That's interesting; I work with a fair number of gemologists in my practice."

They will usually follow with the socially appropriate response and ask you what you do. You reply with your brief answer, but then go on to ask them more about themselves.

"I'm a Financial Services Professional specializing in risk management, wealth accumulation, and wealth preservation. Gemology has always seemed interesting. Do you have an area of specialization?" (Or something to that effect.)

We do not want to get into a lengthy discussion of ourselves but want to listen to learn more about them and create the beginnings of a social bond. Later in the event or even sometime the next day you will follow up.

The Famous Two-Part Question

Now that you have provided a brief description of what you do, how do you follow up with the potential Suspect? Consider the time-tested and proven Two Part Question. It is designed to be used face-to-face in the same initial meeting or at another non-business event. It can also be used in an informal phone conversation. After a brief greeting:

This is the famous Two-Part Question.

"Bill, I enjoyed meeting you the other day (if calling) and to be honest, I couldn't help but wonder what you've done regarding your own insurance planning (or financial planning or financial program)? Would you have any objection to discussing your program with me sometime?"

Responses will fall into one of three categories:

1. The rarest response is, "Yes, I would object." If you do encounter this response, simply reply with the most powerful word in the sales person's arsenal, "I'm curious, *why*?" Then listen, and after that person explains why, use the language for the "No, but" response outlined in the third category that follows.

2. The oddly reverse affirmative, "No, I wouldn't object. That might be helpful." In this case, try to set an appointment.

3. The more common response is, "No, but..." and is usually followed by some kind of put off. For example, "No, I wouldn't object, but it won't do you any good because I'm all taken care of" ... or "I think I'm OK in that department, etc., etc." Most of the time the "No" will be implied and only the reason will be stated.

At this point it is important to understand that no matter what their response, you say the same thing.

"I understand, and obviously this is neither the time nor place to discuss your personal affairs. The thing I would like to do, however, if you don't object too violently (said with humor) is to stop by for a few minutes, share a little about the way I work, and to get your thinking on the subject. Fair enough?"

Whether or not the individual agrees, drop the subject at this point to avoid the appearance of pushing. This was why you purposely selected a casual, non-business setting to ask the initial question. American culture strongly values fairness. So, when you close your comment with, "Does that seem fair enough?" you enhance the probability of getting an affirmative.

Follow Up Promptly

Your follow-up should occur within a week, while the memory of this incident is still fresh in the individual's mind. The follow-up can take place either by phone or in person. When calling, after a brief reference to your previous preliminary conversation, request a specific appointment. If the individual is easily accessible, you may prefer to just drop in during business hours.

Meeting People Quickly at a Networking or Business Event

If you are at a large networking event like a chamber of commerce meeting, your goal is to meet as many people as possible in the limited time available. Often, you only have time to meet people at your immediate table. Here is a method to meet more. Simply go up to people quickly and say the following:

"Pardon me, I would love to meet and have a chance to talk with you in more depth, but due to the size of the meeting and the limited time would it be OK if I just briefly introduced myself, and maybe we could exchange business cards and arrange to talk later at a more convenient time? I'm Chris Dutton. Nice to meet you."

Then exchange cards and follow up with a call within a week. This allows you to maximize the number of business cards you are able to collect at a large meeting and gives you a reason to call.

Final Thoughts on Prospecting Through Personal Observation

Personal observation prospecting is a method that is often overlooked by Financial Services Professionals, yet it can be very effective. It provides the advantage of allowing the Suspect to associate a face with your name. Even something as simple as dropping by offices in a business park, introducing yourself, and dropping off your card can yield results. There is no doubt that referred lead prospecting is the fastest, most cost effective and powerful method of prospecting, but personal observation can be an important addition.

What If You Are New in the Business?

Begin By Sharing Your Approach

What if you're new in the business and haven't yet provided services for your nominator? How can you get started? Easy! Your friends, relatives, and acquaintances (FRAs) can make excellent nominators. By mastering the following language it is possible to obtain referrals to qualified individuals on your very first day in the business.

"Bill, as you know, I recently joined the Diamond Life Insurance Company and am very excited about the opportunity and the professional approach that I'll be using. If you don't mind, I would like to share it with you and get your reaction.

Our business model consists of three steps. First, I meet with individuals who are interested in making intelligent, long-range plans for their financial future. As we discuss their plans and objectives, we use this Confidential Questionnaire to remind us of the things we need to discuss and to keep us on track.

As you say this, place the Fact Finding form right-side up in front of your friend, relative, or acquaintance. If they pick it up or want to look at it, stop until eye contact is re-established. Then continue:

"The second step is for me to take this information back to my office where it is reviewed and analyzed and, if appropriate, a written report is prepared. No two of these are exactly alike, but here is one that has been prepared with the names changed, of course, to give people an idea of what we do." (Present the report.)

"The third step, for our clients, is the preparation of a permanent record which is kept up-to-date through the years through regular face-to-face reviews. This one is similar to those which will be prepared for my clients." (Show sample.)

Then Move to Get an Affirmative

You then move to the first step in the Six Step Prospecting process by obtaining an affirmative, not based upon what you have done, but upon what they think of the approach.

"Now, my first reason for wanting to spend a few minutes with you is to get your reaction to this kind of approach. Does it seem to make sense to you?"

Sometimes your friends, relatives, or acquaintances will misunderstand. Instead of responding to your question, they'll raise an objection to purchasing or to having this service done for them. If that happens, agree with the objection and tell them you didn't make yourself clear. Go through the three steps again, and explain that all you want to know is whether they think the process – the procedure – makes sense. Once they say it does (give you the affirmative) go on by saying:

"Good, I'm glad you feel that this professional approach makes sense because the second reason I wanted to see you today was to ask for your help in evaluating some of these people whose names I have jotted down, to see if, in your opinion, they might conceivably be logical candidates for the service. (No pause.) Starting with your brother-in-law, John, about how old is he?"

Having obtained an affirmative, suggest a name from the prospecting outline and ask a qualification question. Note that there is *no pause at all* between suggesting the name and asking the first qualification question.

Conclusion

When the language of Six Step Prospecting and Three Step Promotion is used properly – when it is *mastered* and *internalized* – there is really no risk in attempting to obtain referrals. Most of the time, nominators will offer assistance in introducing you to others, particularly if a previous nominator introduced you to them. In these circumstances you have both a process for obtaining the names of individuals who meet your selection criteria, and one for turning those names into introductions.

Additionally, the psychological *Principle of Consistency* tells us that after nominators refer or introduce us to people they value, they will have an internal tendency to look for reasons that support their behavior. That is, they will begin to look for reasons why their referral was justified. In short, after they refer you, they will actually begin to see *you* in a more favorable light!

If, on the other hand, your nominator shows hesitation, you have a method of addressing those concerns and getting the conversation back on track. And finally, if they are still concerned, you have a way to gracefully exit the conversation, with your nominator agreeing to introduce you under the right circumstances. Consequently, there really is no downside risk in pursuing referrals – you have nothing to lose and everything to gain in mastering the skills of Six Step Prospecting and Three Step Promotion. Best of luck!

Condensed Six-Step Prospecting Language

1. Get an Affirmative

"Now that you've had a chance to see something of the work I do, tell me frankly, how do you feel about what you've seen so far?"

2. Feed a Name or Category

"Earlier you spoke highly of Barbara Powell and I'd like to share what I do with her. Approximately how old is Barbara?"

3. Qualify the Suspect in Depth

"And what does Barbara do in her career? What is her position at the XYZ Company?

Would you be willing to guess as to what Barbara's ultimate potential might be? ... And what would that mean to her economically? ... What is your estimate of how well she is doing now?"

4. Who Else Comes to Mind?

"If your mind works like mine, as you were telling me about Barbara, perhaps the names of other people flashed through your mind? If that happened, who else came to mind?"

5. Pinpoint

"Now, I'd like to ask you to open your mind wide for a moment and think of five people you know here in the Chicago area. (Pause for a moment.) If you had to identify just one, who in your opinion has the very best opportunity to really make a mark in his or her business or profession, to really rise to the top, who would that person be?"

6. Double-Step Ahead

"From all you have told me, it appears that you know Dennis reasonably well. Is that so?

"Knowing him as well as you do, would you put yourself in his position for just a moment, and think from his point of view. Tell me, who would Dennis be apt to know well here in the Chicago area?"

Condensed Three Step Promotion Language

1. Describe

"Now I'd like to describe the procedure I normally use in introducing myself to a potential Client. I write a brief letter (or email message) outlining the type of work I do. Then, I call to ask the individual for an appointment. That's entirely up to them. When it's appropriate to do so, I ask the person who has told me about the individual to add a brief note of introduction."

2. Challenge

"Looking at these people who we previously discussed and starting with the first one, Barbara Powell, tell me, do you feel that you know Barbara well enough and have a comfortable enough relationship with her that it would be appropriate for you to add a note of introduction?"

3. Summarize and Stress

"Fine, now to summarize. When I get back to my office, I will write letters (or email messages) to these people and will call them. In the cases of those with whom you feel comfortable, I'll send the letters (email messages), which include your note of introduction.

"The important thing I would like to stress is that it is you, and your influence and prestige, that are important. Without them, I'm only a stranger. But with your introduction, the probability of my being able to meet these people under favorable circumstances is greatly increased. Then, it's entirely up to them, of course, as to whether they wish to continue a relationship with me.

"There are two reasons why I hope to meet them. The first is obvious, they sound like respected and interesting people.

"The second reason is perhaps more important. All of these people are going to discuss their financial goals with someone, sometime, and I hope to have the opportunity to participate in that discussion. As you know, I feel strongly about providing quality and service, so I truly appreciate your support."

Chapter 11

Soft Skills for Pre-Approach, Phone Activity, and Approach

The Next Steps in the Sales Cycle

The Pre-approach, Phone Activity, and Approach are the three steps that follow 6-3 Prospecting and Promotion in the Sales Cycle. Once you have obtained the names of Qualified Suspects and – it is hoped – the influence of the nominator, you are ready to proceed with the next steps that lead to the all-important Fact-Finder.

The Pre-Approach

The Objective

The Pre-Approach segment of the Sales Cycle (which includes phone activity) has only one objective – to obtain a face-to-face appointment with your Qualified Suspect on a favorable basis. It is your first personal contact with your Suspect and, therefore, is the first impression you give of yourself and your business. A well conducted pre-approach will set the stage for the Approach that will lead to a Fact Finding Interview and an opened case.

Keys to a Successful Pre-Approach by Mail, Email and Phone

Send a Pre-Approach Letter and Introductory Brochure

Preferably, you will send a company approved pre-approach letter (or a company approved email message), along with a brochure that has been endorsed by a nominator, and then follow up in a timely manner. An introduction from a nominator who has prestige with the Suspect is often all it takes to secure an appointment. When designing a brochure be sure to leave enough blank space on the front for the nominator to be able to write a brief endorsement. Keep the interior of the brochure simple and uncluttered. You can say a little about yourself, but don't try to list all of your accomplishments. The idea is simply to introduce your Pre-Approach phone call. The pre-approach letter or brochure allows you to assume the Suspect is expecting your call and knows its purpose is to arrange for a time for the two of you to get together.

Introducing the services of:

O. Alfred Granum, CLU

Bob,
Al has been a great help to
Mary and me.
He's worth the time.

The Use of Email for the Pre-Approach

More and more people use email today as their primary means of business communication. Email is so fast and efficient that many people use it almost exclusively and often discard unrecognized postal or snail mail without even opening it. Given this trend, many Financial Services Professionals ask the nominator if they know if the Qualified Suspect has a preferred method of communication. They also often ask the Qualified Suspect the same question. If it appears that the Qualified Suspect uses email extensively then it is recommended you send a company approved introductory email message in addition to, or possibly in place of, a letter and brochure.

Some Financial Services Professionals include some brief nominator endorsement comments in the email message. If you were referred, be sure to include the nominator's name in the title of the email or it may not be opened. If you have not been referred, or have no recognizable name associated with the Suspect, you may be better off forgoing the email in your Pre-Approach because it may be perceived as SPAM or junk mail.

Phone Activity

The Objective

Calling for appointments remains a critical skill and crucial activity in building your Clientele. The objective of calling a Qualified Suspect is actually two-fold. The first objective, of course, is to secure a face-to-face appointment. However, if your language is clear and straightforward as to who you are and what you do, the telephone can also be viewed as a way of screening out those Suspects who really have no interest. This can be a tremendous time-saver. With this mind set, you are in control. You are the one deciding who you will see. Remember, only the best get in to see you!

Two Objectives of Phoning:
1. Obtain a face-to-face appointment with those who are receptive.
2. Screen out those with no interest.

Set Standard Calling Times

It is very important to set aside regularly scheduled daily phone times that no one violates – not your Clients, your manager, your assistant, or you. Have yellow Suspect cards prepared and Prospect or Client File folders pulled in advance of your calling time. It is difficult to acquire the critical momentum needed in your phoning activity without proper, prior organization. You should be organized well enough to make thirty-six dials in one hour. (Remember, the thirty-six dials will come from a combination of all file folders of any Prospects or Clients who are listed for that day's phone calls plus that day's 1-31 yellow Suspect cards.) Your Pre-Approach calls, however, will only be to your Qualified Suspects.

Master Your Phone Language

Master the Pre-Approach phone language and a standardized response to objections. The phone scripts discussed in this chapter are brief, straightforward, and to the point. It is purposefully designed this way for several reasons. First, if the message is too long or wordy, the busy Suspect will not take the time to listen and will, instead, cut you off and terminate the conversation. Second, if you are to achieve the amount of dialing necessary to give yourself a fighting chance to get in front of enough people, you must stick to a concise, well-rehearsed script.

Master a concise, well-rehearsed script. You only have one chance to make a good first impression.

Use a Confident, Professional Voice

Confidence comes with the mastery of your phone scripts *as does courage*. Suspects are often more tuned in to *how* you deliver your message than on what you say. They will often grant you an appointment because you sound professional, confident, nonthreatening, and nondefensive. It cannot be emphasized enough – you only have one chance to make a good first impression.

Ask for the Appointment Three Times

Studies show that it is most often during the third request that the individual grants the appointment. This technique alone can mean the difference between mediocre phone results and great calling success.

Remember, you put a tremendous amount of effort into earning and acquiring an introduction to this individual – why not give the same effort to getting in front of him or her?

Keep Records

You are looking for both a high quantity of appointments, as well as high quality. The quantity can best be handled by mastering the Six Step Prospecting and Three Step Promotion skills outlined in the previous chapter. The appropriate quantity of appointments, as well as a self-assessment of the effectiveness of your phone skills, can only be determined by keeping accurate records. Your Reached to Appointments call ratios (as shown in your *Success Manual* and automatically calculated by the *CAM System*) should average at least 50 percent by using the techniques outlined in this book. If they do not, then perform the mastery techniques from Chapter 9 to check if you are properly doing each of the steps outlined.

Categories of Suspects for the Pre-Approach

For Pre-Approach purposes, all Suspects fall into one of only two categories: People we know such as friends, relatives, and acquaintances, and people we don't know yet. Within these two categories are Suspects that we have been referred or introduced to and those we have not. Our Pre-Approach telephone language will vary slightly depending upon which group our Suspect falls into.

Calling Referred Leads

Let's begin with people we don't know yet but have been referred to.

If you have been referred and have sent a Pre-Approach communication, you might consider the following script for your call:

"Hello, Mr. Edwards, this is Sam Baker and I'm with The Diamond Financial Group here in Boston. I sent you a letter the other day in which I was introduced by John Barker (or in which I mentioned John Barker's name). I'm calling now to ask if I might schedule an appointment to see you later this week. Would 3:00 p.m. on Wednesday be convenient?

You may choose to use somewhat different language, but notice that this script is short, crisp, and to the point. Also, it does not hedge or try to obscure what you do or why you are calling. Now, keep in mind that people are always doing something else when they are interrupted by your phone call. Consequently, their first, almost knee-jerk response is to offer a quick objection and try to return to their previous activity. You should expect this and have your response ready.

Responding to the First Objection (Your Second Attempt)

"No, I won't be in town on Wednesday. Is this about insurance?

Your response:

"I see. (Pause.) I had no reason to assume you were in the market for any particular financial product, nor did John so indicate. However, our unique planning service has been of interest to many, particularly in today's tax and economic environment. Will you be in town next week?"

Notice that it is important not to let the conversation dangle. Always end with a question that is designed to schedule the appointment. If he says he will be in town, continue by naming a specific time.

"Could I see you next week at 10:30 a.m. on Monday?"

Responding to the Second Objection (Your Third Try)

"To tell you the truth this is a busy time for me and I already work with a Financial Advisor."

Your response:

"Yes. (Pause.) I understand. Nevertheless, the reasons for my wanting to stop in are, first, to have a chance to meet you and, second, to review our services and get your thinking on the subject. On that basis, would you object to seeing me next Tuesday at 2:00 p.m.?"

Notice that the suggested time is changed as if you are assuming that the objection is to the specific time suggested. But what if he objects a third time?

"The truth is I'm really not interested at this time."

Response to the Third Objection

If the Suspect continues to object, switch to an attempt to stay in touch by saying:

"I see. (Pause.) However, circumstances do have a way of changing. Would you have any objection to my staying in touch with you and checking in again at a later date?"

Qualify and Place in Your OCS

If the Suspect has no objection, proceed slowly, calmly, and smoothly:

"Fine. Let me just verify a bit of preliminary information. Your last name is spelled E-D-W-A-R-D-S? Your first name and initial? Your business address? And telephone number? Company name? Your title? And your birth date? Thank you. Hopefully we'll get an opportunity to meet in the future. Good-bye."

Calling Nonreferred Leads

The Pre-Approach for leads to whom we have not been referred also consists of a preliminary communication followed by a phone call. The phone pattern is almost identical to that used with referred leads except for the elimination of any mention of a nominator. In this way we keep our memorization task simple.

"Mr. Edwards, this is Sam Baker and I'm with The Diamond Financial Group here in Boston. I sent you a letter the other day in which I mentioned our planning services. I'm phoning now to ask if I might schedule an appointment to see you later this week. Would 3:00 p.m. on Wednesday be convenient?"

Responding to the First Objection

"I see. (Pause.) I had no reason to believe you were in the market for any specific financial products just at this time. However, in these days of a constantly changing tax and economic environment, our planning services have been of interest to many. Will you be in town next week?"

If the Suspect says he will, continue by naming a specific time.

"Could I see you next week at 10:30 a.m. on Monday?"

Responding to the Second Objection

"Yes. (Pause.) I Understand. Nevertheless, the reasons for my wanting to stop in are first, to have a chance to meet you and, second, to review our services and get your thinking on the subject. On that basis, would you object to seeing me next Tuesday at 2:00 p.m.?"

Responding to the Third Objection

If the Suspect continues to object after the third try, switch to an attempt to obtain permission to stay in touch:

"I see. (Pause.) However, circumstances do have a way of changing. Would you have any objection to my staying in touch with you and checking again at a later date?"

Qualify and Place in Your OCS

If the Suspect has no objection, go on slowly, calmly, and smoothly:

"Fine. Let me get just a bit of preliminary information. Your last name is spelled E-D-W-A-R-D-S? Your first name and initial? Your business address? Telephone number there? Company name? Your title? And you birth date? Thank you. Hopefully we'll get an opportunity to meet in the future. Good-bye."

Keep Your Responses Simple and Consistent

The responses to objections tend to be about the same no matter what the objection. The language is intentionally designed to be simple and consistent. It is difficult to sound relaxed and confident if you must constantly be on guard to respond in a dozen different ways to the myriad of possible objections. No matter what the objection, you should respond in basically the same manner.

Pre-Approach to Friends, Relatives, and Acquaintances

Friends, relatives, and acquaintances can be excellent potential Clients, yet some Financial Services Professionals are unsure of how to offer their services in a nonthreatening manner. Consider this time-tested and proven pre-approach. It is designed to be used in an early face-to-face encounter on a casual basis at a nonbusiness time or during an informal phone conversation. After a brief greeting:

"Bill, we've known each other for awhile now and as you know, I work with The Diamond Financial Group, and to be honest, I couldn't help wondering what you've done regarding your own planning. Would you have any objection to discussing your life insurance (or other) program sometime?"

This is the famous "Two Part Magic Question"

If the person says "Yes, I'd like that," then proceed to trying to arrange a time. Often, however, not being prepared for the question, the person will offer some socially appropriate evasive answer. Regardless of the objection, your response is always the same:

"I understand, and obviously this is neither the time nor place to discuss your personal affairs. The thing I would like to do, however, if you don't object too violently (said with humor) is to stop by for a few minutes, share a little about the way I work, and to get your thinking on the subject. Fair enough?"

You will recognize that this is the same Two-Part Question we presented in Chapter 10 while discussing Personal Observation Prospecting.

Phone Language for Automatic Contacts

Automatics Revisited

Twice yearly automatic contacts strengthen relationships, capture cross-sales, and lead to increased referrals.

Throughout this book there are references to Birthday Automatics and Review Automatics. The significance of this terminology was clarified earlier in Chapter 3. These automatics are an integral part of the system that enables you to stay in regular touch with all of your Active Prospects and Clients in the Alphabetical section of your OCS Card File.

You are expected to stay in touch with all of them through two personal contacts each year. One of the contacts is initiated shortly before the individual's birthday and an attempt is made to set up a birthday lunch. This contact is known as the Birthday Automatic. The other personal contact is initiated six months following the individual's birthday and is known as the Review Automatic.

Birthday Automatic Phone Language

Many people think this is a selling occupation. This is only partly true. At least equal weight must be given to the prospecting and promotional aspects of the career. For that reason, in addition to the prospecting that is integrated into selling calls as previously discussed, the Birthday Automatic is also designated primarily as a prospecting and promotional get-together.

The phone script is very straightforward. Consider the following:

"Bill, this is Sam Baker of The Diamond Financial Group calling. I know that you have a birthday coming up on the 10th, so I'm calling you for two reasons. First, I want to wish you a great day. (Pause for a response.) Second, I have some things to go over with you and would like to share lunch with you on or about your birthday. The 10th might be a busy day for you. Would the 10th at 11:30 a.m. suit you or would you prefer the day before?"

The Case History Notes indicate the date of the last meeting as well as all other pertinent information. The file folders with the Confidential Questionnaire and Case History Notes should always be open in front of you when calling a Prospect or Client.

Responding to Objections

If there is an objection as to the time or date, try another. If the Prospect objects because he or she is not in the market, stress that this is a Happy Birthday lunch and you have no intention of recommending a purchase unless the situation calls for it. You are interested, however, in getting his or her thoughts on a couple of matters.

Review Automatic Phone Language

Language for Active Clients

Review Automatic contacts occur six months after a Prospect's or Client's birthday. The purpose of the contact for Active Clients is to offer to conduct a review of their financial and insurance program. Additionally, new things are happening all the time in the industry and within most companies. Be prepared to mention some specifics should your Client hesitate about getting together.

The importance of Review of Age-Change contacts: OCS research reveals that 20 percent of a client base, when well served, will buy again in any given year.

Consider the following language for scheduling the appointment:

"Bill, this is Sam Baker with the Diamond Financial Group calling. My records indicate that it is time for us to get together to update your situation. With that in mind, I'd like to schedule an appointment to discuss this with you further. Would Thursday at 2:00 p.m. be okay or would Friday at 3:00 p.m. be better?"

Response to Objections

If your Client is hesitant about meeting, you might consider something like the following:

"I see. (Pause.) Actually, I had no reason to believe you were in the market for any additions to your program just at this time. However, in today's ever changing financial environment many of my better Clients have found that keeping on top of changes is very beneficial, and I think that some of the current ones will interest you. Would Wednesday morning be better?" (Nail things down.)

Contacting Active Prospects for Reviews

The phone language for scheduling a Review appointment with an Active Prospect is basically the same as for an Active Client. Keep in mind that Active Prospects are contacted at this time for the purpose of scheduling an appointment to review the discussion that took place during their Fact Finding Interview. Your objective in this appointment is to determine if the recommendations that have been made are still appropriate and to encourage these Prospects to act!

What about Suspects?

You may have some Suspects in the 1-31 and Monthly sections of the system with whom you talked earlier and who gave you their birthday and permission to stay in touch. Although not an Automatic, if they are financially promising Suspects, you might want to capitalize on your knowledge of their upcoming birthday. Consider simple language such as the following:

"Bill, this is Sam Baker of the Diamond Financial Group calling. You may remember that we spoke several months ago at the suggestion of John Barker. On that occasion the timing wasn't right for us to meet but you did tell me that your birthday was_____.

"So the reason for my call today is twofold: First, I want to wish you a great day. (Pause.) Second, I would like to meet with you for a sandwich or a cup of coffee on or about your birthday. Would the 10th at 11:30 a.m. suit you or might the day before be better?"

Invite Them to Come to Your Office

Be alert to the possibility of inviting Suspects and Prospects into your own office. Get the agreement for the appointment first and then consider the possibility of inviting the Prospect in. Many people enjoy getting out of their offices if the distances involved are not too great. It's surprising what can happen when you ask. A sandwich, salad, and piece of cake in an office are often more appealing than a rushed lunch in a crowded restaurant. And certainly, the setting is much more conducive to a thoughtful discussion.

Have the Script in Front of You

Whatever the phone technique being used, you are strongly urged to compress it to fit one printed sheet and to keep the sheet in front of you as you do your calling. Even with experienced Financial Services Professionals, efficiency tends to fall off dramatically as one strays from proven patterns. For convenience, a condensed sheet of the scripts is provided at the end of this section.

The Three Step Approach

The Objective

The objective of the Approach is to set the stage for a smooth assumed consent transition into the Fact Finding Interview. Additionally, you are there with some additional objectives in mind:

- Demonstrate your competence;

- Gain the Prospect's confidence;

- Establish a professional, down to business style;

- Establish the fact that you work primarily on a personal introduction basis.

Begin Immediately and Be Brief

Create a professional style and a sense of urgency by getting right down to business. The entire approach can easily be done within a few minutes. Having broken the ice with your pre-approach procedure, here is the suggested Three Step Approach language.

"How do you do, Mr. Edwards? My name is Sam Baker. First, I want to thank you for taking the time to meet with me. I know we both have busy schedules. I also want to thank John Barker for introducing us, because I work primarily on a personal introduction basis. I've been looking forward to meeting you because John spoke very highly of you."

People will remember what you initially say or do in an interview.

The Psychological Law of Primacy says that people will remember what you say and do first. It is, therefore, important to begin the approach quickly and in a business-like manner. You also want to teach the Suspect how to do business with you by introducing the idea that you work primarily on a personal introduction basis. You are not asking for referrals; you are not saying that you will be asking. You are merely informing the Prospect as to how you conduct business.

Describe the First Step

"Mr. Edwards, our services consist of three steps. First, I meet with people who are interested in making intelligent, long-range plans for their financial future. As we discuss their plans and objectives, we use this Confidential Questionnaire that reminds us of the things we need to talk about and keeps us on track."

Show the Confidential Questionnaire

As the Confidential Questionnaire is mentioned, open it and place it right-side-up in front of the Prospect. If the Prospect says it looks complicated say, "Yes, we do a thorough job." If the Prospect picks it up or looks at it, stop until eye contact is re-established. When this is done, proceed as follows.

Describe the Second Step

"The second step is for me to take this information back to my office (as the word "take" is uttered, casually reach out and take the Confidential Questionnaire away from the Prospect) where it is reviewed and analyzed and, if appropriate, a written report is prepared. No two of these are exactly alike, but here is one that we prepared, with the names changed of course, to give people like you an idea of what we do."

Show a Sample Report

At this point, place a sample of one of your presentations in front of the individual. Present the report page by page for the Prospect's inspection. This may be done silently, or appropriately brief comments may be made as each page is presented. Conclude by saying:

Describe the Third Step

"The third step, for our Clients, is to periodically review and update the program. As personal and business situations change, and as the marketplace changes, your program may also need to be updated."

Move to the Confidential Questionnaire

"Now, in order for me to determine whether such a report would be appropriate for you, with your permission, (no pause) I'd like to begin by asking you a few questions. You spell your name E-D-W-A-R-D-S? And your first name is Robert? And your middle initial? Do your friends call you Bob? May I?"

Turning the Confidential Questionnaire form so it is right-side-up in front of the Prospect, ask:

"Is this exactly the way you like to have your name used?"

Proceed with Assumed Consent

Note that the interview is started on the assumption that the Prospect would like to have this work done. Remember where you are in the Sales Cycle. You began with a referred lead from a nominator. You then sent a letter briefly outlining your services with a note of introduction from the nominator. Next you called to ask for an appointment. By scheduling the appointment, you may assume that the Prospect had some question or concern in the back of his mind about his financial or insurance program. If the Prospect's mind had been completely closed, he or she never would have let you in.

The Advantage of Strong Pre-Approach and Phone Language

This is the major advantage of separating the Pre-Approach from the Approach. If the Pre-Approach has been successfully negotiated, 80 percent of all Approaches should result in a completed Confidential Questionnaire. However, if the Prospect objects because there isn't time at the moment, schedule a definite date for the future. All other objections are handled as follows.

Eighty percent of all Approach appointments should result in a completed Confidential Questionnaire.

Handling Objections in the Approach

If the Prospect objects by saying he is not interested or by using some other vague response, you must get to the real underlying issue. To do that, simply say in a nondefensive tone:

"That's interesting. Why is that?"

The answer will almost always fall into the pattern of typical objections such as:

- "I'm not in the market..."

- "I've had this done..."

- "This involves too much work for you, particularly when I have no intention of buying..."

- "I wouldn't want to be under any obligation..." etc.

Use a Well Rehearsed Standard Response

As with the Pre-Approach, you should master the following response to these objections and use it consistently. Your response should be so well rehearsed that it sounds completely natural. When you do not have to think about what you are going to say, you can turn all of your attention to your Prospect.

Pause first, to give the appearance of giving thought to the comment, then reply by saying:

"I understand how you feel, Bob, and I certainly appreciate your honesty and your point of view. But, with your permission, I'd like to take a minute to tell you a bit more about our services.

"I know from my records that for every three of these studies I do – and by and large they are done for persons who initially feel much as you do – I find that when the record is written that, over the next year or two, one of the three becomes a Client. So I'm well taken care of.

"But from your point of view, the important thing is that in almost all cases we are able to come up with some constructive suggestions or recommendations. You know, no one has a corner on all of the good ideas and in today's financial environment it pays to be on top of significant changes.

"With that in mind, could I begin by asking you a few questions? (No pause.) Your position here at the company is?" (Again, confidently assume permission for completing the Confidential Questionnaire.)

Staying in Touch

If this doesn't work, and if the reiterated objection cannot be handled graciously, agree and go on to say:

"That's perfectly all right. However, no one knows for sure what the future will bring. Circumstances do have a way of changing. Therefore, with your permission, I would like to stay in touch and check with you again at a later date. Would that be all right?"

Qualify and Place in Your OCS

More often than not, the individual will agree that it would be all right to stay in touch though he may again stress the statement that he has no intention of doing any business with you. Just ignore that part of it and go on by saying:

"Fine. Let me get just a bit of preliminary information. I have your last name spelled as E-D-W-A-R-D-S. Is that correct? And your first name is Robert. What is your middle initial? And your date of birth?"

Be Prepared to Prospect

The Desired Outcomes

Every Approach you make should result in one or more of the following:

1. Completion of a new Confidential Questionnaire.

2. A definite date for the completion of a Confidential Questionnaire.

3. A list of nominated Qualified Suspects.

If They Don't Agree to the Fact Finder Interview, Begin the Six Step Prospecting Process

At the completion of a properly conducted Approach, even if the Suspect refuses the Fact Finder Interview, they have seen enough of your services to be able to respond to the first question of the Six Step Prospecting process outlined in Chapter 10. As you are putting away your sample report, Confidential Questionnaire, and your other tools in preparation for leaving the individual's office, pause for a moment and, almost as an afterthought, say:

"Tell me, Bob, now that you have had an opportunity to see something of the work that we do, tell me, what do you think of our general approach?"

The individual will almost always respond with a positive statement about your services but will indicate that the timing just isn't right for him right now. This gives you the affirmative you need to go on with the appropriate steps of the Six Step Prospecting and Three Step Promotion language we discussed earlier.

The Value of the Double-Step Ahead Question

Can you see how valuable the Double-Step Ahead question (step # 6) is in this instance? Having names or categories to feed to the individual (from the nominator who introduced you in the first place) is extremely helpful in turning an Approach interview, which only resulted in permission to stay in touch, into a productive point earning interview.

Be Prepared and Build Your Clientele

If you are well-prepared and know exactly what you are going to say next, you have the advantage and can have a lot of fun while earning points and taking giant steps in the direction of building your own clientele.

Condensed Three Step Approach Language

For convenience, a condensed single page of the language used on your calls is provided here.

Describe the First Step

"Mr. Edwards, our services consist of three steps. First, I meet with people who are interested in making intelligent, long-range plans for their financial future. As we discuss their plans and objectives we use this Confidential Questionnaire that reminds us of the things we need to talk about and keeps us on track."

Place the Confidential Questionnaire in front of the Prospect. Continue only when eye contact is re-established.

Describe the Second Step

"The second step is for me to take (as the word "take" is uttered, casually reach out and take the Confidential Questionnaire away from the Prospect) this information back to my office where it is reviewed and analyzed and, if appropriate, a written report is prepared. No two of these are exactly alike, but here is one that we prepared, with the names changed of course, to give people like you an idea of what we do."

Show the sample report. This may be done silently, or appropriately brief comments can be made as each page is presented.

Describe the Third Step

"The third step, for our Clients, is to periodically review and update the program. As personal and business situations change, and as the marketplace changes, your program may also need to be updated."

Move to the Confidential Questionnaire

"Now, in order for me to determine whether such a report would be appropriate for you, with your permission, (no pause) I'd like to begin by asking you a few questions. You spell your name E-D-W-A-R-D-S? And your first name is Robert? And your middle initial? Do your friends call you Bob? May I?"

Phone Techniques for Assistants

With a little practice, a good assistant will relieve you of almost all of the necessary phone calls. The assistant's results should be as good as or even better than yours. The assistant has a couple of advantages:

1. Rejections (since they are of someone else) are not as tough to take as they are when you are making the call and being rejected.

2. The assistant can say things to build you up that you might not be able to say yourself.

Birthday Automatic Telephone
Language for Assistants

If an Appointment Is Not Desired

If the Prospect or Client has been seen recently, or if the individual has not been helpful in the past as a nominator, the telephone conversation could be something like this:

"Mr. Edwards? This is Debbie Green, Sam Baker's assistant calling. Mr. Baker knows you have a birthday coming up on the 10th and requested that I to call and wish you a happy birthday and ask if there is anything we can do just now that would be helpful, or if there are any questions that have come up since you last got together on June 15th?"

The Case History indicates the date of the last meeting as well as all other pertinent information. File folders with Confidential Questionnaires and Case History Notes should always be open in front of the individual calling the Prospect or Client!

If an Appointment Is Desired

If, on the other hand, you wish to see the individual for suspecting or other business purposes, the assistant would say something like this:

"Mr. Edwards? This is Debbie Green, Sam Baker's assistant calling. We know that you have a birthday coming up on the 10th so Mr. Baker asked me to call you for two reasons. First, we wish you a happy birthday." (Pause for a response.) "Second, Mr. Baker has some things to go over with you and would like to invite you to share lunch on or about your birthday. Would the 10th at 11:30 a.m. suit you or might the day before be better?"

Additional Considerations

If an objection has to do with the date selected, negotiate for another time. Always try to schedule luncheons at 11:30 a.m. and 1:00 p.m. so the rush hour is avoided and to make it possible to have two lunch meetings some days. Notice that the invitation is worded so that paying the tab is optional.

Review Automatic Telephone Language for Assistants

With a Complete Confidential Questionnaire

Since a complete Confidential Questionnaire interview has almost always been held on some prior occasion, use the following wording:

"Mr. Edwards, this is Debbie Green, Sam Baker's assistant calling. Mr. Baker has noted that it is time to meet and review your situation and he would like to arrange an appointment with you. Would 2:00 p.m. next Wednesday be convenient?"

Without a Complete Confidential Questionnaire

If a complete Confidential Questionnaire interview has not taken place previously, say:

"Mr. Edwards, this is Debbie Green, Sam Baker's assistant calling. Our records show that it has been about six months since you and Mr. Baker last spoke and Mr. Baker would like to arrange an appointment with you to gain a better understanding of your current situation, update our files, and get better acquainted. Would 2:00 p.m. next Wednesday be convenient?"

Any objections, other than an honest one having to do with the specific time suggested, can be handled with the sequence of answers suggested for use when calling new leads.

New Lead Telephone Language for Assistants

You may prefer to call your new Qualified Suspects yourself to determine the level of interest and to dead file those who show none whatsoever. Usually, however, you will be equally successful having your assistant call new leads. The key to success is mastering the phone language so the assistant can be both comfortable and effective. Consider beginning with the following:

"Mr. Edwards, this is Debbie Green, Sam Baker's assistant calling."

If You Have the Nominator's Name Available

Continue with the following:

"He wrote you a letter the other day in which he mentioned John Barker's name. The reason for this call is to ask if you could see him next Wednesday at 2:00 p.m. Will this be convenient for you?"

Without a Nominator's Name

Use the following:

"He wrote you a letter the other day in which he mentioned our _____ service. The reason for this call is to ask if you could see him next Wednesday at 2:00 p.m. Will this be convenient for you?"

Responding to the First Objection

With a nominator's name use the following:

(Pause.) "Mr. Baker has no reason to assume you were in the market for any particular financial product, nor did John Barker so indicate. However, John did feel that you might be interested in the service that we provide. Will you be in town Wednesday?"

Without a Nominator's Name

"I see. (Pause.) As I said, Mr. Baker has no reason to assume that you are in the market for any particular financial product just at this time. However, our unique planning service, particularly with our present tax and economic environment, has been of interest to many individuals in positions similar to your own. Will you be in town Wednesday?" (If he says he will, continue by naming a specific time.) "Could Mr. Baker see you at 10:30 a.m.?"

Responding to the Second Objection

"Well, the reasons for Mr. Baker's wanting to visit with you were, first, to have a chance to meet you and, second, to review our services and get your thinking on the subject. On that basis, would you object to meeting Mr. Baker sometime?" (If he has no objection, continue by naming a specific time.) "Could you see him at 10:30 Thursday morning?"

Response to the Third Objection

If he continues to object, even after the *third try*, switch to an attempt to stay in touch by saying:

"I see. (Pause.) However, circumstances do have a way of changing. Would you have any objection to Mr. Baker staying in touch with you and checking again at a future time?"

Qualify and Place in OCS

"Fine, let me get just a bit of preliminary information. Your last name is spelled E-D-W-A-R-D-S? Your first name and initial? Your business address? And phone number there? Your company name? And your title? And your birth date? Thank you very much. Good bye."

Confirm the Date and Time

Once an appointment has been agreed upon, be sure to repeat the specific time and place, and then ask that he or she have an assistant call you should a conflict arise. The language to be used is as follows:

"Fine, Mr. Edwards. I have the time down on Mr. Baker's calendar as 10:30 a.m. Thursday the 14th. Would you like to just jot his name down on your calendar? It is spelled B-A-K-E-R and the time, again, is 10:30 a.m. Thursday. If you find that you will be out of town, or for some other reason can't keep the appointment, would you be good enough to have your assistant call me. My phone number is 782-0633 and my name is spelled G-R-E-E-N."

Set a Tentative Future Appointment

For the person who is agreeable, but who asks you to call back to make a definite appointment, follow up with this:

"That would be fine. However, Mr. Baker does try to schedule his appointments as far in advance as possible. Therefore, may I schedule a tentative date for, say, two weeks from today at 4:00 p.m.? Would that be alright? Then, if you find that you will be out of town or if for some other reason you can't keep the appointment, please have your assistant call me. My phone number is 782-0633 and my name is spelled G-R-E-E-N."

Condense to One Page

Whatever the telephone technique being used, you are strongly urged to compress it to fit one sheet and to keep the sheet in front of you as you do your calling.

Chapter 12

Fact Finding Interviews

The Two Fundamental Skills

There are two fundamental skills that drive the entire client building process: Referred Lead Prospecting and Complete Fact Finding. Your Prospects will buy from you if they feel a bond or connection with you and trust you. As we have already discussed, the first step in building trust in a relationship is to be referred or introduced by a nominator your Prospect knows, respects and trusts. The next step is a properly conducted Fact Finding Interview.

Bonding Between People

People feel a bond or connection with each other when they have shared important life experiences. When Prospects share the facts of their lives, and their feelings about those facts, they feel that something special has occurred between the two of you. They know that they very seldom share their inner thoughts and feelings with people. When they share them with you, something special takes place.

Consequently, during the Fact Finding Interview, the bonding process will occur between you and the Prospect. At the conclusion of the Fact Finding Interview you will hopefully know more about the Prospect's hopes, dreams, aspirations, concerns and financial situation than any other adviser and, perhaps, even any of their friends. If the interview is handled properly, you will have begun what should become a long and rewarding relationship.

Getting to the "Inner Person"

Get beneath the socially acceptable facade with careful questioning and listening.

It has been said that the real purpose of a quality Fact Finding Interview is to get to the "Inner Person" within the Prospect. That is, to get beneath the socially acceptable façade and find out what is really important or troubling to the Prospect. Without the careful questioning and listening that this entails, you will not get to the inner person; you will not create the bond and you will not establish the vital trust. Without these you will not have a true Client – that is, one who will buy from you repeatedly and freely name you as their trusted financial professional.

Four Objectives of a Good Fact Finding Interview

1. Get the facts;

2. Do some advance suspecting;

3. Reach the inner person

4. Build your prestige.

The Fact Finding Puzzle

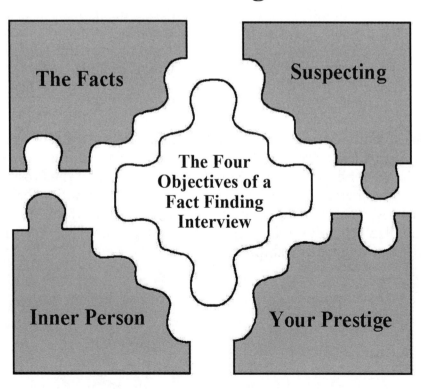

Get the Facts

Obviously, the first priority is to ask every question and obtain all of the factual information. Do not skip anything even if you believe you know the answer. (People will have greater conviction in what they hear themselves say.) When you ask a question, give your Prospect adequate time to reply. Never cut the Prospect short! Show sincere interest and never be judgmental! When the answers on the Confidential Questionnaire are their answers rather than your answers, your Prospects will feel more inwardly motivated to take action on your recommendations.

People have a greater conviction in what they hear themselves say.

Do Some Advance Suspecting

"Advance Suspecting" is the process of identifying people who could become Qualified Suspects. Each time you complete a new Confidential Questionnaire, do some advance suspecting. During the Fact Finding Interview, you will uncover most of the names and categories that you will "feed" the Prospect during your Six Step Prospecting attempt. For example, as you ask about the organizational structure of the firm, jot down any names that are mentioned. Do the same for guardians, attorneys, and relatives as you discuss a will and the disposition of property. There are literally dozens of advance suspecting opportunities throughout the Fact Finding Interview. You must train yourself to constantly look for them.

Reach the Inner Person

In some ways, the term "Fact Finding Interview" is a misnomer. This is because it is just as important to get to the feelings of an individual as it is to acquire facts. Planning for financial security requires character. The Prospect must care about someone or something in order to act. Some people care for their families, some care about themselves, some care about their business success, and some care about the liquidity for the perpetuation of their business or previously accumulated property. Your job is to find out what and whom they care about. Unless they care, they're not likely to act. People are reluctant to share their inner thoughts and cares. Getting people to open up is the ultimate goal of quality Fact Finding.

Your job is to find out what and whom your Prospect cares about.

Build Your Prestige

The final objective of the Fact Finding Interview is to build your own professional prestige by the manner in which you conduct yourself. This includes punctuality, the neatness of your notes, your professional style and your personal appearance. Your Prospects will be impressed by the thoroughness with which you treat every question, and by brief, appropriate references to ownership provisions, wills, trusts and other potential tax-saving devices.

The Psychology of the Fact Finding Interview

The Psychology of Attraction

When conducting a Fact Finding Interview you are not only trying to gather important information, but also trying to create a psychological environment in which the Prospect develops a deeper level of trust, respect, and attraction. Psychologists have long understood that there are four clear principles or guidelines that will help you achieve this.

1. Listen intently to the Prospect

2. Listen for feelings and information that isn't readily shared

3. Remain non-judgmental

4. Stay focused on him or her

Let's look at these principles more carefully.

Listen Intently and Carefully to the Prospect

While it may seem obvious, the importance of maintaining eye contact, and looking at your Prospects attentively and with interest, cannot be overly stressed. Take notes and use nods and verbal acknowledgements as they speak. Reduce all outside distractions such as phone calls.

Listen for the Personal and Feeling Side of What People Say

Prompt, but don't urge, them to share what is important to them. What is important is often private and personal. When people are anxious because they are in debt, or concerned about their childrens' future, or feel stressed because they can't quite seem to get control of their financial world; they tend to try to keep their thoughts and feelings private.

Remain Non-judgmental

Do not make value judgements.

If trust is to be built along with attraction you must listen in a completely non-judgmental manner. Don't make or show any value judgments as you listen. If they are discussing a shortcoming such as the failure to save, or the disappointment of a divorce, listen without any sign of judgment. People feel judged enough today. It is a pleasant surprise and relief for them to be listened to and accepted, rather than judged.

Maintain Focus

There is always a temptation to talk about your accomplishments or your opinions as various topics come up. Stay focused on the Prospect. The interview is about them, not you. You are trying to attract and create trust, not impress. Listen in a quiet and calm manner unless the material is something to be enthusiastic about. If they are describing a personal achievement, then you can show your genuine interest and enthusiasm. Don't engage in "mind reading" and avoid assuming, "I know what you are thinking." Stay tuned to them. Don't be formulating your response as they speak. Don't interrupt unless absolutely necessary.

Avoid the temptation to talk about yourself. The interview is about them, not you.

The bond between people increases when one listens to the other carefully, sincerely and without judgment. You will know you are doing this successfully when your Prospects say things like:

- "He was so easy to talk to."

- "She really listened."

- "He seemed to really care."

- "I think I told him more than I've told anyone in years!"

- "I think she understands us."

The Psychological Principle of Consistency Revisited

Another aspect of the bonding that can occur in a good Fact Finding Interview involves the psychological Principle of Consistency. People seem to have a strong internal desire to keep their thoughts, feelings and behavior consistent with one another as a way of dealing with the ever increasing complexities of life. In an attempt to keep their internal psychological world consistent, people will accept information that supports their views and systematically reject information that does not. How might this desire for internal consistency affect the bonding process in a good Fact Finding Interview?

Most people begin with the assumption about themselves that they are a good judge of other people; a good judge of character. Given this assumption, after a Prospect shares a great deal of personal and private information with you, they face a potential internal conflict. If they view themselves as intelligent and discerning in their dealings with people, and they have just "shared more with you than anyone in the past 20 years," the only consistent conclusion they can reach about you is that you are special. You aren't the run of the mill salesperson.

When people find themselves sharing personal information with you, they come to the internal conclusion that you are special.

They will begin to look for reasons why you are indeed special and, in fact, most likely the person they want to deal with regarding their financial affairs.

Maintaining Trust and Attraction

Once the Fact Finding Interview has been completed and Prospects have begun to place their trust in you, the nature of the relationship changes. The new Clients who have extended their trust now have high expectations of you. In order for them to remain consistent in their feelings toward you, they will want and expect you to do a good job. This trust is not to be taken lightly. You now have the responsibility of honoring their trust by following through on your commitments and doing the best job you can.

Here, again, we see the value of the OCS in helping you to maintain your promised regular contact. If you fail to honor your commitments, the Principle of Consistency can work against you. That is, if Clients feel disappointed or even betrayed, they can become bitter and cynical towards you rather than supportive. A quality Fact Finding Interview creates both exceptional opportunity as well as professional responsibility.

The Art of Questioning and Listening

The Art of Reaching the Inner Person

The Confidential Questionnaire is filled with open-ended questions that will help elicit both facts and feelings.

The art of reaching the inner person involves asking your Prospects questions in such a manner that you will elicit not only facts but feelings as well. In addition to obtaining the factual information, ask open-ended questions, such as:

"What is your opinion of _____?"

"How important is _____ to you?"

"What would you like to see in terms of _____?"

"How do you feel about _____?"

Questions such as these allow you to reach into your Prospect's world to find the emotion that will power the sale.

Emotion Sells It, Logic Pays for It

This simply means that it is emotion that moves the person to the action of buying. However, without a true need being met (the logic of the sale) the emotion will fade and people will ask themselves why they bought. If there isn't a logical reason, then they may lapse the purchase.

Listening Is King

The only way you will reach the inner person is through careful and caring listening. Unfortunately, many in the financial services profession think that "selling" involves marshaling arguments and trying to "convince" the Prospect. The real art of selling involves questioning and listening. When you listen for what is important to your Prospects (emotionally), selling then becomes nothing more than providing solutions that help them to achieve their goals and then motivating them to act.

The art of selling involves skillful questioning and careful nonjudgemental listening.

Again, all questions are asked in a quiet, direct way with absolutely no hint of judgment on your part. If you show judgment, your Prospects will stop telling you their feelings and will start telling you what they think you want to hear or what they feel is socially appropriate to reveal. It is non-judgmental, intimate listening, combined with a genuine sense of caring, that creates the bond that leads to a lifelong Client.

The Law of Reciprocity

The Law of Reciprocity states, "We give first to receive later." When you carefully listen first, your Prospects are more apt to truly listen when you want to guide and explain (close). When you haven't listened, your Prospects feel no internal obligation to reciprocate by listening to you.

A Learned Skill

The art of questioning and listening is a learned skill. Your mission is to become so well versed at this skill that it seems absolutely natural and conversational to your Prospects. Remember that the Fact Finding Interview should be perceived by your Prospects as a dialogue, not an interrogation.

The interview should be perceived as a dialogue, not an interrogation.

Fact Questions

Fact questions, as the name implies, are designed to secure factual information, such as name, address, employer, position and so on. Fact questions are a good way to begin the conversation because they are the types of questions your Prospects expect and will put them into the habit of responding to your questions.

Feeling Questions

These questions usually follow the factual questions and delve into more subjective, personal information. They sound out your Prospect's emotions, opinions, personal plans, pride, doubts and worries. In short, feeling questions help you reach the inner person.

Open Ended Questions

Feeling questions are usually open ended. Open ended questions invite the Prospect to say more about the topic. A closed ended question asks for a "Yes" or "No" answer. Open ended questions often include words such as "think," "feel" or "like." For example, "How do you feel about that?" or "Tell me more about that." Try to ask how rather than what or why.

The Skills of Tagging and Structuring the Future Agenda

When experienced financial professionals conduct Fact Finding Interviews, they are constantly and silently looking for patterns of facts that suggest a particular financial problem or opportunity for their Prospects. These situations, in turn, suggest possible solutions.

It's almost as if you are fitting an internal series of problem templates to the facts shared by the Prospect. In your mind these templates take the form of internal questions. Is this a need for a forced savings product? Is this an education funding need? Is this an executive bonus or deferred compensation opportunity? Etc. Etc. As the problem templates seem to fit the facts, you want to mark or tag these as possible issues in the Prospect's mind. You will want to return to these issues to explore them in more detail.

"Structuring" is simply the process of identifying these for the Prospect as an area of future interest. It involves phrases like, "It sounds like college funding for your children is important for you. This is something we'll want to talk about further." Structuring serves two purposes. First it signals that you are listening to the Prospect and are identifying possible needs. Second, it signals the Prospect that these important topics will be discussed and addressed. This makes the transition to concluding the interview with a Discovery or Summary Agreement much easier and smoother. Tagging and structuring are important skills and contribute substance, structure and momentum to the ongoing sales cycle process.

Mastery Saves You Valuable Time

The art of questioning and listening also requires the mastery of the questions on the Confidential Questionnaire or fact finding form. This will allow you to complete most Fact Finding Interviews in less than one hour. However, if you "wing it," time can easily slip away from you. Staying on time in an organized manner also helps you to build your credibility as a professional.

Starting the Interview

Fact Finding During the Initial Interview

The language of the Three Step Approach is designed to allow you to transition to the fact finding discussion during the initial interview. If your Prospect has the time and the inclination to proceed with the fact finding discussion, then by all means do so. Go as far into the fact finding discussion as is practically possible. This will not only be an efficient use of your time, it will also begin the process of moving the Prospect in the direction of his financial goals.

If your Prospect is married, do not be overly concerned if the spouse is not involved in the initial discussion. In the next chapter, you will learn how to professionally bring the spouse or partner into the fact finding discussion at the earliest practical time. During the initial interview, simply focus on building the momentum of the Sales Cycle.

How Do You Begin?

It is best to begin the actual fact finding process by assuming implied consent. After completing the Three Step Approach language during the initial interview, simply assume consent to begin the fact finding discussion. Look down at your Confidential Questionnaire or other fact finding form with your pen poised for writing and say:

"Now, in order for me to determine whether such a report would be appropriate for you, I'd like to begin by asking a few questions. First of all, do you spell your last name E-D-W-A-R-D-S? And your first name is Robert? And your middle initial? Do your friends call you Bob? May I? Is this exactly the way you like to have your name used?"

The following sequence of questions will follow the Confidential Questionnaire (which can be ordered from The National Underwriter Company). The Confidential Questionnaire is designed to collect the information necessary to complete a basic financial needs analysis report using software available through the Financial Profiles Company, 5421 Avenida Encinas, Carlsbad, CA 92008. However, the questioning techniques found in this chapter are transferable to almost any financial information gathering form.

Personal Data

After recording the full name, turn the Confidential Questionnaire around so the Prospect can see what you have written and ask if the name has been recorded exactly as it should be used. A person's name is very important to him or her. You build your own prestige by showing that you have respect for it.

Personal Data

Client Name: _____ Birth Date: _____

Spouse/Partner Name: _____ Birth Date: _____

Address: _____ Phone: (___)_____

City: _____ State: _____ Zip: _____ Fax: (___)_____

Client SS#: _____ Spouse / Partner SS#: _____

Name to Appear on Reports: _____ E-Mail: _____

The remaining questions in this first section are self-explanatory. Be sure to obtain the complete street address, phone and fax numbers, and e-mail address. When asking for Social Security numbers, you may wish to preface the question with, "Have you verified your Social Security benefits within the past three years?" This is a value added service you may provide your new Clients.

Occupation Section

The occupation section allows you to obtain both factual and feeling information. Begin by obtaining the exact occupational title and the full name, address and phone numbers of the company or firm.

Occupation

Client's Job Title: _____ Employer: _____

Address: _____ Phone: (_____) _____

City _____ State _____ Zip: _____ Fax: (_____) _____

Spouse/Ptnr Job Title: _____ Employer: _____

Address: _____ Phone: (_____) _____

City: _____ State _____ Zip:_____ Fax: (_____) _____

The lower portion of this section provides question prompts that will help you draw out a wealth of information about your Prospect's inner person. Memorize the questions and ask them in the same order every time.

"Have you been with the firm long? Could you give me some idea of how you fit into the organizational structure of your company? What would be your guess as to your chances for advancement and the possibility of your staying with this company permanently? Have you ever thought of going into business for yourself? Would you tell me something about your academic background, Bob, and what you did prior to joining the firm? What do you like to do when you're not working?"

Organizational Structure: _____

Future Career Plans: _____

_____

Academic / Employment Background: _____

_____

Other Interests / Activities: _____

_____

Dependents

The discussion of dependents, particularly children, provides an excellent opportunity to reach the inner person. People are normally proud to talk about their children, so allow ample time for them to do so in this section. In addition to obtaining the factual information, consider the following questions:

"Bob, do you have any children? Could you tell me a little about your son? What is his full name? Does John Cole have a nickname? What is his date of birth? Does John have any special talents we should be planning for, or any other special needs? Are there any plans for additional children? Do you have any other dependents or do you foresee any in the future?

Be sure to give the Prospect sufficient time to answer these questions. Make eye contact as you are listening, and listen with genuine interest. Do not appear impatient to move on. This is very important area of concern.

Dependents

Full Name	Nick Name	Birth Date

Special Considerations: _____

Add'l Children / Dependents: _____

This line of questioning will allow you to identify whether or not additional planning may be needed to accommodate the needs of either gifted or disabled children, children from prior marriages, or partial dependents. These are intimate areas of your Prospect's life – treat them with care and respect.

Education Goals

The line of questioning used for the Dependents section will provide a smooth transition to a discussion of Education Goals. The questions are self-explanatory and should be asked in the order they appear on the form.

You will find the opinions of your Prospects will vary widely on this topic. Some may feel that it is important to send their children to Ivy League colleges, while others may believe that requiring their children to fund some or all of their own education will help to build character. It is important that you listen intently and remain non-judgmental.

Education Goals

What are your thoughts about providing an education or opportunity fund for your children? _____
Have you started such a fund? _____ Could you tell me more about it?

Child's Name	$ Needed / Yr (Today's $)	# of Yrs Needed	Current Savings	Where Saved?	Rate of Monthly Return Savings
_____	_____	_____	_____	_____	_____
_____	_____	_____	_____	_____	_____
_____	_____	_____	_____	_____	_____
_____	_____	_____	_____	_____	_____
_____	_____	_____	_____	_____	_____
_____	_____	_____	_____	_____	_____

Will any other assets be available for college funding, such as gifts from grandparents or scholarship funds?
_____
_____

Accumulation Goals and Emergency Reserves

Having discussed goals for education funding, move on to discuss other short to medium range financial goals and emergency reserves. Once again, the questioning process is self-explanatory. Simply follow the order of the form.

Financial Independence

The objective of the Financial Independence section is to identify the Prospect's feelings about retirement and their related financial goals. The range of responses to these questions will often depend on the age of the Prospect. Younger Prospects may not have concern for, or a clear vision of, retirement. Their focus is often directed toward shorter term accumulation goals.

As people reach middle age, however, retirement planning becomes an important goal. Your mission within this age group is to encourage your Prospects to "paint a picture" of the activities and lifestyle they envision at retirement. Look for the who, what, where, when and why of their retirement picture. This is a picture you will want to play back in future meetings.

Financial Independence

At what age would you like to become financially independent? Client: _____ Spouse/Ptnr: _____

Would you retire then? _____

Could you describe for me the lifestyle you envision at retirement? _____

_____

_____

What is your estimate of the amount of income you would need,
in today's dollars, to fund that lifestlye? _____

How do you feel about your current plan and the progress you are making?

_____

Assets and Liabilities

Having given your Prospect's ample opportunity to share financial goals and aspirations, the next logical step is to discuss the assets and savings programs the Prospect currently has in place to reach these goals. In general, people like to talk about how much they have accumulated, not how little. The residence will often be your Prospect's largest single asset, so bring it up first.

"Now that I have an understanding of your goals and objectives, I'd like to move on to discuss the assets you have working for you. Do you own your home? What is your estimate of its market value? Do you have a mortgage? Do you see yourself staying in this home long-term?"

Move on to discuss other assets such as other real estate holdings, stocks, bonds, certificates of deposit, annuities and life insurance cash values. End with a discussion of the amount of cash in all checking accounts as this will likely be their smallest asset.

Be sure to ask questions that will sound out your Prospect's feelings about their various assets. Their responses might provide clues as to whether certain assets could be used differently to better accomplish their financial goals.

"Bob, what was the purpose of this mutual fund when you purchased it? (Pause for a response) How do you feel about it now?"

After discussing their assets and liabilities, ask your Prospects to identify an assumed portfolio rate of return in the following manner:

"Bob, as you know, each of the assets you have listed earns a different rate of return. For purposes of the report I'm preparing for you, what average rate of return would you be comfortable assuming for your long-term financial goals?"

Assets and Liabilities

Asset Type	Owner	Market Value	Liability	Rate of Return	Monthly Contributions	Notes:
Cash / Checking						
Savings, CD, T-Bills						
Bonds / Income Funds						
Cash Values (Life / Annuity)						
Stocks / Stock Funds						

Asset Type	Owner	Market Value	Liability	Rate of Return	Monthly Contributions	Notes:
Residence					Payment:	Yrs. Remaining: Interest Rate:
Other Real Estate						
Ltd. Partnerships						
Business Interest						
Personal Property						
Other Assets:						
Other Liabilities:		xxxxxxxxx				
		xxxxxxxxx				
		xxxxxxxxx				
		xxxxxxxxx				

Assumed portfolio rate of return: _____%

Retirement plan assets are listed separately from other assets to allow you to identify additional contributions made by your Prospect's employer, as well as your Prospect's assumption for annual increases in retirement plan contributions.

Retirement Plan Assets

Retirement Plan Owner	Market Value	Liability	Rate of Return	Monthly Savings	Company Contribution	Annual % Increase

There is a relationship between all of the questions on the Confidential Questionnaire form. In the Occupation section on the first page, you will have asked about future career plans. If Prospects have indicated that they do not see themselves staying with their current employer permanently, then it is appropriate to now ask about the long-term viability of the corresponding retirement plan assets and contributions.

"Bob, earlier you indicated that Mary is considering a position with Microsystems Corporation. What percentage of her current 401(k) assets are vested? Should we ignore her future contributions to this plan, and the corresponding company match for now? If she moves to Microsystems, we can update the analysis later."

Direct Income Sources

This section of the Confidential Questionnaire is provided to help you identify any additional assets that may be available to satisfy financial goals. It refers to sources of income that would not show up on your Prospect's current balance sheet, such as inheritances, trust fund income or deferred compensation plans.

"Are there any other future sources of income, other than the assets we have just discussed, that might impact your financial independence or that of your survivors?

"Would you tell me something about the circumstances of your parents or grandparents, and your in-laws, Bob, as they might have a bearing on possible inheritances to you, Mary, or John. Do you see this inheritance as a significant part of your estate?"

Direct Income Sources

Will you receive any other source of income in the future, such as an inheritance or trust fund income? (Yes / No)

Client / Spouse	Lump Sum Or Monthly	Age Income to be Received	Amount of Income	PV / FV	Notes

Do you wish to include this assumption in your retirement planning? _____

Estate Planning? _____

Cash Flow

The cash flow portion of the Confidential Questionnaire allows you to identify sources of income, savings objectives, and your Prospect's cash flow picture. Approach the issue of income sources in a direct and matter of fact manner.

"Bob, what will your salary be this year? And Mary's? Do you anticipate any unearned income, such as interest or dividends? And looking ahead to the future, what do you anticipate your income will be two years from now? And Mary's?"

Cash Flow

Annual Income Sources	Two Yrs Ago	Client Current Year	Two Yrs. Forward	Two Yrs. Ago	Spouse/ Partner Current Year	Two Yrs Forward	
Salary							**What percentage of your *future raises* would you like to save or invest?_____**
Self-Employment							
Interest & Dividends							
Pensions/Annuities							**What percentage of your current income are you saving/investing now?_____**
Social Security							
Rental Prop. (Net)							
Pensions/Annuities							
Social Security							**What percentage would you like to be saving/ investing?_____**
Other:							

	Monthly	Annually
TOTAL EXPENSES:	_____	_____
TOTAL TAXES:	_____	_____

This sequence of questions will give you not only current factual information, but will also give you an idea of your Client's income potential in the foreseeable future. It will also set the stage for a discussion of future and current savings and investment objectives. These questions will be reviewed again during future meetings as you attempt to help your Prospects and Clients move in the direction of their financial goals.

"What percentage of your future raises would you like to save or invest? What percentage of your current income are you saving or investing now? And what percentage would you like to be saving or investing?"

Finally, wrap up the Cash Flow section by asking for an estimate of your Prospect's total living expenses and income taxes to be paid. This will give you an idea of the amount of disposable income that is available for their financial goals and objectives.

Concerns Profile

The questions provided in this section will help you to correlate your recommendations with your Prospect's concerns about basic financial risks, such as inflation, taxes, liquidity, or safety. Simply read the introductory paragraph aloud and then pause to ensure that they have understood your instructions. Then read the questions aloud as they appear on the form.

Concerns Profile

In order to help me prepare recommendations that correlate with your financial concerns, I'd like you to rank the following areas of concerns from 1 (very low) through 9 (very high). We are concerned principally with "surplus" money that you have saved or invested, or will save or invest in the future and, of course, inherited money. It is the growth, protection and eventual use of this capital that we are asking you to think about as each financial concern is ranked. Please try to avoid duplicating the same ranking of any of the six concerns.

_____ **Inflation Hedge** How much are you concerned about having your savings dollars and investments keep pace with inflation?

_____ **Tax Advantage** To what extent are you concerned about getting all of the tax relief to which you are legally entitled and which is suitable for you?

_____ **Safety** How much are you concerned about being sure you could get back your own dollars? (High score indicates a desire for safe investments)

_____ **Liquidity** How much are you concerned that your investments can be quickly converted into cash?

_____ **Current Income** How much are you concerned about getting maximum income from your savings and investments this year?

_____ **Family Benefit** To what extent are you concerned that your investment program not be harmful or difficult for your family to manage?

What is your estimate of the long term rate of inflation? _____

If your Prospect happens to provide the same ranking for two areas of concern, do not call it to his attention until he has answered all of the questions. You may then go back to the two areas that are ranked the same for further clarification.

"Thank you, Bob. Now I noticed you ranked two areas the same – safety and family benefit. Of the two, which do you feel is more important to you, being able to get back your own dollars invested, or making sure your investments would not be harmful or difficult for your family to manage?"

Finally, remember to obtain your Prospect's estimate of the long-term rate of inflation.

"Bob, when we discussed your savings goals, we talked about them in terms of today's dollars. However, we must also recognize that inflation exists. Therefore, my analysis will estimate the amount of capital that will be needed to accomplish those same goals in future dollars, at an assumed rate of inflation. What rate would you like to assume as an estimate of the long-term rate of inflation?"

Advisors

The Advisor portion can provide a great deal of information that may be helpful in the future. First, you will have the names of financial, legal and employee benefit advisors should you need to consult them as you are analyzing your Prospect's programs, or helping to settle Client claims. It may also provide a potential source of funds (via income tax refunds) for the accomplishment of financial objectives as well as potential sources of future Suspects.

Using a matter of fact tone, introduce the Advisors section in the following manner:

"I'd like to record the names of a few of your advisors, in case we need to consult any of them as we are analyzing your program. I would, of course, consult with you before doing so. Who prepares your income tax returns? Do you usually receive a tax refund? In what amount? And whom do you consult for legal advice? What is the name of your employee benefits advisor at work? Would it be possible to obtain a copy of your employee benefits booklets and statements? Is there anyone else you consult before making financial decisions?"

Advisors

Tax Returns _____ Do you usually receive a tax refund? Y / N

_____ Amount: _____

Legal Counsel _____

Employee Benefits _____ Benefit Booklet Available? _____

Other_____

Estate Planning

The next section of the Confidential Questionnaire will give you an idea of the estate planning arrangements that have been made to date. It may also provide valuable advance suspecting information. Approach this section in the following manner:

"Bob, I'd like to move on now to a brief discussion of your current estate planning arrangements. If you were to die prematurely, what current plans exist for your estate distribution?"

"Do you have a will? Briefly, what are its provisions? Has a guardian been appointed for John? Is there a contingent guardian? Whom did you appoint as executor? Where do you keep your will and other important family documents? Are there any other family members in the local area who should be notified?"

Again, these are open ended questions that will help you better understand your Prospect's inner person. If your Prospects have not prepared the necessary documents for their estate planning, suggest that they consult their legal advisor for assistance in making these arrangements.

Estate Planning

Current Plans for Estate Distribution _____

_____

Wills / Trusts / _____

_____

Guardians _____

_____

Availability and Location of Family Documents _____

_____

Other Family Members_____

Life Insurance

Next, identify the amounts and types of life insurance policies they have in force. Then go on to ask the questions in the lower section to identify the purpose of those policies and to identify health considerations that may affect their insurability.

> "How did you arrive at the amount of life insurance you own? What do you want your life insurance to do for you? How do you feel about your current program? Are there any health considerations that might affect your insurability? Do you or Mary use tobacco or nicotine products of any type? What about higher risk avocations, such as flying, scuba diving or racing?"

Life Insurance

Company/ Date Issued	Insured	Policy Type	Owner	Beneficiary	Net Death Benefit	Annual Premium	Current Net Cash Value
_____	_____	_____	_____	_____	$_____	$_____	$_____
_____	_____	_____	_____	_____	$_____	$_____	$_____
_____	_____	_____	_____	_____	$_____	$_____	$_____
_____	_____	_____	_____	_____	$_____	$_____	$_____
_____	_____	_____	_____	_____	$_____	$_____	$_____
_____	_____	_____	_____	_____	$_____	$_____	$_____

How did you arrive at the amount of life insurance you own? _____

What do you want your life insurance to do for you? _____

How do you feel about your current program? _____

Are there any health considerations that might affect your estate plans or insurability? _____

_____

Tobacco / Nicotine: _____ Medications: _____

Hospitalization: _____ Aviation / Avocations:_____

Survivor Needs

"Now, in order for me to help you determine whether or not your life insurance coverage is sufficient, I need to understand what you would want Mary's and John's worlds to look like if anything happened to you. Do you think they would want to stay in their home and neighborhood? Should the mortgage be paid off? What about other debts? Should an emergency fund be available? Would you want the same educational plan for John that we discussed earlier? With those things provided, how much total monthly income would they need, from all sources, in today's dollars? Do you anticipate that Mary would continue to work at the same pace as a single parent? Would her employment income remain the same or should we assume that it would be reduced for a period of time?"

Continue with this line of questioning as you complete the Survivor Needs information. Ask the questions in a quiet, calm and nonjudgmental manner. Then ask about the survivor needs of the other spouse (Bob, in this case).

Survivor Needs

	Client's Death	Spouse's (Partner's) Death
Surviving Spouse's Total Monthly Income Needs (Today's $)	$_____	$_____
Surviving Spouse's Anticipated Employment Income (Today's $)	$_____	$_____
Last Expenses	$_____	$_____
Pay Off Mortgage?	$_____	$_____
Pay Off Other Debt / Loans?	$_____	$_____
Fund Education?	$_____	$_____
Emergency Reserve?	$_____	$_____
Charitable / Other Bequests	$_____	$_____

Notes: _____
_____
_____

Be aware that it is important to record pre-tax income needs, if you are using Financial Profiles software. Additionally, when asked about assumptions for last expenses, most Prospects will respond with their estimate of the cost of funeral expenses. Last expenses will also often include miscellaneous medical expenses, probate and legal fees, and possibly taxes. It is recommended that you discuss an estimate of 4% of the estate value with your Prospects to cover these miscellaneous last expenses.

Disability Income Needs

Continue with a discussion of Disability Income Needs by asking the questions as they appear on the Confidential Questionnaire.

Disability

If you were unable to earn an income due to a lengthy illness, or a serious accident, how long would you be able to live from savings or investments? _____

How much after-tax monthly income would be needed to maintain your lifestyle? _____

Would the healthy spouse/partner be able to work full time if one of you were disabled? Should we plan for a reduction of their income? (Yes / No) Percentage Reduction? _____

Do you own disability income insurance? _____

Company / Date of Issue	Insured	Type	Monthly Benefit	Annual Premium	Elimination Period	Benefit Years	COLA
_____	_____	_____	$_____	$_____	_____	_____	Y / N
_____	_____	_____	$_____	$_____	_____	_____	Y / N
_____	_____	_____	$_____	$_____	_____	_____	Y / N
_____	_____	_____	$_____	$_____	_____	_____	Y / N

Disability Insurance Type: G=Group P=Personal O=Overhead Expense

General Insurance

The final portion of the insurance section allows you to verify that your Prospects have the necessary medical insurance coverage and that all of the major assets are insured.

Policy Type	Policy Name	Policy Benefit	Annual Premium	Notes:
Medical Insurance	_____	_____	_____	_____
Long Term Care Insurance	_____	Daily Benefit: __	_____	_____
Homeowners	_____	Elim. Prd.: ____	_____	_____
Liability	_____	Benefit Prd: ___	_____	_____
Auto Insurance	_____	_____	_____	_____

Prioritize Needs and Identify Budget

The Discovery or Summary Agreement

You should now have a fairly thorough understanding of your Prospect's financial situation, their goals, and the motivation behind them. Because several needs have been discussed, however, it is important that you and your Prospect come to an agreement on the priority of their needs. This process of clarifying the content and priority of their agenda is called formulating a Discovery or Summary Agreement. That is, these are the issues that you and your Prospect have "Discovered" during your interview. As you clarify and prioritize these, the resultant agreement is often referred to as either the Discovery Agreement or the Summary Agreement. Consider the following language for doing so.

"Thank you, Bob. As you can see, I've tried to touch on all the areas that have an impact on your family's financial security. Now I need to get your thinking on their order of priority. Let's suppose for a moment that, for whatever reason, you were able to act on only one of these areas of concern in the immediate future. Which would be the most important for you and your family to act upon first? And second?"

Prioritze the goals and needs discussed.

Priority

Of the needs we have just discussed, which do you feel is most important for you and your family to act upon first? Second? Etc. _____

_____

_____

_____

Then go on to identify a budget for addressing the needs that have been discussed. Ask the question directly as it appears on the Confidential Questionnaire.

Budget

What amount of monthly income would you be willing to contribute toward your financial goals?

_____

_____

Test Desire

In an earlier chapter, we said the steps of the Sales Cycle are designed to lead you and your Prospects up the Right triangle. Having taken a complete and thorough Confidential Questionnaire, you have begun the discussion of the Problem portion of the triangle.

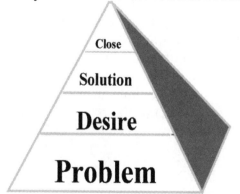

The *Right* Triangle
Anatomy of the Consultative Sales Process

Close

Solution

Desire

Problem

It is equally important to identify the Desire portion before concluding the interview. Consider the following language for doing so.

"Bob, assuming I can find recommendations that you're comfortable with – and that are within the budget you've just given me—tell me, are these goals and concerns important enough for you and Mary to act upon in the fairly immediate future?"

Test desire to take action.

If your Prospects give an affirmative response to the desire question, then you are on your way to a New Client, and they will be on their way to greater financial security! If, on the other hand, your Prospect hesitates, it is best to identify any concerns or obstacles during the Fact Finding Interview.

"Obviously, you have a reason for your hesitation, Bob. Do you mind if I ask what concerns you?"

Remain quiet and allow your Prospect ample time to respond. Then, restate the desire question in the following manner:

"I understand, Bob. That's why I was careful a moment ago to add the qualifying comments of, '...if I can find recommendations you're comfortable with—and that are within the budget we've just discussed.' You see, I'm trying to determine your sense of timing in addressing these issues. If I could meet those qualifications, do you feel you and Mary would be willing to start moving toward these goals in the fairly immediate future?"

The Principle of Consistency Revisited

You will recall that the psychological Principle of Consistency suggests that people have a desire to keep their thoughts, feelings, and behavior consistent with one another. If your Prospects agree to the conditions of the desire question, and if you do your job well in designing solutions that are appropriate and affordable, it will become psychologically inconsistent for them not to take action on your recommendations. So there is nothing to lose, and much to be gained (for you and your Prospect), by testing desire before concluding the Fact Finding Interview.

Scheduling the Next Interview

In most instances, your Prospects will agree to the desire question. Remember that you will be talking to individuals who have been previously qualified through the eyes of a nominator as intelligent, responsible and forward thinking individuals. You should now schedule the Closing Interview for not more than one week away, and at a time that the spouse or partner can be present. Strive to meet at your office during business hours where your reference materials and computer are available.

The "It's Just a Matter of Timing" Exit Language

If they do not agree, then there is little point in spending valuable time preparing and presenting your analysis and recommendations. The following language will allow you and your Prospect to conclude the Fact Finding Interview in a manner that preserves the relationship.

"I see. Bob, it sounds like this is just a matter of timing. Is that right?"

Prospects will almost always agree.

"I understand, and that's perfectly all right. However, situations have a way of changing. Now that I have a better understanding of your situation, would you mind if I checked back with you at a later date?"

Transition to Referred Lead Prospecting

When a Fact Finding Interview is conducted properly, you will almost always have identified the names of potential Suspects (guardians, relatives, business associates, etc.) that can be explored. As such, the conclusion of the meeting is an excellent referred lead prospecting opportunity. As you are putting away your paperwork, pivot to your Six Step Prospecting and Three Step Promotion language.

"Bob, might I ask your thinking on one more topic. I'd like some brief feedback. Now that you've had a chance to see something of the way I work, tell me frankly, what do you think of the process?"

Your Prospects will almost certainly gush with praise for the professional and thorough job you have done. Thank them for their feedback and proceed with your Six Step Prospecting and Three Step Promotion language.

Conclusion

A quality Fact Finding Interview is essential to both the relationship and the sale. It is important that you completely familiarize yourself with the Confidential Questionnaire (or other information gathering form). Practice your questions until they become completely natural and conversational.

Mastering the art of questioning is the primary skill of the Fact Finding Interview. Only then are you free to completely focus your attention on your Prospect. This is what leads to quality recommendations, trust, and a long-term professional relationship. Fact Finding truly is a master skill. Good Luck!

Chapter 13

Closing

Preparing for the Closing Interview

Philosophy of Case Preparation

Having completed the Fact Finding Interview, you should now have a very clear understanding of your Prospect's needs, wants, dreams, and budget. As mentioned in the previous chapter, it is your responsibility to handle this information with the utmost care and respect by designing solutions that meet your Prospect's needs as closely as possible – and within the framework of her budget. In short, it is your role to recommend the combination of solutions and products that you would choose for yourself and your family given the same set of circumstances.

Keep in mind that the objective of the Closing Interview is to motivate the Prospect to take *action* on his financial problems. The work you have done up to this point will be meaningless unless the Prospect is willing to do something to solve the problems that exist.

The Five Steps in Preparing for the Interview

Before you're ready for the close, there are five steps to preparing for the closing interview:

1. Send a follow-up communication (letter or e-mail) after your fact-finding interview that summarizes the key discussion points.

2. Prepare a Decision Interview Outline based upon the *Right* triangle.

3.   Prepare a simple presentation.

4.   Prepare to Prospect.

5.   Prepare yourself emotionally.

Step 1 – Send a Follow-Up Communication

The objective is to <u>motivate</u> your Prospects to <u>act</u> on their financial problems.

Psychological *studies* show that the capacity of a person's short term memory is limited. If material isn't reviewed very soon after it is heard, it will quickly be forgotten. Plus, people today live very busy lives with a constant stream of information competing for their attention. Therefore, it is important for you to send a brief – no longer than one page – summary letter as soon as possible after the Fact Finding Interview. The letter should outline the main points of what you and the Prospect agreed to, as well as the date, time, and place of your next meeting. From this, you will gain three benefits:

1.   Convey accurate information the prospect can share with others (such as a spouse) who was unable to take part in the fact-finding interview

2.   Foster assumed consent

3.   Increase commitment from your prospect

Convey Accurate Information for Sharing with Others Unable to Participate in the Interview

Besides enhancing your professional image, a follow-up letter will accomplish several things for you.

Since most approach and fact finding interviews are held during the day at the prospect's place of business, it's usually not possible to have both spouses or partners present. Scheduling the fact finding interview for a time when both can be present brings extra challenges and often results in a number of cancelled and rescheduled appointments and a loss of enthusiasm...for the prospect and you.

Your follow up letter allows the prospect to accurately share the information from your interview with her spouse in an organized manner that captures the main points of discussion. This brings the other person into the planning process at the earliest practical time... even though he was unable to participate in the interview.

Foster Assumed Consent

The second advantage of a follow-up letter is that it serves as an assurance that you understood what your prospect shared with you and that what she said was important.

The follow-up letter provides the prospect an opportunity to correct any information that you misunderstood. And the lack of feedback after sending your letter indicates the prospect agrees with the information you have presented.

This assumed consent lets you know you're on track and can proceed with the other steps of the sales process.

Increases Prospect Commitment

Finally, the Prospect's level of commitment to the financial goals stated in the letter is increased when he actually sees those goals in writing. He is more likely to see himself as a responsible, future-oriented person who is doing his best to take control of his own destiny and that of his family. This self-perception fosters an implied consent that he is willing to pay the price necessary to act on your recommendations.

Step 2 – Prepare a Decision Interview
Outline Based on the Right Triangle

Take a few minutes to prepare an outline of the major points you wish to cover during the Decision Interview. The outline can be handwritten, but it should be tailored to the needs of each Prospect following the basic format of the *Right* triangle.

The *Right* Triangle

Anatomy of the Consultative Sales Process

Close
Solution
Desire
Problem

That is, after the preliminaries, you will want to address the problem first, then the desire, then the solution, and finally the close. The actual area in each segment of the *Right* triangle represents both the importance of each topic as well as the approximate amount of time you will spend on each.

You will want to use the actual outline as an agenda or discussion guide and will refer to it often during the interview. Your Prospect will be impressed with the forethought you have given to her situation.

An example of a Decision Outline follows.

Decision Outline

I. Preliminaries

    A. Seating Arrangements

    B. Up-Date All

        1. How met

        2. Approach used

II. Problem & Desire

    A. Review the Fact Finder/Confidential Questionnaire

        1. Discuss goals

        2. Any changes?

    B. Present Analysis

        1. Explain and congratulate

        2. Identify shortages

        3. Explore noninsurance solutions

III. Solution – Present Recommendations

    A. Present general recommendations

    B. Present product solution

    C. Questions?

IV. Decision (Close)

  A. Complete paperwork / Obtain check

  B. Clarification (Respond to objections)

  C. Other points

      1. Other purchase options

      2. Prospecting for referred leads

      3. Date for a decision?

Focus on What They Have and What They Want

Remember that your Prospects will buy life insurance and related financial products from *you* because they feel you understand them and you are trying to help them solve their problems. As such, your presentation should focus first on their problem – the difference between what their current plan will provide (what they have) and what they want for their family or business.

Design the Solution to Cover the Full Need

When recommending a life insurance product, make sure the face amount will cover the full amount of their need. You should recommend the product that you believe best fits these parameters:

  1. The face amount matches the need;

  2. It is appropriate for cash value accumulation needs;

  3. The premium fits their budget.

Step 3 – Keep Your Presentation Simple

Too many decisions will equal no decision!

Comprehensive fact finding involves the discussion of a number of financial concerns, ranging from having adequate emergency reserves, to college funding, retirement planning, survivor needs, and more. This is why a discussion of priorities at the conclusion of the Fact Finding Interview is vital to your success with closing.

If you attempt to present an analysis of how well your Prospect is doing in each of the planning areas, and then explain product recommendations for addressing problem areas, your Prospect may be overwhelmed. If you provide too much information, the response you'll likely hear is, "I have to think about it." And it is true! Keep it simple!

To close more business, keep your presentations simple. Limit your discussion to the prospect's highest one or two priorities. Solve these needs first. Save others to address in the future. Asking for too much results in no decision!

Step 4 – Prepare to Prospect

The Closing Interview presents an excellent opportunity for Referred Lead Prospecting – or getting your Prospect to refer you to others who may have similar needs. Review the Confidential Questionnaire and the Case History Notes and then jot down the names and categories that you plan to feed for qualification. This advance planning can help you comfortably and smoothly transition to the Six Step Prospecting and Three Step Promotion language at the end of the Closing Interview.

Step 5 – Prepare Yourself Emotionally

Studies show that difficulties with closing are either caused by problems in your preliminary fact-finding techniques or from your personal anxiety level during the closing interview. The fact-finding problems tend to involve the failure to fully develop the bottom two segments of the *Right* triangle – that is, insufficient clarification of your prospect's problem or desire. If they don't *feel* their problem or the uneasiness of their vulnerability, they're not likely to take action.

A second impediment to successful closing can be your own anxiety level about the sale. This unpleasant emotion can distort your natural ability to deal with people. The suggestions that follow will help you control your anxiety level during the closing interview so you can focus on the task at hand.

You are psychologically prepared to close when you can address these five critical areas.

Be Properly Prepared

Preparing your outline for the closing interview can be a significant help. It is very helpful to answer the following question, which addresses five critical areas: "Why should *this person,* buy *my product, from me, today,* and *with what*? When you are very clear about this answer, your anxiety level will be low and you will be ready to sell. Conversely, your anxiety level will rise in direct proportion to your lack of clarity in answering this question.

Be Ready to Ask for the Business

Sometimes we have doubts about whether we are experienced enough, talented enough, or confident enough to ask for the full dollar amount that the problem requires. In some instances we must be prepared to close above our financial self-image. Remember, you're an expert. Envision yourself as a financial physician whose professional responsibility requires you to present the best medical solution. A competent doctor wouldn't hedge, so you shouldn't either. People don't get better unless they take action – the right action. And you're offering the cure.

Your Prospects' needs may require you to motivate decisions above your current financial self-image.

Remember, if you want business, you have to ask for it. Seems basic, but it's surprising how many people never ask. And guess what? In this case, they will likely get what they ask for... nothing.

Be Ready to Listen

For some of us, as anxiety levels go up, so does our tendency to talk. Worse yet, sometimes our anxiety leads us to become defensive as we continue to marshal responses to arguments that may not even exist in our Prospect's mind. Closing isn't a time to win a debate, but to calmly and persistently present solutions to agreed-upon problems. Slow down and listen.

Fundamentals of the Closing Interview

Today's Financial Services Professional may be involved in presenting an ever widening range of solutions to financial problems. Although you should strive to keep the process you use with each new Prospect basically the same, the problems may lead you to a variety of solutions. With some Prospects, your fact-finding will lead you to insurance solutions. For others it could be annuities, equities, or something else.

As such, it's not feasible in this book to try to demonstrate a Closing Interview for each category of problem or product. What remains critical, however, is an understanding of the time-tested principles that help create a successful Closing Interview, regardless of the type of financial service being recommended.

A Decision Is Your Objective

The Closing Interview is often called the Decision Interview because the objective is to motivate your Prospect to make a decision – to take action on her problems. Again, all of the work you have done for her and the time you have spent with her is meaningless unless she *does something* to solve the problems that exist.

The Importance of Minor Agreements

Minor agreements are sometimes called Trial Closes.

Throughout the Closing Interview you will be attempting to build upon agreement on minor issues that will ultimately lead to an agreement to take action. This technique sets into motion the Psychological Principle of Consistency, which was discussed in Chapter 12.

It's human nature for people to have a strong desire to keep their thoughts, feelings, and behavior aligned or consistent with one another. It's as if we want everything to fit together and make sense. When it doesn't, the resulting inconsistency leads to an unpleasant internal tension or feeling of anxiety. Consequently, when someone commits to a minor agreement, it later becomes inconsistent and anxiety-producing for them not to follow through with the appropriate action. Minor agreements – sometimes called trial closes – lead to action!

Have Both Spouses or Partners Present

Generally, both spouses or partners in a decision-making unit should be present during the Closing Interview. Once you have the respect and trust of both individuals, one or the other may handle future additions to the basic plan. Even if you find that only one person will handle subsequent financial decisions, it is still important that both people be there for the initial Closing Interview.

Schedule Closing Interviews at Your Office

Try to conduct Closing Interviews in your office where your reference works and computer are available. Invite them in during regular business hours, if possible, because successful people tend to conduct most of their professional appointments during the day. If they cannot come in earlier in the day, suggest the end of the work day in your office. However, if you must go to their home, suggest giving them half an hour for a quick meal and then starting your interview at 6:30 p.m. This will give them the balance of the evening to themselves and give you a chance to get home at a reasonable hour.

The Meeting Is Not a Time for Practice

At this point, it should be stressed that you should hold practice sessions in your office or in your own home using colleagues or friends as subjects. Videotape and critique your efforts until you feel comfortable. Remember, you must be free to direct your attention to communication rather than to mechanical details. The purpose of practice is to provide time when you can make mistakes and correct them without the consequences of failure in performance. *Your aim should be to establish habits that will operate without effort.* This will reduce anxiety and allow you to be at your best when it truly matters. If you practice your sales procedures over and over and over again in private, you will be repaid a thousand-fold for your public performances.

Follow the Decision Outline

I. Preliminaries

A. Seating Arrangements

When your prospects arrive at your office, take charge immediately. You should direct the seating arrangements and ask the receptionist to hold all calls to ensure uninterrupted concentration. Generally, you will want your Prospects to sit at a conference table, around a corner either to your right or left. This seating arrangement prevents having the barrier of a desk or table between you and is more conducive to the businesslike, yet helping, atmosphere you wish to establish.

Direct the Seating Even at Their Home

In those situations where it is necessary to conduct the Closing Interview in their home, you should also take charge of the seating arrangement. If both spouses are ready when you arrive, avoid being led to the easy chair at the far side of the room. Remain standing and look around. If a dining room or kitchen table seems convenient, ask permission to use one or the other. You want them to sit up and pay attention during your discussion as it will have a significant impact upon their future.

The preference is to sit at the dining table but if you end up in a more relaxed area while waiting, when both spouses are ready, take the opportunity to arrange a businesslike atmosphere around a table. It's far more convenient, and easy to keep eye contact and share your illustrations, if they are seated side-by-side at a right angle from you. This allows you to watch them both at the same time and makes it possible for them to see your illustrations simultaneously.

Decision Outline

I. Preliminaries
  A. Seating Arrangements
  B. Up-Date All
    1. How met
    2. Approach used

II. Problem & Desire
  A. Review the Fact Finder
    1. Discuss goals
    2. Any changes?
  B. Present Analysis
    1. Explain and congratulate
    2. Identify shortages
    3. Explore non-insurance solutions

III. Solution – Present recommendations
  A. Present general recommendations
  B. Present product solution
  C. Questions?

IV. Decision (Close)
  A. Complete Paperwork / Obtain Check
  B. Clarification (Respond to objections)
  C. Other points
    1. Other purchase options?
    2. Prospecting for referred leads
    3. Date for a decision?

Put It All on the Table – Literally!

When you are seated, place everything that you might need during the course of the interview on the table. Organize your materials in the following order:

1. Decision Outline

2. The Confidential Questionnaire form

3. Your written analysis and recommendations

4. Product recommendations and illustrations

5. Application forms

6. Prospecting Outline

Begin with the Decision Outline

You should refer to the outline at the very beginning by explaining that you have given a great deal of thought to their situation and, to eliminate the possibility of overlooking any significant point, you have taken the time to outline your material specifically for them. Place the outline to one side but refer to it as the interview progresses and even check off the various points as you cover them. Again, the outline should be tailored to each Prospect and it should be in your own handwriting or typed.

B. Update the Spouse

Because most Fact Finding Interviews occur during business hours at the Prospect's place of business, the Closing Interview will often be your first opportunity to meet the spouse or partner. As soon as you place your materials on the table, get down to business! A good way to begin is to bring the person you are meeting for the first time up-to-date. If you were introduced to your Prospect under complimentary circumstances, you might want to emphasize that. Consider the following dialogue:

"Mary, I don't know if you and Bob have had a chance to talk about our last meeting so I'd like to take a moment to bring us all up to date. (Look at both of them.) Would that be okay?

"Recently, Mary, I had the pleasure of doing some work for one of Bob's associates, John Barker. When we finished we talked about people whom John thought might like to have an opportunity to evaluate our work. I asked John who, of all the people he knew, had the very best opportunity to really excel in their careers. Without hesitation, John mentioned the two of you." (Pause to allow time for a response.)

In this situation, we are assuming that you were referred to Bob. You would use the same procedure if you had been referred to Mary.

The Importance of the Pinpoint Question

In the discussion of the Six Step Prospecting and Three Step Promotion language, step number five encouraged the use of the pinpoint question. If you consistently use the closing interview as an opportunity to identify new leads, you can enthusiastically begin your Closing Interviews in the way just described. Not only do you have a better prospect, but you have a tremendous chance to get off to a powerful start by passing on these good words.

Of course, this isn't always possible. In situations where you did not hear about the Prospect in such glowing terms, your introductory language will have to be modified appropriately. Do not get yourself off to the worst of starts by saying anything that isn't true; instead, say something like this:

"Recently, Mary, I had the pleasure of doing some work for John and Helen Barker. When we finished, I explained to them that the type of people who find our planning most helpful are intelligent, have a sense of responsibility, and are oriented toward the future. I asked them if they knew of anyone fitting that description and they told me about the two of you!" (Pause for a response.)

Review the Three Step Approach

After the appropriate introduction, continue by restating an abbreviated Three Step Approach for the other spouse or partner's benefit. The Prospect with whom you did the fact finding is listening, too, and will again be reminded of your procedures. Demonstrate items such as the Confidential Questionnaire you completed about their situation and the proposal that has been prepared specifically for them. Proceed as follows:

"After hearing about Bob, I wrote him a brief letter outlining the services we offer and then called him to ask if he would like to review those services with me. He agreed and we met during the middle of last week.

"At that time, I explained that our services consist of three steps. The first is to meet with individuals who are interested in making intelligent, long-range plans for their financial future.

"We discuss their plans and objectives, and to keep us on track, we have developed this Confidential Questionnaire that reminds us of the things we ought to talk about. This is the one that we actually used in our discussion last week and, as you can see, we tried to touch on everything that would have a bearing on your family's long-range financial success."

Show the Confidential Questionnaire

As you talk about the Confidential Questionnaire, turn it toward the Prospects and open it fully so they can see the thorough job you have done. This is where you learn the importance of preparing a complete – and neat – Confidential Questionnaire. If you present a messy or incomplete document, you'll undermine your own image before you even get started! If the spouse or partner takes it away from you for closer inspection, permit him or her to do so. Stop talking and wait until the individual looks up and reestablishes eye contact with you. Then, reach for it and continue smoothly:

"Next, I explained that the second step would be for me to take this information back to my office to review, analyze, and prepare a written report for you and Bob. That's been completed and I have it here to share with you.

"I went on to explain that the third and final step for a Client is to periodically review and update your program. Our objective is to establish a long-term relationship so that we can always be of service, whatever your needs and however your situation may change."

Notice that you are not attempting to describe the report at this time. You will review the report in detail with them later in the interview.

II. Problem and Desire

A. Review the Confidential Questionnaire

Return to the completed Confidential Questionnaire and say:

"Before we get into the analysis that I have prepared for the two of you, I'd like to go back to the information that was collected and first ask if anything significant has changed since we last met. (This protects you from them changing the premise of the close at the last minute.) I would also like to spend a few minutes getting your thinking, Mary, on some of the major points."

Be sure to ask, "Has anything changed since our last meeting?"

At this point, you will look the person who was not present during the original Fact Finding Interview directly in the eyes and wait for a response that grants permission to proceed. The individual who was not originally present will usually be quietly pleased to be included in this important step of the process and will usually grant permission immediately, either verbally or with a nod. Once you have the go ahead, proceed by picking up the Confidential Questionnaire and begin with the personal information section.

"I have your name listed as Mary Elizabeth Edwards. Is that how you prefer to be addressed, or do you also wish to have your maiden name used? Is there a nickname you wish to go by, or do you prefer to be called Mary?

"Bob explained that you are a software analyst at the Dynasoft Corporation. How long have you been with the firm? Could you give me some idea of how you fit into the organizational structure of the company? How do you like working with the company? What would be your guess as to your chances for advancement and the possibility of staying with this company permanently? Have you ever thought of going into business for yourself?"

If a spouse or partner wasn't involved in the Fact Finding Interview, take the time to get to his or her inner person by reviewing the Confidential Questionnaire.

Get to the *Inner Person* of the Spouse or Partner

As with your original Fact Finding Interview, you are trying to draw the other person out to get them actively involved in the Confidential Questionnaire. *It is important to get to the inner person of both individuals.* Therefore, go through the Confidential Questionnaire and touch on all of the important *feeling* areas to elicit the second individual's opinions about each. Doing this allows you to treat both individuals as equals, with the same opportunity for input into what may be the most important planning process the couple will ever go through in their lives.

As you elicit the thoughts and feelings of the second individual (Mary, in this example), you are also indirectly complimenting the person with whom you took the original fact finding information for being a forward thinking individual who is attempting to manage his or her family's financial future. Additionally, you are beginning the process of acquiring the minor agreements discussed earlier.

Don't Shortcut the Process

The entire process of going through the initial introductions, the abbreviated Three Step Approach, and the review of the Confidential Questionnaire should only take about twenty minutes because you already have all of the factual information. *Do not short cut this process, however, to save time.* If you do this preliminary work well, both individuals will feel good about the process and will realize that you are on their side and are trying to help them accomplish their goals.

On the other hand, if your Prospects indicate a significant change in their planning goals, then go back to fact finding. Do not attempt to present your analysis until you have agreement on the problem and the desire to solve it.

B. Present Your Analysis

Having reviewed the Confidential Questionnaire, you may now move to the next step of the Decision Outline – the presentation of the report you have prepared. The tension has been building as you have reviewed the facts of their situation as well as their feelings. In so doing, you have gained agreement on the bottom two sections of the *Right* triangle – their problems and their desire to solve them.

Introducing the Report

Place the report in front of them with the cover closed. As you do, you may introduce the report in the following manner:

"Bob and Mary, as I promised, I've prepared this written analysis for you. It focuses primarily on the financial goal that Bob indicated would be your highest priority. He indicated that (state the top priority) was your first major concern.

"Now, as we go along together, if there is anything that I fail to make clear, be sure to stop me, okay?"

Notice that the burden of blame, should there be a misunderstanding as you go along, is placed on your own shoulders, not on theirs. Instead of, *"If there's anything you don't understand,"* it's better to phrase it as, *"If there's anything I fail to make clear."*

Place the burden of clear communication on your own shoulders.

As you go through the analysis, try to avoid distracting chatter that makes it difficult for them to visually comprehend the report. Invite them to make comments about these ideas as you discuss them. Be conscious, however, of the passage of time. Up to this point, you have really not embarked upon your true function as a Financial Services Professional, and that is *motivation*. Before moving on to the explanation of the proposal pages, let's review the true objective of this interview – the art of motivation.

You're in the Motivation Business

Your profession is one of motivation. Attorneys, trust officers, and accountants have their specialized functions to perform and may sometimes make up a part of the overall estate planning team. *The Financial Services Professional's primary function is to motivate people to create and protect the estates that will do the jobs they want done for themselves and their families.*

The Financial Services Professional's primary function is to motivate people to create and protect the estates that will do the jobs they want done for themselves and their families.

The preliminary activities at the beginning of the Closing Interview are primarily designed to bring everyone up-to-date and to get the Prospects in the habit of agreeing with you on things that are completely logical and easy to agree to.

The preliminaries also provide an opportunity to build our own prestige and to become acquainted with the spouse or partner. To the extent to which you build prestige and confidence, and get them on your side and in the habit of agreeing with you, you greatly increase the probability of obtaining some definite *action*. Everything you have done so far is just pleasant conversation, for you do not *really* do any good for your Prospects until you motivate them to act on their problems.

Don't lose sight of the fact that you haven't yet done your main job. As a sales-focused individual, your profession is motivation! You'll work on motivating your Prospects during the Closing Interview as you review problems and attempt to create desire to take immediate action.

Explain the Analysis

The next step in the Decision Outline involves the explanation of your analysis. Be sure, however, to congratulate them on what they have accomplished so far, and for having the character and foresight to take control of their financial future.

Then highlight the shortages in their current plan. Pause for a moment to allow your Prospects to absorb the information that is being presented. Do not be alarmed if they are initially surprised by the amount of capital that is needed to accomplish their goals. Few people stop to calculate the magnitude of the economic contribution they will make toward their family's well being and lifestyle.

Explore the Noninsurance Solutions

Generally, most people's financial plan is designed to accumulate enough assets to provide for goals such as a comfortable retirement, children's education, a charitable legacy, or a sufficient estate to protect the family and heirs. Often, the most efficient and certain way to accomplish these goals is through the purchase of life insurance or a combination of life insurance and investments.

In today's financial environment, more and more people are looking to investments as a major contributor to their financial plan. If you are positioning yourself as a full service Financial Services Professional you will need to illustrate how investments will fit into an overall financial plan. In that light, you will need to explore the noninsurance solutions to your Prospect's problems.

The purpose is not to determine what financial vehicle is right or wrong for your Prospects, but, rather, an appropriate strategy for meeting their goals and what the next most important step will be at this time.

You help people ensure their ability to complete their financial goals.

Remember that equity products are often more immediately appealing to your Prospects because they imply wealth accumulation and living benefits. It is important to point out to your Prospects, however, that most successful investment programs require the responsibility of regular investing over time. The question arises as to how you, as their trusted financial advisor, can ensure their ability to complete such a program. Death, disability, a catastrophic medical expense, or the loss of employment could all interrupt the successful completion of their plan. It is the unknown timing of issues such as these that often return the focus of the discussion back to insurance solutions.

III. Solution – Present Recommendations

A. Present General Recommendations

Begin by presenting a summary of general recommendations, allowing ample opportunity for questions and feedback. Depending on the area of planning you are focusing on, your general recommendations may range from "consult an attorney about updating your will" to "consider establishing a tax deductible IRA." If minor agreements have been obtained throughout the explanation of your analysis, your Prospects will normally agree with your general recommendations and you will be positioned to present specific product solutions.

Present the Product Solution

It is not possible to demonstrate all of the language used to explain each specific product illustration within the context of this book. In general, however, follow these guidelines when presenting solutions.

First and foremost, recommend the product you believe best fits your Prospect's requirements, as well as her budget. Recommend the product(s) you would purchase yourself, given your Prospect's circumstances. This allows you to present solutions with conviction and meet any applicable suitability requirements.

Second, remember that emotions are caught, not taught! Though the decision to buy someday can be obtained by teaching, the decision to buy today will be obtained by the Financial Services Professional who is involved, who cares, and who shows it. If you believe in the necessity of owning the products you recommend, you will communicate that conviction emotionally to your Prospects.

Up until this point, the tension in the interview has continued to increase. The Prospects have revisited their current situation, their desires for the future, and how their current plan simply won't get them where they want to go. They have a problem and they now know it. What is more important is their perception that you understand them and their problem. Now is the time to begin to reduce the tension by assuring them that you have a solution that will work and that they can afford.

Now is the time to explain the product you are recommending. Explain how the product functions to help them reach their desired outcome. Notice that the emphasis here is not on all of the features and benefits of the product, but what it delivers as a solution.

Answer Questions

Take as much time as necessary to answer all of your Prospects' questions. Their probability of staying with the investment or insurance program is directly proportional to their level of understanding and trust. They will better understand the product as you explain and answer their questions. They come to trust you because you are willing to take the time to do so, and to do so in a manner that relates to them personally.

IV. Decision (Close)

Closing Statement

After explaining all product recommendations thoroughly, and having answered all questions along the way, you are now ready to ask your Prospects to take action. Now is the time to ask your Prospects to buy. Although this may sound simple, many Financial Services Professionals actually fail to ask the Prospects to buy, while others will fail to ask more than once! Remember, you have not accomplished anything in the way of helping your Prospects until they take action.

There are many ways to ask your Prospects to take action. Most experienced representatives find that an assumptive transition to action is the most natural. You simply move to the paperwork.

The Assumed Consent Close (or Application Close)

Reaching for the applications you placed on the table at the beginning of the interview, say:

"Fine. The next step is to complete the necessary paperwork to apply to put the program in force. I already have most of the necessary information; I simply need to ask you..."

The Direct Question Close

An alternative approach might be the direct question close.

"Bob and Mary, given the strength of this program to solve the needs we've just discussed, is there any reason why we shouldn't complete the paperwork to apply to put the program in force?"

In time – and with practice – you will master these techniques and will be able to complete most Closing Interviews in less than one hour. If you wing it, time can easily slip away from you. Staying on track with an organized approach also helps you to build your prestige as a Financial Services Professional.

Clarification – Responding to Objections or Stalls

If your Prospects agree, finish completing the application(s). Remember that the application is an important legal document. Ask your Prospects to read and verify the entire application before signing it.

However, if resistance occurs at this point you have to be prepared to respond. Objections will normally fall into one of the following categories:

- No need;

- No trust;

- No money;

- No hurry.

The Critical Importance of a Complete Fact Finder

If you have conducted a thorough Fact Finding Interview, you and your Prospects will have agreed upon their needs, their budget, and their motivation. Additionally, if you have done a good job of establishing a helpful and consultative relationship, the trust level should be very high at this point. Your Prospects have just shared their most private feelings and goals with you, as well as information about their finances. They want to trust you and they want to believe that your recommendations are the best.

Most of the time, their objections and stalls are just a way of saying, "Convince me that taking action on this program really is in my best interest." Do not be afraid of objections and stalls because in responding you are simply fulfilling your responsibility as a trusted financial advisor.

The following are suggested methods of replying to the standard responses you are likely to hear from Prospects in your attempt to move them to action. The most common response you will hear is, "You have done a tremendous job! Thank you so much! Now, Mary and I need some time to think about it." Calmly smile and respond in the following manner.

Isolate the Concern

If the solution involves insurance:

"I'm very pleased to hear that you like my recommendations. And I'm glad to hear you are giving this program serious consideration. Just so I'm clear, is it the amount of the coverage, the specific insurance policy I've suggested, or the premium amount that you want to think about?"

If the solution involves the purchase of an equity product:

"I'm very pleased to hear that you like my recommendations. And I'm glad to hear you are giving this program serious consideration. Just so I'm clear, is it the mutual fund company, the specific subaccount I've suggested, or the contribution amount that you want to think about?"

If your Prospects respond with a specific concern, that's great! You may now address it directly. If, on the other hand, they say, "We always talk these things over before making a final decision," then suggest that you go to another room for a few minutes to make a phone call, allowing them to discuss their decision in private. That way, if any questions arise in their decision-making process, you'll be able to answer them.

The Medical Close

If your recommendation involves an insurance product and your Prospects then respond that they need *time* to make a decision, respond in the following manner:

"Again, I'm pleased you are giving this program serious consideration. As I mentioned, I believe it is the ideal policy for your situation. Tell me, premium amounts aside, do you feel this is the type of insurance policy you will want to buy when you make the decision?"

Listen carefully. They will almost always say "Yes" because you have given the impression that you are allowing them to delay the decision until sometime in the future. Then proceed by explaining the underwriting process.

"The fact is, as it stands right now, we are only dealing with a hypothetical premiums and benefit amounts. You see, the actual decision will be based on the insurance company's interpretation of your state of health. They will need to review your doctor's records and may also need a medical (or paramedical) exam.

"This process is known as underwriting a risk, and it often takes several weeks. If you decide you want to modify the policy when it comes back, it can easily be adjusted at that time. "Doesn't this make sense to you?"

Ask Three Times

The closing techniques explained here are designed to allow you to encourage your Prospects to act on their problems at least three times. It is often the second or third attempt that will help your Prospects feel comfortable enough to take action during the first meeting. Again, if you sincerely believe your recommendations are in your Prospects' best interests, you have a responsibility to do your best to get them to make a decision.

Referred Leads – Remember to Prospect

If multiple attempts to convince your Prospects to take action meet with continued resistance, shift gears to Referred Lead Prospecting. Appear to give in and, as you are gathering your materials, ask:

"Tell me, Bob and Mary, now that you have had an opportunity to see how I work, tell me frankly, what do you think?"

Get the affirmative and proceed with the Six Step Prospecting and Three Step Promotion language.

Upon completion of the Closing Interview, your Prospects will have seen the full scope of your services. Whether they buy or not, they will be impressed by the comprehensive nature of your services and the professionalism with which you have handled yourself. So be sure to take a few extra minutes to transition to Referred Lead Prospecting.

Suggest a Date for a Decision

If your Prospects continue to insist that they need more time to think it over, then establish a date for a decision. Schedule an appointment within a few days to prevent the momentum that has been established from waning. Before winding up your interview, suggest a *date for a decision* as follows:

Decision Outline

I. Preliminaries
  A. Seating Arrangements
  B. Up-Date All
    1. How met
    2. Approach used

II. Problem & Desire
  A. Review the Fact Finder
    1. Discuss goals
    2. Any changes?
  B. Present Analysis
    1. Explain and congratulate
    2. Identify shortages
    3. Explore non-insurance solutions

III. Solution – Present recommendations
  A. Present general recommendations
  B. Present product solution
  C. Questions?

IV. Decision (Close)
  A. Complete Paperwork / Obtain Check
  B. Clarification (Respond to objections)
  C. Other points
    1. Other purchase options?
    2. Prospecting for referred leads
    3. Date for a decision?

"You know, Bob and Mary, you have a big investment in this discussion. You have spent a lot of time with me and we have tried to make a thorough appraisal of your situation. This is important. Let's do this – why don't you turn this program over very carefully in your minds during the next few days while the facts are still fresh? Then we will get together briefly to make a final decision.

"Whatever you decide at the time will be fine with me because, after all, this is your program. But I would like to make sure that you have had every opportunity to consider all of the factors involved. Even if your answer is "No" for now, we still should talk about timing and programs for the future. Would you have any objection to a brief meeting at the same time one week from today?"

If a decision cannot be reached, set a definite time for a subsequent appointment within a week.

Work to set a definite time – do not settle for the suggestion that you should call them in a week!

In preparation for the *date of a decision* appointment, run an alternative illustration that you still feel would solve their problem, or make a significant step towards that end. If your Prospects ultimately decide against your initial proposal, you will be prepared to say:

"Okay, but there is something else I thought you might want to consider."

You can then present your alternative illustration and begin the closing cycle anew.

Conclusion

Remember that your first Closing Interview is your best opportunity to turn Prospects into Clients. If it is true that "emotion sells it, and logic pays for it," you will never be able to create as much concern, excitement, and enthusiasm for action as in the first Closing Interview.

Where Does the Emotion Come From?

Nothing convinces like conviction!

Part of the required emotion comes from the Prospects experiencing the anxiety of the vulnerability of their situation. Only through a complete Fact Finding Interview can you learn this and play it back to them in a high integrity fashion. A second source of the emotion comes from your personal sense of mission. "Nothing convinces like conviction." If you really believe that your solution is both essential and the best option, you will convey that sense of urgency that moves people to action. You have to believe first!

Where Does the Logic Come From?

The logic of the purchase comes from the basic facts of the situation. Again, without a complete Fact Finding Interview you cannot establish the logic of the purchase. The more one studies the success or failure of the Closing Interview, the more one is drawn to the conclusion that success begins with the Fact Finding Interview.

Follow the *Right* Triangle to Closing Success

The path to a successful Closing Interview follows the trail up the *Right* triangle. Establish the Problem. Identify the Desire. Develop the Solution. Then, and only then, ask your Prospects to buy.

Once Prospects become Clients – that is, after they purchase a product from you – you will have the opportunity to serve them well. You will also be able to develop the all important, mutually beneficial, long-term relationship that is the source of both professional satisfaction and prosperity.

Success awaits you. You just have to prepare. And ask for it!

The *Right* Triangle
Anatomy of the Consultative Sales Process

Chapter 14

Delivery and Post Sale Service

The Delivery Interview, particularly with a New Client, presents an excetional opportunity to accomplish four things:

1. Help guarantee the persistency of the sale;

2. Set up repeat sales to this Client;

3. Stimulate unsolicited or "walk-in" business;

4. Find another New Client.

Four Objectives

Prior to the Delivery Interview

General Preparation

Get in the habit of always reviewing and double-checking the accuracy of each contract before it is delivered. Nothing is more embarrassing than showing up with a contract or policy different from what your Client purchased. Make sure to take along any additional paperwork that may need to be signed such as a policy delivery receipt.

Review the Confidential Questionnaire and Analysis Report to reacquaint yourself with the details of the Client's situation. It is important that you are clear as to why this purchase is the appropriate next step in the plan, and why it is important to act now.

Prepare a Prospecting Outline

Delivery Interviews are great suspecting opportunities. You should not settle for second best! If you have not already done so, define the minimum specifications of the least acceptable new Suspects you will now accept from a nominator.

The following areas provide a good opportunity for preparing yourself in advance with the names of potential Suspects and should make it possible for you to come up with a satisfactory list in almost every instance.

1. Double-Step Ahead Question

Before you ever met your present Client, you asked the nominator the Double-Step Ahead question, "And who, in addition to yourself, does he or she know well here in the city?"

2. The Confidential Questionnaire

Take time to review the Confidential Questionnaire (Facts form) as it is a virtual goldmine of potential suspects. Several of the most productive areas include business or community connections, the names of relatives or friends, as well as guardians and professional advisors.

Preparation allows you to keep an endless chain of referrals going.

3. The Case History

Search the Case History for hints of names or potential categories mentioned in previous conversations, particulary during the Closing Interview when both spouses or partners were present.

4. A Prompting List

If your Client belongs to a professional or business association, or a company with a published financial report, the Delivery Interview is an excellent time to have them identify potential Suspects from a prepared Prompting List.

Assemble a Policy Folder and Promotional Materials

The objective here is to present your company and policy in the most favorable light. The promotional material included should highlight other available products or services in order to improve the probability of repeat business and referred leads.

Stress the Importance of the Appointment

A Delivery Interview will normally take an uninterrupted hour. Therefore, resist any tendency to be casual in arranging for the appointment. Instead, purposely build it up. The phone call should go something like this:

"Bob, I'm glad to tell you your new program has been issued exactly as applied for. I've been doing a lot of work on your program and, as I look it over, I think you should be proud of what you're doing.

The purpose of my call is to arrange for a time when we can get together in my office where my reference materials are all available. (Try to schedule an appointment.)

"If not here, then let's schedule an uninterrupted hour in your office when you will feel free to close your door and to shut off your phone. We should have that much time to go over everything in detail and to make sure your program is set up exactly the way you want it."

Try to Meet in Your Office

Notice how we stress that this is being done for them. If possible, try to get them to come to your office where you know there will be no interruptions. Or, if you have go to the Client's office, you will have laid the groundwork by telling them that their door is to be closed and the phone shut off. Apply the same rule here as you do for a Closing Interview: don't start it unless the stage is set and the conditions are favorable!

During the Delivery Interview

Guarantee Persistency

The first objective during the Delivery Interview is to do those things that will guarantee the persistency of this sale and tie the Client to you for years to come. First enthusiastically review the policy itself paying particular attention to outstanding points of advantage. Many successful Financial Professionals go through the policy ahead of time and identify those provisions that are important and particularly advantageous. This preparation allows you to cover them more quickly and forcefully than might otherwise be possible. Try to demonstrate that the policy itself, regardless of cost, is one of the finest.

Review the policy enthusiastically.

Review Their Goals and Program

After reviewing the policy, take a moment to reflect on why this purchase was so wise. Review the goals that were expressed during your Fact Finding Interview. Then briefly summarize your analysis and their program. This may also include a list of all insurance policies owned, the ownership and beneficiary designations, face amounts, premium schedules, location of important documents and other vital information.

Reflect on why this was a wise purchase.

It may include a review of their investment portfolio and where they stand in their overall investment and savings program.

Tie Their New Purchase to Their Overall Program

The objective here is to clearly show how this purchase isn't a singular event, but another important stepping stone in the achievement of a coordinated, overall plan. Tie the new purchase to their program by showing specifically what part of the program they have just set in place, and how this brings them one step closer to realizing their financial objectives.

Give Promotional Material

Mention that they are now joining the ranks of the other discerning policyholders and investors of your company. Reinforce the wisdom of their choice by giving them copies of your company's best promotional material.

Set Up the Next Sale to Them

Congratulate them and express your admiration for their foresight, responsibility and discipline.

Recognize their accomplishments thus far and reinforce the wisdom behind their decision. You are one of the few people who will know your Client has made this important decision, so you should congratulate them and express your admiration.

Compliment your New Clients on their foresight, responsibility and discipline. They have shown foresight by creating and implementing a plan for their financial future. They are responsible because their actions reflect a genuine concern for the well being of their family, business or heirs. Finally, they are disciplined because they are willing to forego immediate gratification for the long-term benefits of protection, savings, and investment.

Life Insurance Is a "Character Purchase"

If their purchase included life insurance you should mention that such a purchase is not one of frivolous, conspicuous consumption. People buy life insurance when they love someone enough to face up to their obligations, even at the sacrifice of some present pleasure.

Earned Income Is Not "Financial Success"

You might also point out that substantial earned income is – although desirable – no assurance of financial success. Systematic long-range accumulation through life insurance and investments can go a long way toward securing financial success for your Clients whether they live too long, die too soon, or experience a significant disability.

Introduce the Shortages Remaining in Their Program

After having recognized their accomplishment, bring up any shortages that still exist and say:

"Knowing you as well as I do, I realize that had it been possible, you would have liked to have completed this entire program all at one time. You have done a great job but shortages still exist. Perhaps this would be a good time for us to do some thinking about which shortage is of most concern to you and when you think we should consider doing something about it."

Highlight Additional Funds as the Current Limitation

Their reply may be definite enough to specifically pin down the next sale. As a matter of fact, sometimes the "next sale" occurs then and there! If their reply is not definite or is not satisfactory from your point of view, ask another question. Try to help them to admit that the problem is not that they wouldn't like to have the estate for their family or accumulation program for themselves, but that it's a matter of raising the necessary additional funds.

Sometimes the "next sale" occurs then and there!

"I understand, and I'm sure you're willing to agree that you would like to have the whole program if it were not for the problem of the additional funds that are required, isn't that so?"

Introduce "Pre-Allocation"

If they agree, you can then go on to plant the idea of *"pre-allocation"* of money which should make your repeat sales much easier.

Suggest the discipline of "Pre-Allocating" a fixed percentage of future increases in income until their financial program is complete.

"I can certainly appreciate your situation. In fact, most people today tend to live right up to the edge of their incomes or even a little bit beyond. Even the most successful people with whom I work have the same problem. But it seems to me that part of the reason for their success is that they face up to their problems and then decide to do something about them. They also tend to solve their problems the easy way.

"They recognize that most direct or indirect increases in income tend to be absorbed almost immediately into their standards of living. Once that has occurred, it's tough to cut back. Isn't that so?

"So the people who have done the best jobs of creating the estates which they wanted have been those who have recognized this tendency and have said, in effect, "I'm going to beat it! I'm going to beat it by pre-allocating a definite fixed percentage of my next direct or indirect income increase, say one-half after taxes, until my financial program is complete. Doesn't that make sense?"

Identify Their Next Income Increase

If they agree the idea makes sense, explore when it's reasonable to expect their next direct or indirect increase in income. Ask them to contact you if it comes sooner than anticipated. Make appropriate notes in your Case History and if the anticipated increase will occur reasonably close to an Automatic, let the system remind you of the next contact date. Only in exceptional situations should it be necessary to set them up on a Non-Automatic basis.

Stimulate Unsolicited or "Walk-In" Business

Have you ever wondered why two financial professionals operating in approximately the same way in the same market and rendering similar levels of service experience radically different results as far as "walk-in" business is concerned? Some experience a regular stream of strangers calling to ask them about their insurance or investment programs, while others never receive unsolicited calls.

It's Up to You

Plant the seed for unsolicited referrals.

Assuming you are doing a professional job, you have a choice as to which group of financial professionals you will belong to in the years to come. It's pretty much a matter of selling yourself and your services in a professional manner. If you would like some of this "walk-in" business, be sure to perfect and always include this next portion in your Delivery Interview.

Suggest That You Have Done Them a Favor

"I think it's fair to say that our company qualifies as exceptional. However, quite honestly, I feel that it is my personal knowledge of my Clients and my ongoing concern for them that truly accounts for my value as a professional. I'd like to think that by providing you with quality, I have set in motion a process whose benefits will continue to grow over time."

Ask for a Future Introduction

"In that regard, this is the thought I'd like to leave with you. I don't know exactly when it will be – this afternoon, tomorrow, next week or next month – but I know for sure that it will happen not just once but many times. You'll find yourself either on the periphery of, or right in the middle of, a conversation that has to do with an investment or insurance decision by a friend, business associate, relative, or acquaintance. If the participants seem to be looking for guidance or input, I'd appreciate it if you could direct them my way. I'd love the opportunity to help.

Prospect for the Next Sale to a New Client

Persistency, repeat business, and walk-in sales will all have a large impact on your success and happiness in the financial services business. The first three sections of the Delivery Interview have concerned themselves with those areas. However, your final emphasis on prospecting will not only have a great long-range effect, but it's immediate short-range effect can be fantastic! Referred Lead Prospecting makes it possible to climb your way up the tree of success as you direct your efforts toward your most preferable Qualified Suspect.

The "No's" are always the same, whether the person is one of big potential or small, but there is a tremendous difference in their "Yes's!" Not only that, but the strong introduction from a respected friend or business associate will do a lot to reduce the time lag between the first meeting and the first sale.

Referrals reduce the time lag between the first meeting and the first sale.

You Must Master Referred Lead Prospecting!

As has been emphasized throughout this book, the skill of Referred Lead Prospecting is one of your major competitive advantages. You simply can't afford to be average at this all-important skill. The detailed description of Six Step Prospecting and Three Step Promotion presented in Chapter 10 should have been mastered long before the Delivery Interview! A properly conducted Delivery Interview is one of the best opportunities to keep an endless chain of referrals going.

Master Your Delivery Process

You will no doubt notice that we keep bringing up the word "Master." It isn't enough to be "familiar" or "acquainted" with these delivery and prospecting skills. For maximum effectiveness, they must become second nature to you. Life is not a dress rehearsal. You are in the midst of your career and mastery is required for you to fully optimize your opportunity.

Master the skills of the Delivery Interview Outline that appears on the next page.

Because of the tremendous importance of the material that has been covered in this chapter, a summary Delivery Interview Outline is provided on the page that follows. Practice it until it has been completely mastered! In preparation for an actual delivery, it is also suggested that you create and review your own personalized Delivery Outline.

You will never be embarrassed by being properly prepared. Remember that you teach your Prospects and Clients how to do business with you. If your are prepared, they will respect you and will themselves come prepared for your appointments.

The Delivery Interview Outline

I. Things to Be Done Prior to the Delivery Interview

1. Review the policy (or product) to be delivered for accuracy.

2. Gather any additional paperwork that may need to be signed

3. Assemble the product or policy presentation folder and appropriate company promotional material.

4. Prepare a Prospecting Outline (and possibly Prompting List)

5. Stess the interview's importance when arranging the appointment

II. Things to Be Done During the Delivery Interview

A. Guarantee persistency:

1. Review the product or policy purchased.

2. Review the goals and program.

3. Tie the two together.

4. Introduce company promotional material.

B. Set up the next sale to this Client:

1. Recognize accomplishments thus far.

2. Discuss shortages that still exist.

    a) Which concerns the Client the most?

    b) When might something be done about them?

    c) Is funding the program the problem?

3. Successful people handle the money problem by pre-allocation.

C. Prepare the way for unsolicited or "walk-in" business:

1. Introduce any item of sales literature that shows your company in a favorable light.

2. Review the value of your service.

D. Transition to Referred Lead Prospecting

Post Sale Service

Preparation for Further Sales

From one point of view, the expression "Post Sale Service" is a misnomer. Although it is true that services such as reviews and informational mailings do take place "post" – or after – the first sale, perhaps these are best thought of as "pre-sale" services. This certainly makes sense when you consider that normally only a small portion of Clients' eventual purchases occur at the time of their first purchase. Post sale service actively contributes to future sales and is actually a high form of the expression of enlightened self-interest on the part of the Financial Services Professional.

Post Sale Service actively contributes to future sales.

10-3-1 Again

By the time we make the first sale to a New Client, a significant investment in time has been made. This Client is all you have to show for the average of ten Suspects pre-approached, three interviewed in-depth with the Confidential Questionnaire to acquire the one New Client. Each Client stands at the bottom of the great funnel of effort that was necessary to produce this first sale.

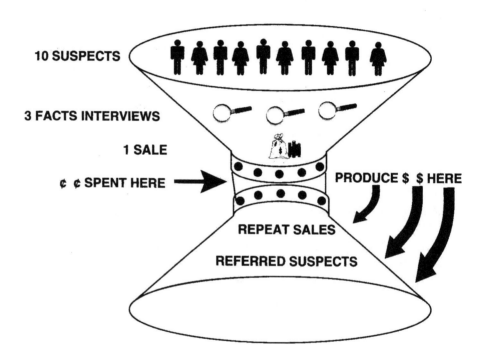

10 SUSPECTS

3 FACTS INTERVIEWS

1 SALE

¢ ¢ SPENT HERE

PRODUCE $ $ HERE

REPEAT SALES

REFERRED SUSPECTS

The Economic Value of a New Client

Take good care of your Clients!

In addition to thinking of our New Client as being at the bottom of a funnel, each should be thought of as being poised at the top of a pyramid of opportunity for repeat sales and referred leads. Consider the substantial first year commissions and potential renewals and trails that can come from an ongoing Client relationship. Statistics reveal that, on average, a New Client will buy five to seven additional insurance products from you as well as additional investment products. Also consider the phenomenal value of their referrals and their potential enthusiastic public relations activity that could result in "walk-in" business for you. A quality New Client can be a virtual gold mine!

Don't Hesitate to Invest in Your Business

Remember these facts and do not hesitate to spend the few dollars that it will cost to dramatize the work already done. The money spent for nicely printed reports, presentation folders personalized with the Client's name, and for a combination lock policy box or an imprinted policy wallet will come back a hundred fold!

Follow Through on Observations and Specific Suggestions

Review your notes and help your Clients get organized by reminding them of the importance of gathering together family records and financial documents. Follow up to see if they made an appointment with an attorney to discuss a will or living trust. This could serve as an opportunity to recommend a competent attorney and, consequently, help develop the attorney as a prospecting center of influence for you.

Make Your Suggestions for Follow-Up

Suggest that they include a list of their policy numbers and investment portfolio contents in their safe deposit box. Remind them that the contracts themselves are to be kept at their home or office. (The box might be sealed at the time of their death). You shouldn't do those things for them, but you can act as a gentle motivator until they get them done. Your Clients will always be pleased with this evidence of your interest in their welfare. Include an appropriate notation to yourself in the Case History so you can follow-up at their next review to be sure they have taken the required action.

Long-Range Cultivation

It is safe to say that "almost nothing" in the way of cultivation mailings is too good for your Active Clients. Birthday cards can be used; sometimes for all members of the family if you have a personal relationship with them. If you use pocket calendars, they may be enclosed with birthday cards to adults and older children. Nicer calendars, if used, should be mailed or delivered in person well before or after the Christmas rush. Consider sending Thanksgiving cards or gifts as another way of differentiating yourself.

You may occasionally send current general advertising material or a competitive comparison. Once a Prospect becomes a Client, do not hesitate to send competitive comparisons because by so doing you are complimenting the Client and reinforcing the feeling that he or she did a smart thing by buying from you.

Treat Your Clients Well

It is not suggested that you must use all of these cultivation pieces. But it is vigorously suggested that you do everything you can for your Clients and that you "treat them right." If you do, you will reap a bountiful harvest of repeat sales, referred contacts, and good friends.

Concentrate your most costly promotional efforts on your proven Clients. In so doing, the program should not become a burden, either from a time or dollar standpoint. For at best, your group of Active Clients will grow, but slowly—say 30 to 50 per year. We are talking about Clients, not just sales!

Be Sure to Maintain Face-to-Face Contact

There is no substitute for face-to-face conversations with Clients.

It would be unfortunate, however, if you lost sight of the fact that there is no satisfactory substitute for face-to-face conversation. Long-range mail cultivation (once you are well established and can afford it) will help to keep your name in front of your Clients. But keeping your name before them will do you little or no good unless you follow through with a regular program of personal visits. If you fail to sustain face-to-face contact with your Clients, you will probably begin to lose them to competitors.

Remember the importance of Birthday Lunches and Periodic Reviews. Everyone appreciates being remembered and treated in a special way. Enhance the power of your Periodic Reviews by bringing a complete and up-to-date printout of the Client's financial analysis. This not only suggests a higher level of post sale service but it also serves as a logical springboard for further program development and sales.

The message of this section on Delivery and Post Sale Service is: You now have a Client. Take good care of the Client. If you do, he or she will take care of you!

Chapter 15

Conclusion

The Three Pillars

Dr. Perry L. Rohrer, founding partner of Rohrer, Hibler & Replogle, consulting psychologists, suggests you establish just a few significant Pillars to guide your efforts. By doing so, most everyday problems – when measured against those Pillars – would tend to solve themselves instead of becoming crises. Following this advice led to the development of the following three Pillars of Motivation, Organization, and Dedication.

Motivation

In every one of your contacts with another individual you either lift him up a little or beat him down a bit. When a Financial Services Professional is injected into an enthusiastic and affirmative environment in which the thing to do is to succeed, his opportunity for success will be materially improved. Conversely, if the atmosphere is negative, critical, and gloomy, that pollution rubs off and diminishes his chances. Eternal vigilance must become an absolute principle.

We are committed to a policy that has no room for the chronically unsuccessful for he or she is not likely to be happy; nor for the malcontent, for he or she could not possibly make an affirmative contribution. Only those who have great potential for the business should be provided the opportunity to free the abilities that lie within them. Those who are unwilling or unable to harness his or her capabilities should be encouraged to move on.

Goethe put it well: "...we are so constituted by nature that we are prone to compare ourselves with others; and our happiness or misery depends very much on the objects and persons around us. On this account, nothing is more dangerous than solitude; there, our imagination, always disposed to rise, taking a new flight on the wings of fancy, pictures to us a chain of beings of whom we seem the most inferior. All things appear greater than they really are, and all seem superior to us..."

The key to motivation is affirmative association. If you surround yourself with stimulating people and inspirational things – and as you do your reciprocal part to uplift and improve – your life also becomes richer and more satisfying.

Organization

Meticulous analysis of 150,000 Suspects and 45,000 new Facts have proven that a successful Financial Services Professional eventually acquires one New Client from each three people who will confide in that Financial Services Professional. No Financial Services Professional we know of, no matter how substantial the volume or distinguished the honors, has done significantly better than to obtain one New Client from three individuals who have disclosed the Facts on themselves. This truth is the Pillar of our organizational endeavor. It follows that:

1. Each new Financial Services Professional must do sufficient suspecting to obtain enough Facts so that New Clients resulting from sales to one-third will build a clientele to the desired level at a rate satisfactory to the Financial Services Professional and compatible with the high standards of the agency or firm.

2. Each established Financial Services Professional must do sufficient suspecting to obtain enough new Facts so that New Clients, developed from sales to one-third of them, will make up for the attrition caused by selection, upgrading, moves, deaths, and saturation.

3. The ratio of Clients to Facts appears to be fixed at about one to three. But the commission and the challenge and the excitement of the case correspond directly with the potential of the Qualified Suspect. These are within the control of the Financial Services Professionals. Therefore, the Financial Services Professionals must prepare themselves professionally to deal with exciting people, and they and they alone must find them.

Good Clients buy many times and lead you to others like them. But, they won't last forever, and so they must be replaced. The optimum for an established Financial Services Professional is to process enough Suspects annually to generate 150 new Fact Finding Interviews with Prospects, 50 of whom will ultimately become New Clients. For the new Financial Services Professional, the optimum is 300 new Fact Finding Interviews the first year, 250 the second year, 200 the third, and 150 every year thereafter.

Dedication to Urgency

Many Financial Services Professionals could be hired and taught to find good Suspects, to telephone them for appointments, to change three of ten Suspects to Prospects by getting Facts, and to prepare and present proposals. The Prospects would love it! They'd appreciate the education and would gush with praise for the polite, employee teacher. They would vow eternal allegiance and promise to buy...someday; but not today.

For emotions are caught, not taught! And though the decision to buy someday can be obtained by teaching, the decision to buy today will be obtained most surely by helping the Prospect catch the enthusiasm projected emotionally by the Financial Services Professional who is involved, who cares, and who shows it.

If Financial Services Professionals expect to receive affirmative action at the end of the close, they must do their part by demonstrating urgency from the very beginning. The work of today must be finished today, and tomorrow's plans must be made tonight if momentum is to be sustained. As was said at the beginning of the Oregon Trail, "Choose your rut with care; you'll be in it for the next 1800 miles!" From the very beginning of our relationships with new Suspects, we must project urgency if we are to deserve prompt action in our attempts to change them from Suspects to Prospects to Clients.

It's Called Financial "Services" for a Reason

Great financial services companies exist to serve their Clients, be they policyowners and their beneficiaries or investors. The Financial Services Professional and the assistant, the general agent or manager, the file clerk, the president, and the janitor – all are servants of, and in the final analysis are paid by, the Clients. The financial services firm serves by keeping the firm's staff and field force alive and vital for present and future generations. Our personal dedication must be to so guard physical and mental health as to be able to radiate the enthusiasm that comes from being constructively excited. The best will be dedicated to people and their problems – not to inanimate things.

Pillars are not indestructible. All weather with age and topple in time. However, having been erected by design and with toil and sacrifice, they are not to be circumvented lightly or casually overthrown. Motivation… Organization…Dedication…all have stood the tests of time. Consider Dr. Rohrer's suggestion. Erect your own pillars and measure your own problems against them; you may find that many will solve themselves when you do so and more of the best of you will be available to deal creatively with the opportunities of your life.

It's Time to Convert to the One Card System

Now that you've completed this book, it's time to take action.

Many of you may currently be using another system, but ready to take your business to higher levels. To do so, you will need to convert from whatever you are currently using.

Steps for Conversion to the One Card System

It is recommended you set up the original system, use it, and learn it for ninety days. Once you have a solid grasp of the system, you can explore other options. The following is a step-by-step guide to converting your practice to the One Card System, summarized from information presented throughout this book.

First of all—stop! Do *not* try to phase into the OCS over a period of weeks or months. You will not achieve the full power of the One Card System by using only pieces of it. Reserve two or three days, usually over a weekend, to do *nothing* other than convert your practice to the OCS.

Determine the Actual Quantity and Quality of Your Current Clientele

1. Determine whether your existing Clients are active or inactive.

    *   To determine whether the Clients are active or inactive, ask yourself, "Do I expect them to buy again? Am I willing to contact them twice per year?" If so, the Clients are considered to be active.

2. Set up new file folders for Active Clients.

    •   Remember that a Client is a *paying entity, an account, a checkbook,* or a *source of funds.* You will often have more than one sale within a paying entity or account.

    •   Set up new file folders for each Active Client. Create a Case History sheet for each file folder. Transfer miscellaneous notes you have on the clients to the Case History Notes or Confidential Questionnaire form. Discard any unnecessary papers.

3. Create white cards for Active Clients.

    •   If the Client is active, create a white OCS card for that entity. Keep in mind, white cards should contain the name, date of birth (for the primary decision maker), and the source and date of the lead *only.* All monthly tabs are to be removed from the top of the card except the one corresponding to the birth month of the individual.

    •   Place the white OCS cards behind the Additions tab of the OCS Card File box. (You will later tabulate the number of Active Client and Prospect cards – white cards – that you have in your system.) Remember that the initial goal of a Financial Services Professional who adopts the One Card System will be to build the number of active white cards (Prospects and Clients) to the level of 500. The white cards represent the number of *active relationships* a representative has in his/her system.

    •   If the Client is determined to be inactive, place the Client file folder in a file drawer marked Inactive Client Files. These entities will no longer be aggressively contacted twice per year. Instead, they may be placed on a passive contact status, such as an annual review letter/email and checklist. If the Client responds due to a change in his or her situation the Client may once again be placed into active status, at which time a white card will be created and placed in the OCS Card File box. Many experienced professionals have assistants place service calls to Inactive Clients on a bi-annual basis.

Update the One Thousand Clients Book

1. If you wish to have a complete record of *all* Active Clients, record the names and corresponding information of all Active Clients in the *One Thousand Clients* book. (Be sure to record age, income and occupation, and FYC data *as it was at the time the individual or entity became a Client*. Estimated future FYC should be calculated from the current date.)

2. Now outline the characteristics of your Least Acceptable New Suspect that you will knowingly allow into your system. Record your new characteristics on the page marked Least Acceptable New Suspects in your *One Thousand Clients* book.

3. Calculate the total future FYC anticipated from your Active Clients. *This figure is a more accurate representation of the true value of your clientele than annual FYC.*

Determine Your Quantity of Active Prospects

1. Here you will follow the same basic procedure as with your Client files – that is, go through every Prospect File folder. (These are individuals with whom you have completed Fact Finding and Closing Interviews but have not yet acted on your recommendations.)

2. Determine whether the individual (entity) has a high probability of taking action in the future. Discard (or store) the file folders of those entities whom you *do not* believe have a high probability of purchasing. In other words, get rid of the dead wood.

3. Those individuals (entities) whom you *do* believe have a good probability of taking action in the future will now be considered Active Prospects. (Keep in mind that Active Prospects are to be contacted twice yearly in the One Card System, so be selective.) File folders should be cleaned of miscellaneous papers and Case History Notes sheets should be prepared.

4. A white OCS card should be prepared for each Active Prospect and should be placed behind the Additions tab of the OCS Card File box.

Prepare Your OCS Card File

1. Update the OCS Control Card and file all white cards in the A-Z section. The specific steps are listed below.

- White OCS cards for all of your Active Prospects and Clients should now be in the Card File box behind the Additions tab.

- Count the total number of white cards behind the Additions tab and record that total on your OCS Control card located in the very back of the box. This card will be updated monthly and will indicate the number of active relationships you have in your system. An agent new to the system should strive to acquire 500 relationships (active white cards) in his or her system as soon as possible. This is a *relationship* business!

- Now file the white cards alphabetically into the A-Z section of the box. The white cards will remain there until one of two things happens:

    1. A Prospect is rejected from the system due to repeated negative contact.

    2. A Client becomes saturated or otherwise satisfied, and is moved to Inactive status.

2. Add Qualified Suspects to the System.

- Go through all leads you have for potential Prospects. Record all information for each individual (entity) on yellow Suspect cards.

- An individual (entity) is considered a Qualified Suspect when you know the name, age, occupation, approximate income, address, and <u>daytime</u> telephone number. These individuals may be placed into the 1-31 section of the box for immediate contact, or the Monthly section if they have recently been contacted and have given permission to stay in touch.

- *Do not* record the names of these Qualified Suspects in the *Success Manual Section* of your *Productivity Planner*. The purpose of recording Qualified Suspects in the *Success Manual* is to reward yourself for *new* prospecting (suspecting) activities from this point forward.

Prepare Your Productivity Planner

You will now want to prepare your *OCS Productivity Planner* (as explained in Chapter 7). Depending on the time of month that you convert over to the One Card System, you will either be preparing for the current month or the upcoming month.

- **Month at a Glance Pages.** Record nonselling events, such as training sessions, office or firm meetings, conferences, holidays, etc. Determine the number of field days you have in the month. Divide the number of field days into your monthly OCS Activity and Efficiency Point objective (100 points per month for experienced representatives). The resulting number will be your *daily* point goal for the month. Record this goal lower Monthly Planning Process section for the Month at a Glance page corresponding to this month.

- **Weekly Appointment Slots.** Mark out nonselling times from the Month at a Glance pages and record them in the weekly section of the Planner. Strive to fill the remaining open slots! (You will be using these pages to schedule appointments when calling or when you are in the field.)

- **Automatic Contacts.** As previously mentioned, the One Card System is designed to build relationships through twice yearly contact of Active Prospects and Clients. The Automatic Contacts area helps to facilitate this automatic contact.

- **Birthday Automatics.** You will want to contact all Active Clients and Prospects who have birthdays during the month as recorded in the Birthdays section for each day. These meetings provide excellent prospecting opportunities.

Go to the A-Z section of the OCS Card File box. You can easily identify – from the exposed monthly tabs – all of the individuals who will have birthdays in the upcoming month. Simply pull the appropriate cards up – not out – from the box and then alphabetically enter the names and birthdays in the Birthdays section of the Automatic Contacts, adjacent to the corresponding Month at a Glance page. By listing the names alphabetically, it will be easier to locate a name when updating the Results column throughout the month.

When you have completed this task you will notice that the names are listed alphabetically. A Results column is also provided to allow you to quickly assess your effectiveness during these excellent prospecting opportunities.

Now transfer the names of these individuals to the top section of the Daily Pages, planning for contact to occur at least one week prior to the birthday. Names and birthdays *only* are to be listed. Do not record telephone numbers here as the names prompt you to pull the file folder on the appropriate day to find the telephone number and review the

Case History and Facts form. Record the results of the call or contact in the Case History Sheet.

- **Review Automatics.** You will list the names of Active Prospects and Clients who may need periodic reviews for insurance or investment purposes in the applicable column on the Automatic Contacts page adjacent to the corresponding Month at a Glance page.

The process for listing Review Automatics is the same. Simply go to the Alphabetical section of the OCS Card File box and look for cards with exposed birth month tabs that are six months prior to the month you are planning. Pull the white cards *up, but not out of,* the box and list the names of these individuals in the Reviews and Other column.

The names (only) of these individuals should also be transferred to the Automatic Contacts section for the applicable day in the *Productivity Planner.*

Again, a Results column is provided for the Reviews and Other column to allow you to quickly assess your effectiveness during these business producing opportunities.

Congratulations, You Have Now Converted Your Practice to the OCS!

Your system is now ready to go when you begin work the next business morning. When you arrive at the office:

- Turn to the appropriate Daily Page of your *OCS Productivity Planner.*

- Pull the file folders of those Clients and Prospects listed on your daily pages. You will also pull yellow Qualified Suspect cards from the appropriate 1-31 tab of the OCS Card File box. A combination of 36 file folders and yellow cards should be on your desk.

- You will begin calling at your set time, starting with Clients and Prospects first to warm up. Note the results of contacts on the Case History sheet of the file folder.

- Next you will call those individuals represented by yellow Suspect cards in an attempt to either schedule an initial appointment, obtain permission to stay in touch, or discard them from the system. Use the lower section of the yellow card to make notations of the conversation or attempts to contact as Suspect.

- As you call, you will schedule appointments using the Appointment section of your *OCS Productivity Planner*. Endeavor to fill *all* of the highlighted revenue-producing appointment slots for the upcoming week. You will also have some spill over into the next week, which is good!

- Record the results of your dialing in the grid below the Automatic Contacts section for the applicable day in your *OCS Productivity Planner*. Use the dot and check codes listed on the divider tabs of the *Planner*.

- After your dialing session, strive to practice Rule #1, which is to see people or work to see people from 10:30 a.m. until 5:00 p.m. at least three days a week. That is, endeavor to do nothing other than conducting appointments or scheduling appointments during these hours. Take your yellow cards with you into the field. If an appointment cancels, get on the phone and dial! Strive to fill those highlighted revenue producing slots!

- Record you accomplishments in your *OCS Productivity Planner* as you go.

- Reserve the end of the day for the handling of mail and e-mail to prevent distractions.

- Each evening, *post* the results of the day in the *Success Manual* section. *Plan* the next day in an effort to maximize point earning activities. Remember, the *Success Manual* and point system are designed to drive and reinforce client building activities. Let the system *run you*. You will be more productive, with less stress as a result!

After effectively implementing the original system, you'll be ready to succeed with OCS through the use of a variety of automated tools. Good luck!

Index

M

N

O

P

Q

R